DISTURBED

IN

THEIR

NESTS

DISTURBED

IN

THEIR

NESTS

**A JOURNEY FROM
SUDAN'S DINKALAND TO
SAN DIEGO'S CITY HEIGHTS**

ALEPHONSION DENG
AND JUDY A. BERNSTEIN

BLACK
STONE
PUBLISHING

Copyright © 2018 by Alephonsion Deng and Judy A. Bernstein
Published in 2018 by Blackstone Publishing
Cover and book design by Kathryn Galloway English

Printed in the United States of America

First edition: 2018
ISBN 978-1-9825-4622-9
Biography & Autobiography / Personal Memoirs

1 3 5 7 9 10 8 6 4 2

CIP data for this book is available
from the Library of Congress

Blackstone Publishing
31 Mistletoe Rd.
Ashland, OR 97520

www.BlackstonePublishing.com

Dedicated to all refugees

PART ONE

AUGUST 2, 2001–SEPTEMBER 2, 2001

DESTINY TREE

Alepho

KENYA

In 2001, nothing was more important to me than the board beneath the big acacia tree in the middle of Kakuma Refugee Camp. There, they posted the list of lucky boys who would leave the camp for a new life in America.

Since the program had begun a year earlier, three thousand Lost Boys of Sudan, as the United Nations named us, had already boarded a plane bound for the land of opportunity. My turn had not yet come.

Now it was August. Another week, another list, another chance.

I made my way down Kakuma Road, past row after row of mud huts, light bouncing off their flattened-oilcan roofs. Heat seared my calloused feet. Boys emerged from their huts, some holding hands, all walking in that determined way, eager to know their fates at the board.

There was no opportunity in Kakuma camp. No future. Everyone wanted to leave. But war still raged back in Sudan, and other countries wouldn't have us. The resettlement program to America was our only hope.

There'd been some weeks when no list went up on the board under the tree, no plane landed on the dirt strip outside camp, and no one left for their new life. When that happened, I focused on school because I knew the resettlement program could end before my chance came. I'd also heard that some boys' files had been stolen and sold, and I worried that at any time my file could go missing too. But once I had an education, no one could take that away.

It was possible I'd never be able to leave Kakuma camp. Life had taught me to keep my expectations calm, because when dreams did not come true it was disappointing. Disappointment could turn to sadness, and sadness made everything seem futile. It could even endanger lives, for young men with nothing to hope for and nothing to lose can be dangerous indeed.

At the sound of footsteps, I turned and looked back over my shoulder. Benson, my brother, caught up to me on the road. His turn had not yet come either.

"Who will stand in the ration line tomorrow?" he asked in Dinka, our native language.

We took turns getting up at four in the morning and standing in line all day. "I will," I said. "Because if my name is on the board, I will be gone."

He laughed a nervous laugh. "Do you think if your name is there today, you will be in America tomorrow?"

I smiled. We joked because that was our way of coping with our situation, but my stomach burned with hunger. Every two weeks all the refugees lined up in the scorching sun for the dried corn distribution. The corn still had to be ground, so a percentage of our ration was needed to pay the grinder. Then we all collected firewood; the corn required hours of cooking to be edible. Once a day, in the afternoon, my brother and I ate together from a large pot. We'd been surviving on that one meal we called *asida* for nine years, always making sure that we didn't eat too much any one day, or we wouldn't have enough to last until the next ration day. We always ran out though. We called those foodless days *black days*.

Today was a black day. But not even the mud we collected from the stream would have settled my stomach. Not even asida—nothing would help until I saw my name on the board.

We walked along the road, each lost in his thoughts. Would this be our day? Would we be together, or separated for years again, maybe this time forever? We didn't share words the rest of our way to the destiny tree.

● ● ●

When I was five, war separated Benson from me. That night, when our village was attacked, my mother shook me awake. "Alepho, Alepho, wake up!" She sounded frightened. I heard distant thunder. Something was not right. "You must go with your brother now!"

My eldest brother grabbed my hand and dragged me through the door. Outside, thunder roared and lit the sky at the same time. What was this? Was it getting closer?

We went out into the tall elephant grass, and when I tried to ask questions my brother hushed me. There was a loud noise, popping sounds from the next village. Frightened, I waited with my brothers.

Suddenly, men on horseback with flaming torches raced through our village. Sharp pops whistled and split the air. People fell. There was an explosion.

"Stay down," my brother said when he saw that I was reaching my neck out, trying to see what was happening to our homes.

So, we crouched. My heart battered my chest. "Is this the danger?" My father had warned me that if danger came, I must run.

"Yes," my brother said and gripped my hand tighter.

With each explosion, the black sky lit up like day. Where were our mother, our father, and the rest of our family? Sobs shook my body. "I want to go home."

"We can't. It's not safe," he told me.

"What about Benson?" He was at my oldest sister's house in another village two hours' walk away.

"I don't know."

I couldn't see our village to understand what was happening. I reached to part the grass. My older brother grabbed my hand back and wouldn't let go. "Stay down. They will see us." We remained like that, huddled in the stalks. My body didn't stop shaking all night.

Hours later, a dull orange lit the horizon. The explosions and screaming had stopped.

I said, "It's quiet. Can we go home now?"

"Soon."

We slept a little in the grass and waited until the sun came up, then crawled from the bush.

In the distance, smoke sat over the area where our village lay. The silence put fear in me. Was my family still alive?

As we crept closer, our eyes wide and searching for danger, I heard crying. We came to a hut. Its roof, now black burned grass, had fallen inside. Outside, a family clung to each other huddled over a child. I couldn't look at his injured leg.

I pulled from my brother's grasp and ran past other huts, some burned, some still with their roofs.

Ours came into view. The roof was there. Our mother was in front with my baby brother at her breast. My father stood beside her. They'd survived the attack. They were alive.

I'd never been so happy in my life. I fell into their arms. Tears poured down our cheeks.

We remained there together the whole day, weeping, with smoke and ash all around us. My father went off to help others, but came back often to check on us.

At the end of the day, as the sun sank and the light was nearly gone, a figure stumbled out of the darkness. My oldest sister. Her mouth moved but no sound came out. My father rushed to meet her, and she collapsed into his arms.

"Oh, Ma! Da!" she cried. "We can't find Benson."

● ● ●

Benson had been seven when he'd disappeared that day.

Now, fourteen years later, we were in Kakuma camp, back together, but for how long?

We reached the shade of the old acacia. A large crowd of Lost Boys were gathered. The representative from the International Organization for Migration (IOM) pushed his way through the crowd to the board. His stapler banged up a list of names. The boys jostled for position and chattered like weaver birds.

"You go," I told Benson. As my older brother, he should know his fate first.

Benson shoved his way into the crowd. Boys who had gotten to the list first slumped away in disappointment. With twelve thousand boys still waiting to go and less than a hundred on the list each week, hope was small for each of us.

Benson made it to the board. His finger moved down the

page, pausing to read each line. It stopped at the bottom and Benson leaned in close, holding his finger on a name.

I pushed through the others. Benson turned to me and smiled. I leaned over a fellow Lost Boy. There, below Benson's finger: *Deng, Benson Athiin.* Just as we had imagined it for so long.

But where was my name? It wasn't on the list.

"Wait," Benson said, "another page is coming."

I closed my eyes and imagined my name on that white sheet. I willed it to be there. I couldn't lose my brother again.

Boys pushed and shoved to see if their names were on the list. I held my ground beside Benson. I wouldn't leave until all the pages had been posted.

The stapler tacked up another page. My turn to lean in. First name at the top: *Deng, Alephonsion Awer.*

Our chance had arrived.

"San Diego," Benson said. "Where is that?"

"I don't know." What I did know was that it was in America, and we were both going. My brother and I would be together. That was all that mattered.

THE BIG BIRD

Alepho

Since the resettlement of the Lost Boys had begun, rumors about American life had flown around Kakuma camp. No one had been there but everyone was an expert. America was the land of the free: free from starvation and thirst, free to drive a car, free to do whatever you wanted.

News spread that I would soon be leaving. People offered advice. A friend came to my hut and said, "To walk barefoot in America is embarrassing." He gave me his black shoes. They were old and raggedy and felt strange on my feet, but I was proud and thankful to have my first pair of shoes.

Elders told me, "Come back and help your country."

Others cautioned, "Stay away from women."

One man gave me important information. He said, "If you meet a really rich sponsor, you get three pillows that hold inside the money for you to live and go to school. If you meet a sponsor who is not that rich, you get one pillow. The poorest man in America is like the richest in Africa. The poor ones give you only one pillow."

I'd never seen a pillow before, but this made sense. In the camp they gave us food, but it was only enough to not starve. In America they would give us a house, a car, and an education. Clearly my future depended on my sponsor and the pillows full of cash.

When the day came to leave, the IOM gave each of us boys a sweater, sweatpants, white canvas shoes, and a large plastic bag with the letters IOM on the side to keep with us as we traveled to our destination.

Benson and I lined up at the fence around the camp, joyous to be on our way, yet sad. Our little brother, Peter, who had been left behind so many times in other camps, watched from the crowd. Despair filled his eyes. They said his file was missing and that he was no longer even in the process. His hope was gone. When would I see him again? I had to do something to help him, but I couldn't do anything here in Kakuma Refugee Camp. As soon as I arrived in the US, I would ask my sponsor how to bring Peter to America, too.

A roar came from overhead and a plane touched down on the dirt strip outside camp, stirring dust into the air. The people gathered at the runway. They made a big deal out of me, Benson, and our cousin Lino.

Our other cousins Joseph and Benjamin were still in the process, waiting to find their names on that tree, and we hoped they would be joining us someday.

The plane gaped its belly for us fortunate boys to enter. My heart pounded as I moved up the boarding line and began to climb the stairs. The crowd shouted and waved from below like I was the president. I waved back, hoping they couldn't see how scared I was to fly.

People inside directed us to our seats and demonstrated the safety belts.

An engine rumbled. A propeller turned, then another, and a roar filled the cabin. I was pushed back against the seat when the plane sped down the dirt strip, bumping and shaking like a tractor trailer. I held my breath and gripped the chair.

The plane lifted off the earth. Flying smoothly as a big bird, we headed toward the sky.

I peered out the window at the vast land that had taken me years to cross on foot but now sped by in minutes.

When we were children, after Benson disappeared during the attack on our village, our father had searched for him for a year. More attacks came to our area after that. It was dangerous, but he never stopped looking for his missing son. One day, while my father was out searching, we received news that he had been killed. How was that possible?

A man such as my father, a great man, was dead. It didn't make sense to me. When a huge male lion killed our goats, my father fought the lion to the death and won. He was a hero in our village. How could he die? He was too big and strong to get killed. I couldn't imagine that my father wouldn't be there, that I'd never again follow him when he worked or hear his stories. I'd never feel as safe without my father.

At six years old, I'd already lost my brother and my father.

Two years after Benson went missing, during another attack, I fled from my burning village alone into the night, as before. But that time the enemy remained in our area and I couldn't return home. Neither could I find my family, and so my thousand-mile journey to escape war began. For three years after fleeing my village, I dodged bombs, lions, and death. Along the way, I met other boys like me, and sometimes we walked together.

Then I arrived in a small town called Kidepo in southern Sudan, chasing a story that a much-older brother I'd never met lived there. A skinny boy with a crooked arm came out of a hut. I'd passed thousands of boys by then, but seeing this boy made my heart leap like a rabbit. Benson had broken his arm as a small child and it had not healed properly. We hadn't seen each other in five years, but I knew right away this was my brother Benson.

We hugged and tears ran down our faces. The most joyous moment of our lives. We promised to always stay together.

Within mere days, bombs had thrust us apart again. We found each other weeks later but were taken to a terrible place called Natinga, a secret camp hidden in the mountains where the rebels trained boys for military service, punishing any attempt at escape with severe beatings.

If Benson hadn't been with me, I would have died in Natinga. For three months I suffered from yellow fever that left me shivering and shriveling on the ground. Benson kept me alive by making soup from leaves and grass. He carried me to the bush to relieve myself.

When a truck came to take away the sick boys, he lifted my twig body into the back. "I will find you," he said and waved goodbye.

Eventually I reached Kakuma Refugee Camp in Kenya. I received medicine and food. My strength returned, but all I could think about was Benson. Could he get out of Natinga? He was tall enough to carry a Kalashnikov rifle. Would he be forced to fight with the soldiers?

Months later, Benson staggered into our camp. He'd escaped Natinga and crossed a treacherous desert, drinking his own urine to survive. We were back together at last.

Kakuma was safer, but with a hundred thousand people in the camp, sixteen thousand of them boys like us, we never had enough water or food. We stood in lines from morning until night. People fought. It seemed that I couldn't escape fighting. I'd wearied of fleeing from place to place to place; I wanted to build my life. But no future existed for me in Kakuma, and war still raged back home in Sudan. You cannot stay where there's war or you will not survive. Nine years passed with no hope—until my resettlement came.

Now, I was flying to my new life in America with my brother Benson and my cousin Lino.

• • •

In Nairobi, they transferred us to a plane like a big white bird. On the seat in front of me was my own video screen. I'd seen some movies in the camp. Some Ethiopians in the camp had made their huts into theaters with video machines and TVs run by car batteries. But I didn't know how to run my own video.

A white man sat beside me. I observed him to learn what I should do. He put on the earphones. I'd seen a few people with earphones in the camp and put on mine. He pushed buttons on a square thing, and the screen in front of him came on. I pushed buttons. A loud scratchy noise came into my earphones and white and black lines raced across my screen. What was this? A picture of America? Was it raining there?

I pushed a button again. People on the screen talked. Some kind of a show. There was laughter, but I couldn't see who was laughing. The actors talked so fast that I didn't understand a single word except the title: *Everybody Loves Raymond*. If this was how they spoke, how would I communicate in America? They talked in such complicated English. I'd been learning English in the camp, but now what I had been doing seemed like not much more than making letters in the dirt.

I switched to another show. Two teams played a game like

soccer but used sticks and glided across shiny white ground, barely moving their feet. I had never seen such things. How did they run like that? They had on big clothes and round things covered their heads. They wore funny shoes. What kind of people were they?

Time passed and everyone around me slept. I kept pushing more buttons and found a basketball game. I knew this sport; we'd played basketball in the camp. I relaxed and enjoyed the screen.

The plane bumped hard. My belly jumped and I grabbed the armrests. What was happening? We were still up in the sky. Had the plane hit something up here? Another plane?

No one else moved. The white man beside me didn't even open his eyes. I calmed down, but every time the plane bumped, I held on.

How long before the plane landed? Fear kept me from sleep and even from moving. People walked in the aisle between the seats, but I stayed in mine because I didn't want to fall out.

They gave us a tray with strange-looking food. Green leaves with orange strips and a red berry on top. Next to it a square thing made of metal. The man beside me peeled back the silver paper. Steam rose. Chicken with rice. In the camp, asida was the food I knew. I hadn't had chicken in many years. My stomach was eager. I ate all of the airplane food. Some of it tasted pretty good.

After they cleared the food trays, a flight attendant came down the aisle announcing, "Dessert. Dessert."

Desert? *Oh no.* Just like in war, we had to leave. My heart raced. I grabbed my bag and stood. Where would we go, up here in the sky?

The white man didn't move and looked irritated. I started toward the exit at the back. Surely, they would tell us where to go. But no one else moved. People looked at me funny. Someone asked if I was lost. Why weren't they preparing to leave the plane? Why weren't they frightened?

The flight attendant came closer to the back, where I stood and offered a dish. "Would you like dessert? Ice cream or cake?"

This was dessert? No wonder other passengers looked confused at me standing there.

I returned to my seat, relieved, and accepted a white square of cake. I'd never tasted anything that sweet. Another Sudanese boy across the aisle took a bite and spat it out. The white people looked at him like, *That is rude.*

I forced down my whole piece. I wasn't going to disappoint any Americans. For a long time my ears buzzed and my body twitched from that white square.

Later that night I had my first glimpse of America. New York City. Lights reached out to the horizon and climbed into the sky like tall trees. I'd never seen so many lights in my life.

At the airport terminal, officials led us to an area with chairs. "Sit here and wait for your next flight."

We watched the people rushing by. The women walked strangely, and their shoes went *kik-kak, kik-kak* on the floor. "Why are they in such a hurry?" I asked Benson. "They have all of their things with them. Are they migrating?"

He looked at me like, *Don't ask your silly questions.* He didn't know either.

I had never seen so many white people. We didn't have white people in my village. The first time I ever saw a white person was in a town on my journey, after I'd left my home. I became sick and some villagers took me to a clinic. The person who checked me was a white lady with smooth yellow hair. Her blue eyes mesmerized me like a witch. She made me well.

Now that I was in New York, it was clear there were more white people in the world. I couldn't stop looking at them, and they looked back at me with an expression that said, *You have two legs and two eyes, but you look different.* I wore pants and a shirt like everyone else. Did I look different?

I noticed that people didn't talk to one another. Why didn't they sit down and have a conversation? Was this the nature of Americans? Back home, people took time to do things—unless they were fleeing danger.

I needed to use the bathroom. I walked through the terminal searching for a sign that said TOILET. A lot of people went in and out of a door that said RESTROOMS, but I wasn't about to go in there. In Africa they kept dead people in rest rooms until they buried them. Did so many people die on airplanes that they needed a special room at the airport?

I returned to my brother and cousin. "There is no toilet."

Another Lost Boy pointed back where I came from. "In America it is called a restroom."

I returned to the restroom and entered. During orientation in the camp they had taught us about flushing toilets. I had never seen one before the airport in Kenya. I was happy that the lever worked as I'd been told. When I finished, I watched to see what the white people did next. After they washed their hands, they put them near a noisy machine and rubbed them together. I did the same. *Whoosh!* I jumped back. What was this? Warm air? I looked into the hole to see where it came from and tried again. I felt like an American when I came out of that toilet and wanted to show the others how it all worked.

After several hours, and several more trips to the restroom, we boarded the plane to San Diego. Soon I would see my city of destiny and know my future.

THE PILLOW IS EVERYTHING

Alepho

SAN DIEGO, CALIFORNIA

Benson, Lino, and I arrived in San Diego late at night, after traveling for nearly two days. They told us that someone would be picking us up in a car. No one had ever picked us up before. The only people I'd seen picked up in cars were leaders, men of caliber, or the educated. The majority of people walked on their natural feet—no shoes, no cars. My chest swelled at the idea of riding in a private vehicle. I had become special and important.

Inside the airport terminal people held up papers with names on them. We looked through the crowd for a white person holding our names.

Benson pointed. "Look. There."

Our names were on the paper, but the man holding it wasn't American. I said to Benson, "Our sponsor is a poor Sudanese."

"Shhh," Benson said.

The man greeted us. "Hi, I'm Diar Diar." He spoke Dinka, but with an accent from Bor, a region west of ours.

I whispered to Benson, "We are not lucky."

We followed him out of the terminal and through a field of cars that stood like cows in a herd.

I asked Diar, "Will we get our cars soon?"

"Maybe in two or three months."

Diar drove out of the car field. Roads went in every direction. How did Diar know where to drive? Red lights and white lights came at us fast. I became dizzy.

Finally the car stopped at a tall building. Was this our sponsor's house? If so, clearly our sponsor was rich. I grew excited.

We carried our bags up steps that connected to the outside of the building. I'd never climbed stairs to a building before. The steps had air between each one and felt strong but I stepped softly so as not to break one and fall through to the ground. Why did they put the entrance to the house at the top? What kept these upper rooms from falling down on the ones below? I didn't feel safe up there.

Diar knocked on a door. Two Lost Boys opened it. Sudanese again? When were we going to meet our American sponsor?

Diar introduced us. "Daniel and James have been in America for several months."

Then Diar showed us around. "This is the room for sitting with a television." In the kitchen he explained how to turn on the water, light the stove for cooking, and put food in the refrigerator. Why would I want my food to be cold?

Diar took us to a small room beside the kitchen. "This is the toilet."

I whispered to Benson, "How can someone use this room for a toilet when it is so close to the cooking?" It didn't seem clean to me. Benson nodded in agreement.

There were two other rooms. Daniel and James slept in one

with two beds. Our bedroom had three beds. At the end of each was a white puffy thing. Was this the pillow? People in the camp had told us that Americans kept their money in pillows. The money in the pillow would help us in our new life so that we could go to school and get an education. I'd promised my friends back in the camp that I'd send them money when I received my pillow. I claimed the bed with the puffiest pillow and impatiently waited for Diar to leave so I could look inside.

Then Diar said, "It is late. Goodbye for tonight. I will see you tomorrow."

Benson and Lino went to the sitting room; they didn't seem concerned about their pillows. Didn't they know? I walked back to my bed and lifted mine. Not heavy. Perhaps money was light? Or maybe we did have a rich sponsor, and Diar had taken our other two pillows. In the camp we'd always suspected the Kenyans took most of our food and gave us only a little. Diar had dropped us off and disappeared. How could we trust him?

I took my pillow into the bathroom and closed the door. I patted it. Yes, yes, I was a big winner. The outer cover opened at one end, but the inside cover was sealed. That meant there must be money. I used my teeth to make a hole and widened it with my hands. I searched inside until I reached the bottom. White fluffy stuff flew all over. No money. My heart dropped. How would I live and go to school? My friends back in the camp would think I had lied to them and taken the money for myself.

After that, I began to question other things I'd been told in the camp. If no one worked in America and everything was done by machines, who built the machines? I had enough common sense to ask that. I still believed that we would receive our own car and house. After all, they had given us food in the refugee camp, so here had to be the same, just more. I really needed to meet my sponsor.

That person would surely set me on my path for a future in America.

The next day Diar picked us up. His quickness interested me. In the camp I had not been exposed to doing things fast. Most days we waited in line at the water tap for hours. And every two weeks we arrived at the food ration line before sunrise and were lucky to receive any food at all by the end of the day. Back in my village, if a traveler arrived at our house, we let him rest for a few days before putting him to errands.

As Diar drove, even in daylight, I thought we were going in circles because all the buildings were square and tall and all the streets looked the same. The land was flat. There were no hills or trees or rocks to mark the land or tell where you'd been. How would he find our way back?

We arrived at a place where Diar said we could get a food-stamp card. I'd been told that in America you needed only your green card and that bought anything.

I asked Diar, "When do we get our green card?"

"It takes more than a year to get the green card."

A year? How could I wait a year? I wanted to buy things and send them to my friends in the refugee camp. There had been nothing in my pillow. How was I going to survive in America?

By the time we reached the house again my head throbbed, my stomach swirled from the car motion, and I still hadn't met my sponsor.

• • •

We stayed in the house all the next day. Our house was nice and clean and had a soft floor called carpet. One thing still bothered me though: the inside bathroom. That seemed unclean. In the camp we took care of business in the bushes, not inside our huts. You could make the loudest noise and no one would care. How would I do that in the house? And where did the water carrying the waste go?

I was surprised that no one came to greet us at the house. In Africa, when people find out that you have just arrived, they come from very far away to visit you. Here, the other doors of the big house were closed. When evening came, lights shined from inside other rooms, but still no one invited us to a meal or even talked to us.

The second day my energy was restored. I told James, "I want to see the whole house and greet our sponsor and the people in this village."

"No," he said. "This is an apartment building, not a house. In America you can't go walking about knocking on people's doors if you don't know them. That's trespassing. They call 911 and the police come and take you to jail."

"Why? I only want to greet them."

I doubted what James told me. Maybe he wanted me to fear people in America and think of them as selfish individuals.

We stayed inside again. There was a lot of food in the apartment—more than I'd ever seen. Bags and boxes of things I didn't know.

James said, "Chips are good. You eat them with sauce."

I tried one but it didn't taste good to me. I wasn't used to so many choices. In the camp we all received an equal share of food every two weeks, and it was always the same thing: corn and wheat that we had ground and then cooked with water to make asida. I had been so tired of asida but now I missed it.

I didn't like just sitting in the house doing nothing. I needed to meet my sponsor.

Finally, on Monday, Joseph Jok, a Sudanese man who worked for the International Rescue Committee, picked us up at our apartment. "Today, you are going to meet a nice lady who will help you to know the town."

Finally, I would meet my sponsor.

Benson warned Lino and me. "You must be respectful when we meet the sponsor. Don't ask too many questions. You can follow my lead."

Benson was older than both of us. I respected that, but he was acting as a chief and I was my own person. We were in America now. Everything was different and we needed to follow the American way. The important thing was that we were about to meet our sponsor.

WE WANT AMERICAN

Judy

AUGUST 13, 2001

At the San Diego offices of the International Rescue Committee (IRC) they directed my son and me to a couch, where we waited to meet three Lost Boys of Sudan.

I'd read an article about these young refugees that had piqued my interest and grabbed my heart. I hadn't forgotten about them when Joseph Jok, a caseworker at the IRC and a grad student I'd mentored at the university, mentioned to me that some of them would be coming to San Diego. He asked if I'd like to meet the new arrivals and show them around. I did, and I especially wanted our twelve-year-old son, Cliff, to share that experience.

"Can we go to lunch before the tour?" Cliff asked from his perch on the couch.

It was the third time he'd asked that question. Not because he was hungry, but because he'd heard that these young men had never had a soda with ice from a machine. That was unimaginable to him, and he was eager to demonstrate such a miraculous invention. They'd never used a light switch, a phone, or a fork either, but that hadn't seized Cliff's interest like the soda had.

Joseph had called Friday to let me know that three Lost Boys had just arrived. Two weeks remained before Cliff returned to school, leaving enough time for a few days of touring the city, visiting the ocean or the mountains, and perhaps SeaWorld or our world-famous zoo. And, of course, getting sodas.

"Yes, lunch first," I reassured him.

Cliff had many other questions that I did my best to answer.

"How old are they?"

"Two are nineteen, one is twenty-one."

"Do they speak English?"

"Hopefully some that they learned in the camp."

In preparation for our meeting of cultures, I'd put on the television segment of *60 Minutes* about the Lost Boys of Sudan. I wanted Cliff to see it. Bob Simon, the host, described the young boys' horrific journey across a thousand miles, barefoot and without parents. I could see that Cliff was moved by their story. Who wouldn't be? My eyes teared as emaciated boys, holding tattered books they'd carried for years, explained how they wanted to come to America, work sixteen-hour days, and get an education to become doctors, lawyers, and teachers. Their bodies were frail, in obvious need of food and medical care, but their spirits weren't broken. In clips from the refugee camp where they had languished for ten years, they played soccer without shoes. I couldn't do anything about their loss of homes and family, but shoes were within my power. After lunch and the sodas, my plan for our first day together included getting them each a new pair.

As excited as Cliff was, I was twice as nervous. By every measurement, these young men and I were as different as we could be from one another. They'd come from halfway around the globe and a culture entirely foreign to me. They'd lost their homes and families, survived a war and years in a refugee camp. I'd lived all of my years in safety and comfort in the same city. They were beginning a new life, and I was in the middle of mine. They were male; I was female. They had nothing, and I had everything a person needs. They had the blackest skin I'd ever seen, and I was one tint this side of albino. It seemed that the only thing we'd have in common was English, and even that was questionable.

On the television segment, some Lost Boys spoke in heavily accented English, and Bob Simon had to repeat most things so that the audience could understand. Even then I suspected the producer had sought out the young men with the best command of English in the first place. He had sixteen thousand to choose from.

I wondered too, would they be more like boys or men? Would they be sad and homesick or delighted to be here? They'd witnessed and endured things that adults never recover from. An April 1, 2001, *New York Times Magazine* article characterized them as "among the most badly war-traumatized children ever examined." What would I do if they were withdrawn, unstable, or depressed? Joseph had assured me that the boys Cliff and I would meet today were happy and normal. I was skeptical. Normal (whatever that meant) maybe, but happy?

Relax, I told myself as we waited on the couch to meet them, *we're just showing them around town for a couple of days, not adopting them*. Cliff would get to know people from a very different place. To experience this cultural opportunity we didn't even need to travel around the world. All we had to do was drive less than an hour down the freeway.

Fifteen minutes later Joseph walked into the IRC offices with three tall, exceptionally thin young men with short-cropped hair and flawless black skin. Their shirts, buttoned to their chins, were tucked into pants with hems far too high above cheap canvas shoes.

They approached, smiling. I should have asked Joseph about basic protocol. In my work and recent travels I'd met a Buddhist monk, an Orthodox rabbi, and a Muslim man, all of whom had declined my outstretched hand. An awkward feeling.

I whispered to Cliff, "I'm not sure if it is their custom to shake hands. Especially with women."

He gave me a look like, *So what am I supposed to do?*

Joseph introduced the three as Benson, Lino, and Alephonsion. I repeated each name and shook their hands quickly, hoping that if touching a woman was uncomfortable, at least their discomfort would be brief. I struggled with the name of the last one.

"Call him Alepho," Benson said.

They smiled eagerly when I introduced Cliff.

Joseph said, "I told the boys we would go for something to eat. I'll come too."

"I'm glad you're coming too, Joseph." His presence was a relief for me. At least we could communicate adequately.

Joseph smiled. "There's an Ethiopian restaurant nearby."

I couldn't see Cliff's face, but I could imagine his reaction. An Ethiopian restaurant was unlikely to have a soda machine. That would be the biggest disappointment.

The three young men didn't look too thrilled either.

"Would you like to try American food?" I asked, hoping I wasn't stepping on Joseph's toes.

"Yes, yes, we want American," they chimed in unison, and I smiled. This would be easier than I'd thought.

THE HANDSHAKE

Alepho

A few days after our arrival in San Diego, Joseph Jok drove us to the IRC. I'd begun to see that life in America was not as simple as the people in the camp had told us. Daniel and James had been here for three months, and they said that they still had many things to learn. I didn't want to wait two or three months. I wanted to begin my American life right away, but I needed someone who could show me the culture, explain what to do and where to go, and help me begin my new life. I longed for an American guide. And finally, the day had come when I would meet my sponsor.

We entered the IRC offices. A white lady with yellow hair waited there with her young son. I said to myself, *Oh, this is going to be good, she looks American.*

The lady stood up. "She is skinny," I said to Benson in Dinka. Benson made his eyes narrow which meant to stop talking.

But this was important. I ignored his warning. "That means she is not rich and does not have status."

Benson shushed me.

Even though Benson was older, I didn't listen. "I want a strong sponsor."

Benson ignored me.

Joseph Jok walked over and we followed. Joseph introduced the lady as Judy and told her our names.

The lady gave me her hand really quick and took it away without holding my hand. She didn't seem interested in meeting me.

She did the same thing to Benson and Lino. Her hand didn't want to collaborate with our hands. This was not a good sign. Back home, if someone really liked you they shook your hand for minutes and looked at you to make a connection.

"That was rude," I said to Benson. "She isn't rich and she doesn't like us." I had been so excited to meet our American sponsor, but this lady was not happy to meet us.

"Quiet," Benson said.

"I'm just saying, did you see how she shook our hands? It was like there was something in her hand that she doesn't want us to touch."

The lady named Judy was smiling and talking with Joseph. She introduced us to her son, Cliff.

Cliff didn't shake our hands at all. He just raised his hand up and said, "Oh, hi."

CHICKEN

Judy

Benson and Alepho climbed into the back seat of our Ford Explorer and Cliff instructed them on the use of the seat belts. Lino rode with Joseph in his car, and we headed out to find an American restaurant.

"How was the plane ride?" I asked.

"Two days," Benson answered. "Very long."

"Did you like the food?"

"I liked it," Alepho replied.

"I did not eat," Benson said. "Just drink soda."

For two days? "Which kind of soda do you like?"

"Sprite" and "Coke" were the immediate responses from the back seat.

These were not the questions I wanted to ask. Not the kind of answers I was really seeking either. I wanted to know things that were more revealing: *Where are your families? What did you eat on your journey across the desert? Were there really crocodiles and lions? How did you survive all that time at such a tender age?*

I followed Joseph for several miles through east San Diego, an area I hadn't visited in forty or more years, back when the Sears store had been the highlight. Although born and raised in San Diego, I'd seldom ventured this far east of the main downtown area since my husband Paul and I had moved north to a more rural neighborhood shortly after we'd married, nearly thirty years earlier.

The old Sears store was nowhere to be seen, but we passed shops for tailors and motor parts, an occasional adult bookstore, and many boarded-up doors. The grocery stores weren't big supermarkets, but more the size of barbershops. There wasn't a fast-food place in sight.

Cliff initiated conversation with Benson and Alepho more than he typically did with older American teens. I concentrated on keeping up with Joseph, who finally pulled into a Burger King—the first American restaurant I'd seen in the neighborhood.

"There used to be a McDonald's nearby," Joseph said as we headed across the parking lot. "But it went out of business."

Out of business? That was a first. New McDonald's restaurants seemed to sprout everywhere.

Benson hurried ahead and opened the door for me. That simple gesture caused so many things to run through my mind. Who'd taught him such niceties? He'd been in a refugee camp without a mother since he was Cliff's age. Was opening doors for women a universal courtesy? And had I been conscientious enough about teaching Cliff those things?

We stood in the line. "They have different kinds of sandwiches," I explained.

"What is sandwich?" Benson wanted to know. He seemed to be the group's spokesperson.

I pointed to the menu above. "See the pictures up there?"

They studied them. "What is hamburger?" Benson asked.

"Hamburger is beef. You know, cow. They grind it up and make a patty. Like a cookie. And put it between two pieces of bread." Bewilderment set in on their faces. Or disgust. I wasn't sure. Joseph smiled. He didn't want to interfere. I waved to other customers to go ahead of us and simplified the choices. "Beef, chicken, or fish?"

"Wow," Lino said without exclamation.

"Chicken," Alepho said.

"Chicken," Lino chimed in. Benson only wanted a soda. I tried to persuade him to order more, but he declined. Maybe once he saw the food, he would change his mind.

The cashier handed cups to each of them. Alepho looked inside.

"Over here," Cliff said.

The big moment my son had been waiting for. While Cliff led the three young men to the soda machine, Joseph and I staked out a table. Heads above the crowd, the three formed a semicircle around Cliff and watched his every move. Alepho stepped up to try it first. He held his cup under a nozzle but nothing happened. Cliff showed him how to push the cup against the lever. Alepho jumped back when the ice burst from the machine into his cup. Joseph observed like a proud father.

I'd first met Joseph Jok when he was a graduate student at San Diego State University, and we'd worked together on a project to create a sewing center for the newly arrived Sudanese refugee women. Besides grad school, Joseph also worked full time at the IRC as a caseworker, assisting refugees in creating new lives for themselves. Since the arrival of the Lost Boys, he'd been busy. Their needs were great—from paperwork to medical care and housing—and his work hours didn't stop at sundown or respect weekends.

I'd learned in our time together that Joseph also held a doctorate in veterinary medicine from Alexandria University in

Egypt. However, that foreign degree didn't allow him to practice in the US. To be licensed here, he would have to pass additional boards and complete an internship—a feat that was financially impossible while supporting a wife and kids. His job at the IRC provided income, but watching how he cared about these young men, I suspected money was not the only reason he worked with refugees. Helping these Lost Boys as much as Joseph had been doing would surely cut into a person's private life. And from what we'd just experienced getting lunch, they would need a lot of help.

FANCY FOOD AT THE KING'S RESTAURANT

Alepho

After we met Judy and her son in the IRC offices, we followed them to her car. It was clean and looked like a kind of Land Rover. "It is new," I said to Benson. "Maybe she is rich even though she is skinny."

Benson and I entered the back seat of Judy's car. Cliff helped us fasten the seat belts. Lino rode with Joseph, and we followed Joseph's car. I couldn't tell which buildings were houses and which ones were stores. There were shops in Kakuma camp that people built within their shelters. Here it was different; all the buildings looked like houses. People drove their cars from place to place and no one walked. In Kakuma everyone walked. The streets had a different smell than our dirt roads. The cars went by without making any smoke. The cars in African cities made smoke.

"The cars go all day," I said to Benson. "They never stop. Where are they going?" Would I be doing the same thing one day?

Joseph stopped the car in the road. We stopped too. A red light was above. What did that mean? Danger? Cars still moved on the other side coming from that direction. The light turned green and both cars went. How did the light know when to stop some vehicles and allow the other vehicles to go? Were they controlled by a person or was there life in them?

While Judy was driving, sometimes she looked at me in the mirror. My suspicions about her were once again aroused when she began asking questions. She asked about our plane flight and what kind of soda we liked. I said, "Coca-Cola," but I didn't know. I was thinking, *Why is she asking a lot of questions? This is not right. Is she investigating us?* I was raised in a way that you voluntarily speak about who you are. When you exchange greetings, you say you are the son of so and so. But people do not ask you more than that.

Joseph stopped his car in a place with other cars and we did too. We went inside a building that said Burger King. So this was a special place for a king to eat. My suspicions eased. I knew then that our sponsor must be wealthy.

Inside it smelled like fancy food. How many more kingly things were we going to be having?

We went into a line. The people standing in front of us weren't skinny like us, and they didn't say anything to us.

Judy asked, "What would you like to eat?" She pointed to a board with bright pictures. They were good for someone who didn't know how to read. I read names, but I didn't recognize the types of food or the pictures either. I wanted asida but nothing in the pictures looked like asida. She explained kinds of food that I didn't understand. This restaurant made me nervous. People looked at me as if I were a tree. Could they see that I didn't know what kind of food sparked my interest? I felt ashamed that I didn't know what to order from the menu.

Judy said, "Beef, fish, or chicken."

I didn't see a picture of a chicken on the menu. We knew chicken, though; we'd had it a few times in the camp. "Chicken," I said.

I told Benson, "I want other things too."

"Get small food and a small drink," Benson warned. "We have to find out if it is free."

Benson ordered only a soda but I knew he was hungry. He was just worried about spending the sponsor's money.

"America is a free country," I told him. "She has a green card and she will get us free food with that."

Judy paid with money.

"You see," said Benson, "everything is not free."

The restaurant person gave us each an empty cup.

Cliff said, "Over here." I followed him to a machine. I had tried one of these machines at the airport in New York, but this one worked differently. He instructed us to watch. His cup filled with soda. I tried what Cliff did, but it didn't work.

Cliff said, "If you want ice, push your cup against this lever."

Chunks burst into my cup. I jumped back. The machine in New York had not done that! Cliff showed me how to put Coke in the cup as well. When I was done, I wanted to show everyone else, but Benson was not willing to watch even though he didn't know what he was doing.

We went to the table and sat down. I drank my soda through the straw. Sweet, fizzy, and cold. Too cold. My teeth hurt and my face ached, but I didn't want to let anyone know this thing was affecting me.

"Is this alcohol?" Lino asked. "I feel drunk."

I said, "I feel drunk too. This American soda makes you feel high." We had never had alcohol but we had seen drunks in the camp. "In America soda is designed differently. It's not like any other soda."

A young man brought food to our table. Judy gave us boxes of brown sticks. Where was the chicken?

She explained, "The fat ones are chicken and the thin ones are potatoes."

I tried one and said to Benson in Dinka, "The chicken over here doesn't even taste like chicken."

Benson said, "It's probably better than our chicken."

"I don't think I'm going to eat this."

Benson forcefully replied, "You are not going to throw away food. You have to eat it."

Cliff opened a little packet of sauce and dipped his food in it before taking a bite.

I opened all of the packets and put the chicken in each one. Some were sweet and others were sour. They tasted strange but I forced them down.

"This is how you learn," I said.

The food was weird but I felt so special eating at a place for kings and rich people. Would it be like this forever in America?

WHAT IS ON TEETH?

Judy

Benson nibbled at a few fries and sipped his soda. High cheek-bones and upward-slanting eyes gave him a perpetually cheerful expression. His bright yellow nylon mesh shirt fit his sunny personality and helped me to distinguish him from Alepho, who wore a serious expression. But he looked so much like Benson, I wondered if they were brothers.

Benson talked a lot, but he didn't look at me when he spoke. I wondered if that was polite in his culture. Joseph did look directly at me, but he had been here longer. They spoke among themselves quite a bit in their own language. I enjoyed watching their expressions. Sometimes it was laughter, other times they seemed to be instructing or chastising each other.

"What language are they speaking?" I asked Joseph.

"Dinka."

I wanted to be privy to their comments. Joseph was, and he seemed to be enjoying what they said. What did they think of all this?

Alepho was the most eager eater; he even sampled all of the dipping sauces. At once. Between bites he pointed to Cliff's mouth. "What is on teeth?"

"Braces. They make your teeth straight."

"Wow," Lino said.

"Look good," Alepho added.

Sweet of him to say, but did they really look attractive to him? "They take them off after a year. Then the teeth will be straight without a gap."

"Dinka girls with gap in teeth are worth more cows."

Cliff threw me a guarded look of surprise.

"How do you like the potato fries?" I asked.

Lino sat up straight. "Potatoes are good food."

"Yes, you're right, but fries aren't so good for you."

They looked at me with startled expressions, as though they'd just eaten a poisonous plant. "But only if you eat too much and get fat."

Before I spoke, I needed to consider context. I felt guilty that their first meal with us was fast food. But, they'd come from a place where eating the wrong thing could be deadly. From what I understood of their experiences, food wasn't measured by how healthy it was, only if you had enough to survive.

"A lot of fat Americans," Benson said in a sincere tone with a big smile on his face, like he'd just paid us a huge compliment.

Cliff burst out laughing. Joseph smiled. The three newcomers looked puzzled.

Joseph said, "It's not good to get too fat. It's okay to eat here sometimes but not all the time."

I could have spent all day just listening to them, but I'd promised Joseph we'd show them San Diego. "What shall we do next?" I wanted to get them shoes, but there wasn't enough time left in the day to both tour and shop. Hopefully we could get together a second time.

"We want to sign up for school," Alepho said.

School wasn't on our to-do list; we were just tour guides for a couple days. At nineteen and older, they weren't eligible for our traditional high schools. I had no idea where they could attend.

Joseph came to my rescue. "We'll do that another day. Let's go see their apartment so you know where they live."

In the parking lot Alepho came up close to me. "We speak English," he said. His voice was deep and serious. "Your accent is just difficult for us."

What? I thought our conversations had been going well. Had I directed my questions to Joseph too much? Spoken too quickly? Clearly Cliff wasn't the only one learning from this experience. Standing in the parking lot of a Burger King, I felt like a foreigner in my own land.

THE APARTMENT

Judy

Joseph continued eastward, and we followed through an area with which I was familiar from news reports of its crime and gang violence. Cliff was turned in his seat talking to Benson and Alepho in the back. I'd been concerned he would be too shy to interact, but it had ended up quite the opposite.

Joseph pulled into a small parking lot, and we climbed to the second floor of a six-unit apartment building. Joseph invited us to sit on one of the two couches in the living room. Cliff sat beside me. We had a clear view of the kitchen with its old freestanding refrigerator, a stove and oven combination that predated me, and chipped cabinets with one of the doors hanging from a single hinge.

"How many people live here?" I asked.

"Five boys."

The term "boy" made me uncomfortable. Joseph used it, however, and they continually referred to each other that way. "By themselves?" When I'd first heard that Lost Boys would be living together in small groups in the inner city, I wondered how well they would do. Especially alone. Even kids with family support were at high risk in neighborhoods like this. "Joseph," I whispered, "this neighborhood. Aren't you concerned?"

He smiled. "Not too much. They are good boys."

They seemed like good boys, but Joseph was a relative newcomer too, and a family man. Did he know about the gangs and crime in this area?

"I'm sure they're great boys. But is it safe here?"

"Mentors will be very helpful to them."

This was the second time he'd mentioned mentors. What exactly did he mean by that in terms of refugees? Was it an official role? I'd heard of sponsors, but the guys were already here, and IRC was taking care of the basics.

I didn't respond to Joseph. I couldn't and wouldn't commit to something like mentoring now. Cliff still needed me around after school and weekends were for family. My free time on weekdays was dedicated to completing my novel. I was already involved with United Cerebral Palsy and the San Dieguito River Valley Conservancy. In recent months, I'd been trying to add focus and discipline to my life, not distractions, which was why a day or two as a tour guide around the city had made perfect sense in the first place.

Benson went into a bedroom and returned with two books, one small and thick and the other large and thin. Obviously they were precious by the way he cradled them. I recalled a scene in the *60 Minutes* segment detailing how some boys had carried books all the way from a camp in Ethiopia.

He extended the smaller one toward me. "Dinka Bible."

No bigger than my palm with a dingy, white cover, it lay lightly in my hand, yet was weighty with symbolism. From what I'd learned about the situation in Sudan, the beliefs within that cover had inspired so much hatred that two million of his countrymen had been killed.

"Are you Christian?" Alepho wanted to know.

He sure asked probing questions. "My grandmother was Episcopalian, sort of, but my parents didn't go to church. When I married my husband, Paul, I converted to Judaism." I wanted to say that I thought religion should be more like pizza. Some people could prefer a thin crispy crust, others the doughy deep dish with extra cheese, and others not at all, yet everyone could still be friends. But I realized that pizza as a metaphor might not work.

The three just looked at me.

"I believe that all religions have some good things to offer," I added. "They have so many things in common. It's a shame there are wars over the differences."

They nodded. Benson handed me the larger book. "Manifesto of the SPLA. Sudanese People's Liberation Army."

I knew so little about the history and politics of Sudan. I thumbed through the pages. "What language is this?"

"Dinka," Benson said. "Please read."

"I can't read Dinka."

"You can do it," they said.

The words were short and I read them aloud using the logical phonetics of Spanish, the only other language I knew. They listened politely. I thought I was doing well until I came to the second line. They roared in laughter. I laughed too. Formalities had been shoved aside, and these serious, proper, young gentlemen were suddenly gleeful.

"Please," I said, "teach me to say something correctly in Dinka."

Benson said something I couldn't begin to repeat.

"How about 'thank you'? Can you teach me how to say that?

Please, can you write it on a piece of paper so I can see it?" As a visual learner, not to mention that math was my strength and language my weakness, my only hope was to see something written.

He wrote, *yin ca leec.*

"*Yin ka leek,*" I said.

"*Yin sha laish,*" he corrected.

I repeated it several times. At least I would be able to thank them in their language.

Alepho pointed to a dusty, discolored computer monitor and an old central processing unit on the table. "Can you make that work?"

My background was in the computer industry, but resurrecting and reconnecting such antiquated computer components was beyond my skills or desire. It probably couldn't do much anyway. The difficulty of using its limited functions would only discourage them. It impressed me, though, that he sensed the value of a computer on only his third day in America.

A man came out from one of the bedrooms and extended his hand. "Hello, I'm James."

He was the same height and coloring as the others but appeared a bit older. We shook hands and made introductions.

"How long have you been in the US?" I asked.

"Three month."

As he spoke his forehead wrinkled along five faint lines that radiated up from between his brows.

"Can you find job for me?" James asked.

"I don't know this area too well. Have you put applications into businesses?" Not wanting to be rude, but eager for a second look at his forehead, I let my gaze float an inch above his eyes. He wasn't looking at me anyway.

"I work, you see, and it is good, but I need other job. Sometimes one, maybe two ..."

I didn't understand the rest of his sentence, but it gave me a chance to look at the pattern of scars like sun rays that radiated up to his hairline and gave him an intense, serious expression. It looked intentional. I wondered what it represented and how he got it.

"What do you do at work?" I worried about Benson, Lino, and Alepho finding jobs. They were too young and new to America to face this harsh reality so soon. From what Joseph had told me, federal funding paid for the first three months, but after that refugees like the Lost Boys were pretty much on their own. Daunting expectations for boys who were not only young and alone, but who also came from such a different world. Good thing the three newcomers had been placed with older roommates who had been here a little longer.

James responded, "Set up tables and chairs for hotel banquet. Good work, but only one or two day."

Only one or two days of work per week. Now I understood. Considering the job probably paid minimum wage, that would be impossible to survive on in Southern California, no matter how thrifty one's lifestyle.

Yet I was no more prepared for James' request than I had been for Alepho wanting to sign up for school. I looked to Joseph for rescue, but he was quite obviously waiting to see what I said.

"I go everywhere," James said. "I go downtown. Everywhere. They say, 'No jobs. No jobs.'"

"The IRC has job development," Joseph interjected. "They will help you."

I added, "Yes, the IRC knows more than I do."

We exchanged names. I gave them my cell phone number and wrote down the number to the phone in their apartment. Alepho wrote something on a scrap of paper and showed it to me. The words "size" and "seize" in neat handwriting.

"We do not have dictionary," he said. "I understand meaning of these words, but how does one pronounce them?"

I sounded out each word. Their extensive vocabulary surprised me. They seemed to have less difficulty understanding me than I did them. "We must get you a dictionary," I said, happy to agree to something I could provide. The day was passing quickly, but I still wanted to buy them new shoes and maybe some new clothes. I worried they'd get beat up wearing the clothing they had: pants four inches too short, one pair a yellow plaid like someone's old golf hand-me-downs. I didn't want to insult anyone; it was a matter of safety.

"Joseph, can we go somewhere and let them pick out new shirts and pants?"

"Sure."

"Would you like to go to a store?" I asked them.

"We want to register for school and find a job."

"The IRC will help you with that," said Joseph. "And your mentor will too. Let's go to the store today. Walmart has good prices."

WALMART

Judy

Cliff talked with the guys while I drove. The afternoon was flying by too quickly. Showing them San Diego would be entertaining and educational for all of us, but I was realizing they had more urgent needs and desires. Clearly the advice and connections of a mature native would be invaluable, but that native wasn't me. I lived forty minutes north of the city, and had been out of the business world since Cliff was born. Sure, I felt an urge to help them, but I wasn't equipped for the duties and responsibilities of mentoring. I couldn't help with the two things they'd already asked, school and work. I had no idea what else might be entailed.

Yet, I could see they needed guidance and wondered if the mentor they did get would give it to them.

We parked on the edge of Walmart's crowded lot. I asked Joseph, "Would they mind if I take a picture?"

He smiled. "It's okay."

I pulled a camera from my purse. "I'd like to take a photo."

They leapt into a group and grabbed Cliff to pose with them. "Get the cars in the picture," they instructed. I took several shots of very enthusiastic subjects.

Inside the store, they craned their necks upward. Benson stretched both arms toward the ceiling. "A royal palace. Is this the store for the whole United States?"

Not quite. Probably the oldest, smallest Walmart in San Diego. "There are many like this."

He looked at me with disbelief.

With each thing we did, I better fathomed how little they understood of the world outside the refugee camp.

We found pants and shirts for each of them. Lino, who towered over six feet yet had only a thirty-inch waist, insisted on the forty-four-inch belt. He pointed out that the extra leather for the same price was a good value. Then he politely asked, "Can you allow us some shoes?"

The others spoke sharply to him in Dinka.

"Shoes are why we came," I said. "Let's have a look."

The style and size selections in the shoe department initially overwhelmed them, but eventually they started trying on shoes. Benson made his selection first.

Cliff asked, "May I take Benson to get some pencils?"

In the car, Benson had told Cliff that he liked to draw with colored pencils. While the others finished selecting shoes, Cliff and Benson started down the aisle together on a quest for colored pencils. Even though Cliff didn't come much above Benson's waist, I could see that he was confident and fully in control. Halfway down the aisle, Benson reached out a long graceful arm and put it around Cliff's shoulders. Tiny bumps rippled along my arms. I wished my camera could have captured that moment. I stared after them, burning the scene into my mind. Even when they'd disappeared around the corner, I didn't turn back to the others. My welling tears might have confused them.

The rest of us meandered through aisles and all of the things must have been strange to them. We caught up with Cliff and Benson in the school-supplies area. Now Alepho and Lino were interested too. "Would you like a composition book and some pens?"

Their eyes lit up. "Yes. We want to write down everything we see."

After much deliberation and quite a bit of discussion in Dinka, they each chose a small pocket-sized notebook.

"You don't want something larger?"

Benson asked, "If we write, will you help with our English?"

"Of course. That would be a pleasure."

I handed my credit card to the person at the register, grateful that I could afford things to help these boys. While I paid at the checkout, Alepho went over to a ten-foot-tall stack of boxes of strawberry SlimFast. I'd already demonstrated how a can opener worked (even though they didn't know what a can was) and tried to explain so many other things that my American world was beginning to look ridiculous even to me. I did *not* want to explain diet food.

"What is this?" he asked. His shoulder bones jutted out beneath his shirt. Like the others, he was close to six feet tall yet probably weighed less than me.

I sighed. "You drink this to get thin."

He nodded with an expression that wasn't sarcastic or judgmental, just pleased that he'd understood correctly what he'd been reading.

The others joined us. Their bewildered looks prompted me to explain further. "Remember what I said about eating too much of the food at the restaurant and what you said about Americans being fat?"

They nodded.

"Once they get fat they eat this to get thin again."

My own words embarrassed me. How many hungry people could be fed with what Americans spent to get thin again?

AMERICAN SMELL

Alepho

We called it the American smell. Everywhere we went, the new clothes, inside the cars, in our apartment, each place had scents that were different than anything in Africa. My mind was fine-tuned to smells. They created a lot of questions in me.

I asked Judy to sign us up for school and help us find a job. She didn't give me an answer to that question, but she and Joseph said they would take us to a store. We arrived at a place that was like a city inside a building.

Benson said, "Stay together. There are cities within cities. You don't want to get lost and go into another city."

I wanted Benson to be there with me, but I didn't want him to tell me to do this and not that. I was like a young cat wanting to explore this new world. I had a hunger to learn things quickly, to figure out how things worked, because I knew that understanding helped a lot in surviving. There were so many things I didn't understand here.

Judy asked, "Would you like to pick out some new clothes?"

The clothes we'd been given in Kenya smelled new, but these in America smelled better. They smelled fancy.

After we picked out the clothes, we walked around this huge store. What were all of these things? Did people buy them? We came to a row of objects that looked like guns.

"Guns," Lino said in Dinka.

Benson said, "They don't look like guns."

"These are American guns," I explained. "I saw these short, round guns in American movies. They are more modern than ours. They look small but when they shoot they destroy a lot."

Movies in the camp had given me clues about things here. We used to grow okra near the water tap and sell it until we had saved up five shillings to go to the Ethiopian area, where some people had a television and a tape machine that ran on car batteries. Another world happened on that little screen. I saw *Double Impact* and *Broken Arrow*. *Predator* had a very scary thing that ate people, but it lived in the jungle, so I wasn't worried about it here in the city. Benson usually saw movies first; he liked finding things out. He saw a movie about Buddha. I didn't know about Buddha until he told me. We saw *Rambo*. My friends thought the fighting was good. They said his moves were skilled. I wondered about that. Why did people say America was a peaceful country if it produced such skilled fighters? Maybe the fighting was only in a small part of America, not the whole country.

Later another kind of movie came to the camp. People were fooled by the cover of the tape they put on the outside to show what the movie was about. They had titles like *Hot Game* but the cover didn't show what happened in the movie. People went to see it and asked, "Is this what white people are doing? Are things like this considered normal for movies in other parts of the world?"

Some people just left. I was careful to not waste my money on these films. I liked movies with spaceships and flying objects that made me wonder how a human being could create something that was heavy yet still flew.

I wanted the kind of strength and brains that I saw in the movies. For years, in the refugee camp, I had had headaches because of too little food. I couldn't focus. A constant daze surrounded me. My schooling was affected. Being with friends was difficult. I wished the pain would go to another part of my body. Anywhere but my head. When you've suffered for a long time, the suffering becomes part of you.

Eating a handful of cooked cornmeal once a day was not enough. I'd been to the clinic in the camp. They prescribed aspirin, but it did nothing to alleviate the pain. I'd hoped that in America that pain would leave me. Happiness would be the day I didn't have a headache.

Now that I would have food in America, my interest in education was cemented. Without the constant hunger, I would be able to learn. I could build my life on my education. Education would allow me to belong in the world like a letter belongs in the alphabet. No one is better than the other, each one does a different thing in society. Which letter was I? What could I do? That was what I was determined to find out.

Movies showed me what was outside the camp. After the movies, we had often discussed what was real or not. I leaned toward believing things were real and that they were somewhere else in the world. If not, how could they take pictures of them? People came to our camp with cameras, so I knew about cameras, and they took pictures of real things.

"I am going to ask about these guns," Lino said.

"Don't ask too many questions," Benson warned.

Lino asked Judy anyway. We went close to listen for her answer. Judy said, "No, no, those aren't guns. They dry your hair."

We looked at each other. Why would someone want to dry their hair?

Judy said, "When your hair gets wet, that's the way to get rid of the water."

James had shown us a white cloth in the bathroom at the house. "After you shower you wipe your body with this cloth."

I took a shower, wiped my body with that cloth and little white things stuck all over my skin. In the camp after our shower, we waited a minute or two, put on our clothes, and came out of the bath shelter.

America was very sophisticated. I needed education to understand all of these things around me. How did these things come about? What I was seeing made my schooling in the camp seem so small. I felt puny and worried.

In the refugee camp, it was natural for me to always go about with a pen and a paper to record things. Here in America, I was seeing so many new things, learning so many new things, that I needed to write them down.

Judy took us to an area in the store where Benson and Cliff were looking at many sizes and colors of composition books and pens, like nothing I'd ever seen before. In the camp, we usually tore a piece of paper into pieces to share. I looked at all of the composition books and decided on the biggest one.

Benson said, "You need to look at the price and see what it is. If it is less, that is the one you need to get." He showed me the number on the one I'd picked out. "No, no, don't be greedy. You must get the small one for less money."

I put the big one back and picked a small one. We went to the front of the building. Judy pulled out a card and gave it to the person. Her green card. Food in a king's restaurant wasn't free because it was special, but things here were free. I wished Benson hadn't stopped me from getting the bigger notebook.

A tall stack of boxes that read SLIMFAST caught my interest. What was that? Did it make people run faster? Be smarter? It seemed that in America, if you wanted to be big or small, you took certain medication to alter you. In the *Predator* movie, Arnold Schwarzenegger had a huge gun, and he was able to hold it with only one hand while the gun fired. Could SlimFast give me that kind of strength?

"What is this?" I asked Judy.

She paused and looked like I had asked her about an American secret she didn't want to share with me.

She said, "You drink this to get thin."

Why would someone want to be thin? Didn't they want to be healthy and look rich and powerful? I was disappointed. I wanted to get big and strong and fat. We saw some people in the store who were really big. They walked slowly. Some even rode in chairs with wheels. "Wow, that one is really rich," we said.

In the car on the way back to the house we talked about the things we had seen that day. When one of us asked, "Why would anyone want to dry their hair?" we all laughed. I was so excited and so happy. I'd been picked up in a car and taken to an eating place for kings and to a store where rich people bought things. I had new clothes, a writing book, and a pen. What an amazing day.

Judy drove us back to the house. We got out with Joseph. Judy and Cliff stayed in their car. "*Yin ca leec,*" she said with an American accent. "Goodbye." Then they left, and I was stunned.

Why did she leave us so quickly like that? I thought she was our sponsor.

DRIVING HOME

Judy

We'd nearly reached home before Cliff said a word. "What do mentors do?" he asked.

"They do things like counselors. Parents are mentors to their children. But sometimes other people can be mentors too. Like a special teacher."

"Are the guys orphans?"

"I'm not sure. They may not know if their parents are still alive. They're orphans here in the US, that's for sure."

I had questions like that too, and many more. They'd endured such terror as young children, it didn't feel right asking. They seemed so cheerful. Did they ever talk about the past? Or had they put it out of their minds?

"Mom, we didn't get them the dictionary. They need one."

"Oh, you're right. Darn."

"Are you going to be their mentor?"

Part of me wanted to call Joseph, ask more about this mentoring. When Joseph had mentioned mentoring earlier, I didn't think I wanted any part of it. Now, I was feeling tempted. *Slow down,* I told myself. Making an impulsive or casual commitment would be unfair and selfish. Showing newcomers around town was one thing. Assisting with education, jobs, health care, and immigration issues was another. What did refugee status mean anyway? I knew so little about the whole process I didn't even know what I didn't know. I wasn't a social worker. My naive mistakes could be at *their* expense. No rush. I could mentor someone in a few months when my novel was finished and Cliff was back in school. Joseph had said other boys would be coming. Thousands were still in the camp.

"That's a big decision," I replied. "A lot of responsibility. I may not know how to do all the things they need."

"You can do it, Mom."

Oh boy, he wasn't helping. But I liked that he'd enjoyed himself so much he wanted me to commit.

Nevertheless, Benson, Alepho, and Lino had been shorted our first day when our time ran out. Maybe before summer was over in two weeks, I could take them to the zoo or the beach or a ball game. I hoped Cliff would want to come.

"Mom, when can we take them to get a dictionary?"

I smiled. "I'll call Joseph when we get home."

• • •

It was after five when I dialed Joseph's extension. He picked up on the first ring.

"Hi, it's Judy."

"I know."

"We didn't get to do much today. Can we show them around again?"

I sensed Joseph's warm smile through the phone. He probably knew this would happen.

"Yes," he said. "The same three boys? That would be fine."

I almost asked what the responsibilities of a mentor were, but was still afraid it might imply more than I was ready to do. "When?"

He ran through a list of things they needed to get done. "Is Thursday good?"

"Thursday is fine." Truth was, I'd probably have made any day fine.

WHAT IS THE MEANING OF FREE?

Alepho

The next day we waited in the apartment all day, but Judy and her son did not come back. Joseph came in the afternoon. "Where is our sponsor?" I asked.

"She will come again," Joseph said.

"When?"

"In two days."

When it came to learning, I was greedy. I wanted to learn about America in one day. America was the land of the free, where everyone aspired to be the best they could be. My life's work would be a testimony to what freedom could do for an individual. I wanted to be an explorer of the vast mysteries. A warrior of life.

I took in as much as my mind could handle. Thankfully I had the notebook. Things needed for survival had to be written down in my guidebook. My American life skills.

Joseph said, "I am taking you to get your ID."

"What is ID?" I asked.

"It is important to have an ID to identify who you are."

"Won't people just look at the person of me to know who I am?"

"It doesn't work that way. You need proof of who you are and a residence address."

That didn't make sense to me. I never had an ID in my life. I was known as the son of Deng Akuectoc, and that was enough.

Benson said, "There are millions of names to be memorized and no one is willing to do such a mundane task as memorizing the names of all the citizens."

Millions of Americans would not know there was a person by the name of Alephonsion Deng who lived in the United States, and I wouldn't know them. Strange. Back in Sudan, everyone in my village, and even distant villages, knew one another. In the camp, there were thousands, but we saw each other so often, we at least knew what family or tribe or country everyone came from and that was enough. We had a ration card to get food but we didn't need an ID to know who we were.

After the DMV, we went to the Social Security office. We wrote on paper forms that had places to put your name, address, and zip code.

"What is the function of a zip code?"

Joseph tried his best to explain things. "Zip code is for mailing letters. Now they will give you your social security number for your tax ID."

I knew about taxes but one did not need a number back home. A tax collector came to the open-air market and approached the seller and said we need this amount of money from you. Tax was collected by hand.

Joseph said, "You must carry these cards in your pockets at all times, wherever you go. Don't lose them or you'll have to pay money to replace them."

In the camp, we had only the ration card. Here we had many, and it was only our first week. I wrote down my new responsibilities in my guidebook. I had to be mindful to keep these small cards all of the time.

By the end of the day I was confused and overwhelmed. We had an I-94 number, a zip code number, a DMV ID number, and a social security number. These mathematical number sets were my new name. Did people take time to know you in America?

WHAT HAPPENED THERE?

Judy

Questions about Sudan peppered my thoughts. *What had happened to the girls? Their parents? How far did the boys walk? What was the refugee camp like?*

"Let's look up some information on the internet," I told Cliff.

We searched "Sudan History" on my computer.

The situation in Sudan was termed a civil war that began in 1983 and still wasn't over. Almost twenty years—the boys' entire lives. Two million Sudanese in the south had died and five million had been displaced. "Like our civil war?" Cliff asked.

Good question. "I don't know. Sounds like most of the dying was in the south."

A northern Arab, Muslim government fought the black animist and Christian south.

"Race and religion, that's typical," I commented. They'd been neighbors for a thousand years. What had happened in 1983 to spark such a horrible conflict? I read on. Huge oil reserves located in the south but controlled by the north funded the war.

"Of course: oil."

How often was oil behind it all? I hoped no Sudanese oil went into my gas tank. Surely, we wouldn't buy oil from a government who seized land and killed its own people like some drug cartel?

Many boys had been outside their villages tending herds of cattle and goats when the attacks came. Their parents were killed. Their sisters sold into slavery.

"Like real slaves?" Cliff asked.

"I guess like real slaves." Cliff was probably referring to the American slavery of the past. I doubted he'd heard too much about the various types of modern-day slavery, like sex trafficking or captive domestic workers. The girls sold in Sudan had probably suffered from all aspects of slavery. Personally, I'd never known anyone who had been directly affected by any form of it.

We read on. Tens of thousands of boys had fled. Maybe half survived the hundreds of miles' journey to Ethiopia. Two years later, the new Ethiopian government drove them out of Ethiopia and back into Sudan at gunpoint. They swam the Gilo River. A thousand boys shot, drowned, or eaten by crocodiles.

Cliff's eyes widened. "Crocodiles? Did Benson swim that river?"

"I don't know." I thought it was interesting he asked about Benson specifically. They seemed to have bonded over colored pencils.

Once back in Sudan and right in the midst of the ongoing civil war, the boys began another trek south. Finally they'd reached Kenya. Sixteen thousand of them languished there for nine years in a camp called Kakuma. From the photos, Kakuma was one really dusty, desolate place.

I felt pride in America, glad that our country had recognized these boys' dire situation and taken action. I gave Cliff a hug, thinking about the boys' mothers. I felt awful for them. How did they endure all this? Their daughters sold. Their husbands murdered. Their sons, only little boys, fleeing alone into a war. Had their mothers survived? How would they know?

I regularly devoured two newspapers a day, read *Newsweek* and *Time* magazines, watched the TV news, and listened to public radio in the car. Why hadn't I heard about this whole situation in Sudan while it was happening? Or had I heard but not paid attention to a disaster so far away and unlikely to impact me?

Cliff and I moved to the family room and again watched the *60 Minutes* segment. Having just spent a day with three Lost Boys, the show hit me in a whole new way. More personally. More like a mother. Today's charming incidents when they were learning about American conveniences wouldn't be so humorous when they went looking for work. Within three months they'd need to have jobs, begin paying for rent and food, and make good on the $850 they already owed the US government for their plane tickets here. Where would they find either time or money for education?

At one point in the segment, a Lost Boy stood on a busy city street in America. He put his hand to his brow and looked up and around at the tall buildings with a confused expression. He was searching for a job.

I turned off the television. The boys who had come to the US would be more likely to survive than those left behind, but they would face challenges. I recalled Benson, Alepho, and Lino standing in the IRC office—hope brimming in their eyes, enthusiasm in their handshakes, all eager to begin their new lives. Who knew what they'd heard about America? Cars, houses, a comfortable life? All of it was possible, but first they needed more education. And before that, they needed jobs. That would be difficult now that the tourist season was ending and the California economy was in a slump. Every day the news carried stories of executives taking jobs at car washes and fast-food places just to put food in their own kids' mouths. How was a never-before-employed, unskilled teenager with an accent, who didn't drive and was just learning to turn on a faucet and a light switch, going to compete for employment?

"Can we take them to the zoo?" Cliff asked.

"Maybe the zoo, or the beach. Let's ask them what they would like most. Did you hear what they said when they wanted those composition books and pens at Walmart? They said it was to write down what they saw. Let's get them each a disposable camera so they can take pictures too."

"Cool."

COAL-BLACK PERSON

Alepho

My new shoes from Walmart seemed able to travel a long distance. The next day I decided to walk to the IRC office to test them out. When we had driven places, I tried to remember everything I saw and how to get there, but each place looked the same as all the others.

I set out from the house and followed the bus route that Joseph had explained, walking from Euclid Avenue to University Avenue. Then I walked until I reached the big sign that read NORTH PARK and turned right onto Thirtieth Street and walked north until I reached the IRC office. The trip took two hours. I turned around and headed home. Without a dirt trail, big tree, or hill to look for, I had to be mindful to spot the proper street signs. I made it back home. When everything is new, a small accomplishment feels good.

No one spoke to me the entire way. I greeted each person but it was like they either didn't hear me or they ignored me. That puzzled me. Maybe they didn't understand my English. Did

American people not like me because I was much darker than everybody else? Perhaps a coal-black person wasn't welcome.

When I reached the apartment, I told Benson, "American people did not respond to my greetings. They looked at me like I had an elephant tusk on me. Maybe they are unhappy. But I think they might be just rude."

Benson said, "Don't judge people if you do not know them or have no connection with them. Maybe you are being rude to Americans. You don't know if it is acceptable to greet first. If you don't know then why are you greeting them? You are the stranger. You should wait for them to greet you first."

I could not answer my brother well. He always assessed everything first to know if it was right or wrong. His scrutiny and advice did not always sit well with me.

I asked James, who had been in America longer. "This is the way Americans are," he said. "Do not put it badly in your mind. You are also an American by being on American soil."

I wanted to connect with my fellow Americans. Back home, it was through a greeting that you connected with people. I told myself not to be discouraged. I had found my way through the city. I would find a way to connect to the people.

POURING WORDS

Judy

Eighteen was the cutoff age to be admitted to California high schools. Alepho and Lino were nineteen, Benson twenty-one. Joseph had told me that Daniel and James were studying for their GED, or high school equivalency exam, in preparation for entering college. They did well on the math, science, and English parts, but American history and literature remained a challenge. Not surprising. I stopped by a local bookstore and selected a few books and a dictionary that I thought might be helpful for their preparation.

A recently cast-off computer system sat in our garage. Paul liked new technology the way some people liked new haircuts. "Can I have that?" I asked him.

He smiled. "Of course. Got any special plans for it?"

I'd originally considered donating it to Joseph's sewing center for the Sudanese women, but the center wasn't ready for it yet. I emailed Joseph and told him that I wanted to give it to Benson,

Alepho, and Lino. Joseph agreed. I sensed he would have been too polite to say so even if he didn't.

Paul helped me put the system together, and we loaded it into the back of my Explorer.

Wednesday night I couldn't sleep. At midnight, I gave up and went to my office. After checking email, I decided to make a few notes. I'd never kept a diary or journal before but there had been something so unique and powerful about my first day's experience with three Lost Boys of Sudan that I didn't want to forget any details.

For five years I'd been working on a historical novel about a slave called Esteban who had crossed the American continent three hundred years before Lewis and Clark. In fact, it was Esteban's story that had piqued my interest in the Lost Boys in the first place. However, working on my novel was laborious. A page a day could be a stellar pace for me. But when writing about my experiences with Benson, Alepho, and Lino, the words poured onto the screen. I returned to bed just before dawn.

Upon waking I found Cliff ready to hit the road. "When are we going to leave?" he asked several times. That translated to "I'm excited" in preteen-speak.

• • •

At the IRC, Joseph took us upstairs to a room filled with computers. The boys were each working on one. Oh good, now they could practice what they learned in class at home.

Cliff and I gave them some choices of things we could do.

It was unanimous: "See the ocean."

I didn't care what we did or where we went as long as they were able to experience more of San Diego than they had the first time we'd been together. And time was short. The next day I'd be leaving town for two weeks. When we returned, Cliff would start school. The thought this might be the last time we would see them distressed me.

"Great idea. The ocean it will be. I just want to make one quick stop on our way."

The town of City Heights lay between the IRC office and the boys' apartment. City Heights had a brand-new library and community center. I wanted to get them library cards.

"You can come here anytime," I explained as we toured the facility and adjacent recreational areas. "You can play soccer, read, swim, or use the computers."

"I can't swim," Alepho said.

I found that curious. How had he dodged those crocs in the Gilo River?

I'd anticipated a bureaucratic hassle getting the library cards because of their refugee status, but it turned out to be easy. Once again, the day was speeding by, nearly noon already. No sense in ending up at the beach with empty stomachs. We headed toward an adjacent mall. To Cliff's delight, the only dining choice was McDonald's.

While crossing the parking lot, I asked, "Did you know each other before coming here?" Perhaps in a camp of a hundred thousand they hadn't met.

"Benson is my older brother," Alepho said with an impatient expression. "Lino is cousin."

Brother? No wonder I confused the two sometimes. Had someone said that and I missed it?

I hesitated before my next question. Was "do" or "did" the proper way to ask such a thing? I decided to be positive. "Do you have other brothers or sisters?"

"Yes," Benson said. "Our younger brother, Peter, is still in Kakuma camp."

"When will he be coming here?"

Benson didn't look at me. "He was supposed to come to US first, but his file is lost."

A bureaucratic error and brothers were separated by half a world. That must have robbed them of much of the joy in coming here. I wanted to know more, but we were at the front of the ordering line and getting impatient looks from the people behind us. Alepho decided on a cheeseburger. Benson and Lino wanted only sodas. Worrying like a mother that they'd be hungry later, and slightly perturbed that they weren't willing to eat at the times I planned, I encouraged them to try something. No luck.

At the table, I unwrapped my fish sandwich and, because I couldn't get it out of my mind, asked, "Do you think they'll find your brother's file?"

Alepho's brows knitted. "It is not lost," he said. "It was stolen."

A stolen file. That sounded hopeless. How did a refugee file get stolen? Why would anyone want it? And what could they do about that from here?

"People steal them," Benson said, as though reading my mind, "and sell them to rich men." There was outrage in Benson's voice, but he averted his eyes. I worried I was intruding on painful stuff they'd rather not have to talk about.

I took a bite of my sandwich. "Sure you don't want something to eat?" Oh jeez, how stupid did that sound?

"Our uncle needs help," Benson added.

"Help?" I mumbled. "What happened?"

"His brother was killed. He takes care of the family now. They are hungry."

The bite became a dry wad in my mouth. I wanted to know about the rest of their family but I was afraid to ask. Cliff hadn't said a word. I wrapped up the fish sandwich and snuck it into the trash. "Let's go see the Pacific Ocean."

CROCODILES?

Judy

We drove from the mall parking lot onto a wide boulevard.

"Oohs" and "aahs" erupted from the back seat. "Is this freeway?"

"This is just an avenue, but it leads to the freeway. You'll know when we get there."

A multilevel interchange loomed ahead. I pointed it out. We rose to the top of the on-ramp. They peered out the window and chatted in Dinka.

What I saw ahead was not so exciting: a freeway packed with crawling cars.

"Traffic," I grumbled.

They exclaimed all at once, "*Rush Hour* Jackie Chan!"

Cliff turned around and said, "*Rush Hour 2* is coming out."

How in the world did they see or know about the first one? "Did you see the first movie?"

"In Kakuma. Five shillings. We grow okra and sell it."

What? My visual image of refugee camps came from newsreels of crowded white tents in desolate places. Not vegetable gardens and movie theaters.

We entered the freeway at a creep. Frustration filled me. I wanted them to experience it at full speed. We also needed to get to the beach and still have time for the park or a museum.

Cliff pointed out Qualcomm Stadium.

"We would like to go there," one of them said.

A baseball game. A potentially fun possibility. Hot dogs, popcorn, and sodas, of course—the whole American experience.

The traffic moved at a snail's pace. The boys fired questions from the back seat about car dealerships, malls, and many other things I hadn't paid attention to in years. After commuting to work for twenty years, a freeway at anything but full speed made me antsy and irritable.

A truck cut in front of us. I stifled an obscenity and considered hitting the horn. The truck attempted another lane change and the cars in the next two lanes released a chorus of honks.

"Are they angry?" Benson asked.

"Yes."

"Why?"

Good question. Everyone moved so slowly that his lane changes hadn't really affected anyone.

"People are just in a hurry," I said, glad I hadn't joined the honkers.

Cliff pointed out boarders swooping and diving at a skate park. "That's my favorite sport."

I realized the slow pace was making the drive more interesting for them and giving Cliff time to explain things. I turned on the radio. As they delighted in their new world, Bob Marley's "Legends" played in the background. An epiphany enveloped me like the coolness from the air conditioner. Why was I in such a rush to get to the beach? I'd been so focused on my plan that I'd nearly missed these precious moments. These boys had fled naked on bloody feet, hoping to stay ahead of another bomb falling from the sky. What was it like for them to be traveling in a cushioned seat, safe in a belt, water in hand, music all around, with cool air and new clothes? I thought I had insight, gratitude, and balance, yet I'd forgotten the simple pleasure and appreciation of traveling in a car. Unless I was about to give birth—and that wasn't going to happen—I vowed to never be impatient about traffic again. I would turn on the music and relax.

The freeway cleared. We passed downtown San Diego and headed onto the soaring blue arc that is the Coronado Bridge. At its apex, which was high enough for almost any ship to pass beneath, aircraft carriers and battleships came into view, skirted by delicate white-sailed boats.

They leaned toward the windows and gestured and rattled on in Dinka.

Beyond Coronado Island, the ocean spread to infinity in a silver haze.

"Ooh. Is that Pacific Ocean?" Benson asked.

"Yes, that's it. We'll go down where you can touch it."

"We've never seen ocean close up," Benson said.

I'd begun to be able to distinguish their voices. Alepho's was deep and quiet. Benson had a slightly different accent, and Lino was a man of few words but spoke the loudest and clearest when he did.

Benson went on. "We saw the Red Sea at night when we left Sudan. We saw the ocean from the plane when we came to New York. But it was night when we came to San Diego."

"Are there crocodiles?" Alepho asked.

I almost chuckled at the idea, but stopped myself as the *60*

Minutes segment came to mind. I looked at their faces in the rearview mirror. They would have been younger than Cliff when they'd had to cross the Gilo River.

"The beaches are safe," I said. Caution about sharks could wait.

Since Coronado Island links to the mainland it is technically a peninsula. We drove south on the aptly named Silver Strand, a long sliver of beach that rejoins the continent close to the border with Mexico, past high-rise condos, gated communities, and mansions with docks and yachts. I pulled into a public beach and parked the car.

A strong onshore breeze carried a fine mist that was as palpable as it was visible, cooling the hot August day. The lustiness of the living ocean ripened the air.

Our first-time visitors lifted their heads and sucked the foreign aroma into their nostrils. I did the same. Wonderful memories of fishing with my dad or walking along the pier came to mind. It smelled like home to me. How was it for them?

I brought out the three disposable cameras and explained how to take photos.

"Do you have photos of family?" Alepho asked.

"Yes. I will bring some next time."

We headed across the broad beach, through deep sand. Long-limbed Lino took off at a lope with the ground-covering strides of a Thoroughbred colt. He reached the surf's edge when a wave was in full retreat and bent to touch the water. A new wave pounded toward him and he scurried back toward us. When the line of water slowed to a halt on the dry sand, he touched the white foam and exclaimed, "Wow!"

I'd been hoping for that response.

We all ceremoniously dipped our fingers into the earth's greatest body of water. Even though I'd grown up on the Pacific

Ocean, in all my years I had never experienced it quite so fully as in that moment.

They snapped pictures, mostly of Cliff. Lino held his camera at cockeyed angles and fired and reloaded like a machine gun. He'd taken all his photos within the first few minutes as though it were a race. Benson looked through his viewfinder and moved forward and backward, up and down, carefully considering his composition, just like an artist. Alepho, the observer, as I'd begun to think of him, was distracted by the washed-up shells and seaweed. He hadn't taken more than one or two pictures.

The beach wasn't crowded. Kites floated in the air and a few sunbathers had established their territories equidistant from each other. Cliff wrote CLIFF WAS HERE in giant letters in the wet sand. I took a picture.

Benson pulled out his notepad and wrote or drew something. He gestured toward the water. "Are there dolphins?"

"Yes, and whales too."

"The sea mammals."

Alepho pointed at a beached kelp float almost the size of a soccer ball with a twenty-foot tail.

"It's just a plant," I said. "You can touch it. It's called kelp and grows out in the ocean. Those balls make its branches float." He looked relieved. Cliff jumped on one and it burst open.

Noisy gulls called and circled above us.

"I saw seagulls in a book," Alepho said, "but I never saw them in person. We do have many pelicans in Africa."

From their comments, their educational background seemed broad and their curiosity limitless. They possessed so much hope and promise, but I feared our inner-city living might suck it out of them like a vacuum. They'd survived a war; did that equip them to thrive in a ghetto?

We walked south, passing people sprawled in the sun. Some wore the latest trend in swimwear: thongs. The guys chatted away in Dinka as though the sea life deposited by the surf held their interest more than the barely covered women. Maybe they were too shy to acknowledge the bare buttocks? Still I didn't want to embarrass them by asking what Dinka women wore.

I shared some safety tips. "Swim where there are lifeguards. Watch for dangerous currents and jellyfish. A few beaches might have sharks but the lifeguards are careful to warn people."

"Is it allowed to take people's pictures?" Alepho asked.

"It's polite to ask them first if you would like to do that."

He pointed toward some waders in the far distance. He wanted a photograph of Americans at the beach just like a tourist on safari wanted to capture the Maasai.

"That is fine. You only need to ask permission if they are close."

We stood for a while, looking out toward the horizon. What were they feeling? A war had stolen everything except their lives. Now they'd been plopped into a foreign land with strange people and languages and objects they'd never dreamed existed. Did they look back and think of their loved ones stranded in some godforsaken camp, or worse, back in the war? Did they wonder if they'd ever see Sudan or even Africa again? Were they hopeful or homesick?

We headed away from the water; gooseflesh pimpled their skin. They were so thin.

Back in the sun-heated car, I wanted air-conditioning, but they rubbed their arms and sighed in pleasure at the warmth. A large chunk of the day remained. "Shall we go to the park?"

A brief discussion in Dinka ensued. "Yes," Benson said. "That would be very good."

SMELLS LIKE SEWAGE

Alepho

Judy said that we would go see the ocean. I couldn't wait. I'd read about the oceans. I couldn't imagine something so big. My father had told me there was a huge lake to the west of Dinkaland where white people lived. I think that huge lake might have been an ocean.

Judy drove across a very high bridge. "That is the ocean out there," she said. It didn't look like the water bodies that I had seen. I couldn't see any water, just fuzzy white clouds on the ground.

Judy stopped the car. We got out. What was that smell? People said they loved the smell of the ocean. This smelled like washed-up sewage.

We started across a wide sandy area. The ground looked beautiful, but the air was cold and the not-fresh smell made me uncomfortable in my body.

The sand sloped down. Then I saw the ocean. The blue water had a white mist hanging over it. It was so close. We had just passed by houses. Why did people build houses so near to this vast water? If the water decided to come out in flood season it would wash all those houses away. I was glad the house they gave us was far from this huge water. If they gave me one here for free, I wouldn't take it.

We walked down the slope. "The water is coming," I said, stopping. Lino was already next to it. The water rose up. Lino ran away. The water fell down in a crash and white foam spread across the sand. The water did that again, like it was trying to come on land but it couldn't.

Judy gave us each a little box. "This is a camera. It takes photos."

It didn't look like the camera she'd used before. In the camp we had sometimes gone to the Ethiopian area, where people held a large black box and took a picture of us. The way that thing made the picture on a piece of paper baffled me. How was it possible? I had never seen something like that until I arrived in Kakuma camp.

When we were at Walmart and Judy took our picture with Cliff, she told us to smile. We were smiling anyway to be there. But in the camp, we just stood there. I thought you were supposed to act how you were feeling. I hadn't felt like smiling back in the camp.

Judy explained how to use the camera. Point it, push the button, and twist the knob. As I held it in my hand, I felt educated. If I went back to the camp holding this thing in my hand, people would respect me. People didn't know the name of a camera or how to use one. I would have this mysterious thing and only I could explain it because I was educated. If I pointed it at them, they wouldn't know what I was doing.

We walked down the beach. Cliff dug his heel into the sand and wrote CLIFF WAS HERE in huge letters. At school in the camp, I'd learned how to write in the sand. We smoothed a place in the dirt in front of the rock we sat on and that was our paper. Our finger was the pen and we made symbols that represented sounds.

Down the beach, strange brown things that looked like pythons with cobra heads coiled on the wet sand. I stood back and pointed at them.

Judy said, "That's kelp. It's a plant."

I'd seen plants in the Nile River that were like grass. This one had round things, big as the soccer balls we'd made from old rags.

Cliff jumped on a ball. It burst open and water drained out. Instinctively, I had thought one should not touch them, but Cliff knew that it was okay because this was his land. He had taken the initiative. We were the kids here even though he was smaller and younger. I followed him and burst one of the kelp balls, too, feeling relief that it wasn't dangerous and that I wasn't destroying something precious to his culture.

I became used to the smell of the ocean, but was still cold. The place was beautiful. But even if they offered for me to live there, I wouldn't say yes because of the danger from the water.

Up on the dry sand, a woman lay on a small rug in tiny underwear. Farther down the beach, I saw another woman like this. The people I'd seen in movies, the UN workers who came to the camp, and the people in San Diego all wore clothes. Why were these women showing their bodies? Was it so that a man could see they looked good and if he admired them, they could begin to court?

I wanted to share my thoughts with Judy, but she might think, *Oh, this boy just got out of a refugee camp and he's having all kinds of judgments about us.* When you are not sure about a culture or environment, you are always afraid to say the wrong thing. I had to control my tongue so that I did not make my host uncomfortable. We had all been doing a lot of that controlling to be sensitive to Judy and her culture.

I said to Benson in Dinka, "What an interesting display. They take everything off except just covering those vital places."

In our village, women left their tops bare from the waist up. Their bottoms and legs were covered with a decorated sheepskin or goatskin that had been put through a process that made it soft and tender instead of itchy. Sometimes they added other decorations like beads. The skirt was long enough to cover their legs. Once they were seven or eight years old, girls never got naked. The reason was not that men lusted after them. Men were taught not to lust. The reason was because the women respected themselves.

Men wore wild animal skins for celebrations. When I was born, clothes were available but not everyone could afford clothing, so men often went naked. Boys were usually naked. I'd been naked when I left my village.

In the refugee camp, everyone wore clothes.

I said to Benson, "It is strange they do this here. These people are rich, they drive nice cars, everything looks clean, and they have nice houses. Where is the place that people meet each other?" In our village, young people gathered at cattle camp. Boys and girls went there as teens to meet each other. "If there is no other place, maybe this is the place you show yourself."

Lino said, "I don't know, but it looks to me like there is nothing else that is left to cover actually. They are really naked."

Judy said, "Let's go to the park."

I wasn't sure what a park would be. We all said, "Yes, let's go."

The car was warm. I stopped shivering, but a headache was coming so I didn't talk. Talking makes headaches worse.

The park was green with plants and big trees. I saw that a park was a place for nature, where it was not paved over like the city, but it was so small. You could walk across it in less than an hour. Why didn't they give nature big lands? In the park they had rules too. You couldn't pee or spit like in the nature areas in Africa.

People walked around. Was this American entertainment? I found my entertainment in nature too. I liked the trees, mountains, and rivers. But more open, not squeezed.

We went to a place Judy called a museum. There were animal skeletons and some had fur and looked alive, but they were dead. Dinosaurs as well. What interested me was all the information and scientific names they put on the wall. Even though I had a bad headache, all that information gave me joy.

EATING MUD

Judy

I took the shortest route to the park, which meant climbing the steep Laurel Street hill that had terrified me as a child when my mother was learning to drive a manual transmission. No doubt it scared her too. The car angled sharply upward and the engine roared. We were thrown back against the seats.

"Wow," Lino exclaimed.

Across the bridge we entered Balboa Park and parked the car.

"Benson is hungry," Cliff said.

We needed to get our stomachs on the same time clock or eating would be our main activity.

"Is there a McDonald's?" Benson asked.

He got me on that one. I'd told them that McDonald's was everywhere in the world. "No, not right here. By everywhere I meant to say they are in most countries."

He looked at me and tilted his head. "Not in Sudan."

I didn't know, but it sounded likely. We walked toward a

little café, passing a photo display of San Diego over the last hundred years.

"Did you study American history?" I asked, knowing they would eventually have to face it on the GED test.

"No. We want to learn American history," Benson said. "Very important. We want to know all about America. We are Americans now."

Their enthusiasm was contagious and made seeing my own world in a whole new way fascinating and so enjoyable.

Alepho wanted a sandwich. Lino settled on Greek pasta salad and Benson only wanted a soda. Wasn't he the hungry one? He hadn't yet chosen to eat with us except sodas. What was that about?

The sandwich arrived. Alepho picked off the top piece of wheat bread slathered in mayonnaise, folded it in half and took a bite.

Yuck. He wasn't going to like sandwiches, but I didn't want to comment so I picked up mine altogether and took a bite. He watched, put his bread back on top and lifted the whole thing to his mouth.

"What is this?" He pointed inside the sandwich.

Cliff laughed. Greens weren't his favorite either.

"Lettuce," I said. "Green leaves."

Alepho looked suspicious.

"It's safe and good for you. What did you eat in the Kenyan camp? Any fish, chicken or beef?" Didn't one need some kind of protein to survive?

"Fish no good, make you sick. No chicken or beef. Three kilos of grain and corn every two weeks."

Three kilos. Almost seven pounds. Spread over fourteen days came out to about a cup a day. I imagined Cliff trying to figure out how to live off that. They were thin but looked strong. White teeth. Healthy gums. So far, I hadn't sensed any resistance to my probing questions about the camp, but they hadn't elaborated either. As eager as I was to understand how small boys survived a thousand-mile walk through the African wilderness, they were trauma victims and our relationship was new. It was hard to know what to ask, yet disinterest felt uncaring.

"What did you eat when you first left home, when you were walking?"

They all talked at once.

"Fruits growing in the wild," Benson said.

"Nothing to eat," Lino added.

Cliff glanced at me uncomfortably.

Alepho said, "To keep our stomachs from hurting, we ate mud."

TONY HAWK

Judy

We walked around the park and poked our heads into a few museums. They seemed tired. Perhaps bored.

On the way home Alepho slept. He didn't look well. He'd eaten more than any of them. I hoped the café food hadn't made him ill. I wasn't sure what was best for any of them at this point.

We brought the computer components up to their apartment. Cliff hooked them up and plugged them in. Images of a man skateboarding filled the screen—Cliff's wallpaper.

"Who is that?"

"Tony Hawk," Cliff said. "Very famous American."

"Tony Hawk," they repeated, as though he might be on the American history portion of the GED test. Benson got out his notebook.

I'd brought a bag of large composition books and journals Paul had collected from conferences over the years and some pens and handed them out.

"I want to practice my writing," Alepho said. "Will you correct my English?"

"Yes, of course."

I'd also thrown in the paperbacks and dictionary I'd bought at the store. Alepho sat down with *To Kill a Mockingbird* and began reading it at once. I'd suspected he was a reader.

I glanced into the kitchen. Empty red Coca-Cola cans overflowed the trash, filled large clear trash bags and climbed the wall in stacks. There was no evidence of food or discarded food wrapping, not even bags of chips. I wanted to open the refrigerator to see if they'd bought any real food but that would have been downright rude.

"You like Coke?"

"Yes," they exclaimed.

"Did you drink it in Kenya?"

"Very expensive in Kenya."

Not cheap here either. I hoped they had enough money left to buy food. They'd certainly budgeted their corn ration in the camp, but this was probably their first experience budgeting money to buy essentials. At least their indulgence was only soda.

"Benson, I'd love to see your artwork sometime."

He brought out several drawings and showed them first to Cliff. Cliff turned to me. "Look at these."

Benson's colors were vibrant and his images bold. In the first picture a boy tended cows. Each cow had unique markings rendered in vivid orange, brown, black, and white. His sense of composition and color was excellent. The second and third drawings were villages of mud wall huts with women cooking and children running around.

"These are wonderful."

Benson had a hint of surprise in his eyes and he grinned. I

pointed to a girl in the picture. "What happened to the girls from the villages?"

"There are Lost Girls," Alepho said.

"Where are they?"

"They are in the camp, but there are not so many as the boys. Maybe only like one thousand. Most were killed in the villages because they couldn't leave by themselves like the boys." His voice rose, his tone indignant. "Some of the girls they take as slaves. That is why we run, because we don't want to go in the northern army or be taken as slaves. When they raid the villages, they take the young girls and boys back with them to the north to work in the houses. My cousin Deng was a house slave. He wash the people and sleep with the goats. Very, very bad for him."

House slave? People still had slaves? The girls' duties no doubt went beyond washing. Boys too, for that matter. "Do you think some of the Lost Girls will come here?"

"I don't know. Maybe some will come."

Benson brought out a fourth drawing. A tank billowed smoke from the big gun on the front. An explosion in a village sent brown people fleeing or lying dead. In the foreground, a man outfitted in camouflage aimed a gun. The man was undeniably white.

"Is he a good or bad man?" I asked.

"Bad man. He is from the north."

The shooter's gun was some type of automatic weapon.

"Did your father have a gun?"

"No. My father fight with spear."

Machine guns against spears. Lopsided civil war. Sounded more like genocide.

The time to leave grew near. I gave Lino an eighth-grade algebra workbook. They looked through it together. "We did that work in the fourth term." They all beamed.

Interesting. What did "term" equate to here?

"What will you do for the weekend?" I asked.

They looked at me strangely.

"You know, for fun. Saturday and Sunday."

That didn't seem to clarify my question.

"We will be here." Benson had a perplexed look on his face.

I explained that we would be gone for two weeks. We said our goodbyes and headed out. On the way home Cliff was excited—bouncing around in the seat and waving to cars that passed by. Was this my self-conscious twelve-year-old? When we hit heavy Friday-night traffic, I smiled and whispered to myself, "*Rush Hour*, Jackie Chan."

Cliff said, "Lino explained quadratic equations to me. He can say his times tables up to twenty-six."

Somehow the camp didn't have enough food, but the education system didn't seem to lack.

I hoped for more traffic so my time alone with Cliff could last longer. I loved to travel, but this day had rivaled any I'd passed in a foreign country. I hadn't spent thousands of dollars or journeyed days to get there either. I hadn't even used up a tank of gas.

At the back of my mind, I was still wondering what I should do. I had two weeks to think about it.

LOOK INTO MY EYES

Alepho

Judy brought us a computer. Our excitement was that of children receiving their first toy. The problem was, we didn't know how to use the computer. Cliff set it up and demonstrated how to turn it on and shut it down and showed me how to move a thing he called a mouse on the table. That made the little arrow move about on the computer screen. He left it on for us to play with when he was gone.

When they left, Lino shut the computer down by pushing the power button. Benson said, "Judy said it destroys a computer to do that. You must always shut it down with the mouse."

Benson was always keen and warning everybody about taking care of things. He didn't say much, but when he did, he meant it. His word choice was short, simple, precise, truthful, and to the point. No more, no less.

We watched television most of the days when we weren't doing business with Joseph or taking classes at IRC. I could see from the television that there were two ways that people came to know you in America. If you did something good that attracted the admiration of people or if you committed a crime that was widely broadcast in the news.

Daniel and James worried and talked all the time of the requirements for a refugee to have a job within three months. They had been in America longer than that. They had jobs, but their jobs only gave them one or two days of work. They said that wasn't enough to make their livings. I began to worry about where to look for a job. I saw people working everywhere, but how did they get that job?

The IRC programs helped prepare us for the baby steps of our new life in America. We had English class taught by a beautiful American woman who showed us how to ask and answer questions with an Americanized English tone. Another young American woman taught us job-readiness techniques. She said, "When you go to a job interview, first and foremost, dress professionally. Smile and greet them with high energy and attitude. Look the interviewer in the eyes when you answer questions."

The eye-contact thing seemed strange to me. Especially if the person giving me an interview was older than me. In my country, a young person could not hold straight eye contact with an older person. When I was young, I was not allowed to look at my parents' eyes for long intervals. That was disrespectful to the elders. Adults are viewed as almost gods and must be revered highly. A child who does not look into the eyes of an adult is regarded as respectful, sensible, and perhaps has an understanding of life.

When the job teacher noticed that we wouldn't look into her eyes when we had a conversation, it seemed inappropriate for her to correct us. Was it to be the same with Judy? I did not know what was going on in their minds, but it felt rude to be looking into their eyes. How would I look into the eyes of the most powerful person, a company president or boss, while being interviewed?

The teacher said, "Looking into the eyes determines if you are being truthful or lying. The eyes are the windows to the soul of a human being."

I couldn't know people by looking into their eyes. I could only know them through their words and actions.

I practiced, but I was shy. Every time I looked into her eyes I broke out laughing.

"I can't look in the eyes," I said.

"Why not?"

"It is aggressive to look in a person's eyes." Like I was trying to extract something from them.

"If you don't make eye contact with the person you are talking to, they will think you are hiding something."

We all practiced more and looked into her eyes. Pretty soon, all three of us were laughing together, it was so hard to look into her eyes. The job teacher smiled, but she wanted us to be serious, so we tried to stop laughing.

The teacher said, "Next you must learn that in America, smiling is the point of contact. Make sure you always smile. Use your beautiful African smiles. That gets Americans' attention."

We practiced and acted those things out in class. I smiled forcefully, but it felt awkward showing my teeth. The teacher said, "That is good. Flashing a smile will impress people and they will smile back at you." My grin felt like a cat who had swallowed a bird.

The teacher said, "To be courteous you should say who you are."

Americans seemed to think people automatically knew how to flush a toilet, turn on a light, and greet people. I had to learn those things and I needed our sponsor to show us.

BIG FAMILY

Judy

Upon our return from the trip, I called the guys' apartment, eager to see them again. Cliff was already back in school. Alepho answered. "We are about to take the bus to the IRC office."

"If you want to wait, I can drive you there."

Benson greeted me at the door with a warm smile and hand-shake. I hugged him and went inside. They all reached out to shake hands but I hugged them instead, I was so happy to see them. They seemed a little uncomfortable, but I decided getting used to hugs was part of their acculturation.

They wore the new pants, belts, and shoes we'd bought at Walmart.

"You guys look very nice. How is everything going? I brought a few family photos to share with you."

Some of the photos had been taken on our recent trip to Lake Havasu, but they were more interested in one that had been taken in our driveway. "That was my father's eightieth birthday party with all of my brothers, sisters, spouses, cousins, aunts, and uncles."

There were at least twenty-five of us in the photo. They asked me to explain each person.

"Big family," Benson said.

"Yes," I said, wondering if I'd just reminded him that his family, for the most part, had been destroyed.

It must have triggered something because they began telling me about fleeing their villages. The night Benson and Lino left, Alepho was five. He left two years later when his village was attacked again.

"When did you meet up?"

"In 1992."

"Five years. Wow. That must have been something to see your brother after so much time."

Alepho said, "He look so different, but still he was my brother."

"Very much crying and joyfulness," Benson added.

"I can imagine." But I really couldn't. I couldn't imagine being separated from family so young and for so many years because of a war. All that time not knowing who was alive. Or dead. I couldn't imagine wondering if I'd ever have family again or begin to know what it must feel like to find a brother after all those years.

"I have headaches and nightmares," Alepho said.

I'd heard that could be a symptom of post-traumatic stress disorder. "Joseph told me he was getting you some medicine for your stomach. Is it feeling better?"

"No. I lose my appetite."

"Did you have this when you were in Kakuma?"

"It is worse here."

"Then you must tell Joseph."

"I must wait for card."

What card? He was asking for help and I was already lost.

Alepho brought out a *Newsweek* magazine.

"Did you like reading it?" I asked.

"Yes, it is good book. I learn many things about America."

"Great. I will bring you more like it."

"Yesterday I read about a pedophile."

He said it without emotion or humor and not looking at me. They seldom looked at me. *Wonderful. A pedophile. Welcome to America.* I was embarrassed but also had a protective feeling, like he shouldn't have been exposed to those weaknesses in our society yet. A silly response. Surely, it was no different in Africa. He was a grown man who had been through a war. Even Cliff was probably aware of those sorts.

He opened the magazine to an article called "Out of Africa."

"This is about us," he said.

The Lost Boys article that I'd read several months earlier. "I read that last May," I told him, trying to make eye contact. "That is how I knew some of your story." I wanted to read it again. The details would have more meaning now.

He smiled and glanced at my eyes before looking down again. I'd ask Joseph about that. Even if it was uncomfortable for them, they needed to change that habit of looking down or away when they spoke. It wouldn't serve them in any situation here.

"I was told that in America it is important to look into a person's eyes," he said, as if reading my mind. "That is not acceptable in Sudan."

He didn't look at me again. "I'm sorry if I made you uncomfortable. Here, it is good to look people in the eyes. It shows that you have interest in what the person is saying."

"I'm learning that," he said with another glance into my eyes. His attempts to adapt were admirable. "Must one call before visiting?"

He could jump from one subject to another faster than I could conceive of a thoughtful answer. "That is polite, yes."

"I want to be a doctor," he said.

We talked about their education, English classes, GED test, and going to college. We understood each other better each time we met, but our conversations were like talking over an old-fashioned long-distance line, where there's a time lapse while the transmission travels the cable. They often paused after a sentence, and I was too quick to interject or answer, not realizing they weren't done. I overran their words. Worse, when two, or even all of them, talked at once, they just went on talking at the same time, in the same tone, not raising their volume to compete with one another and forcing me to decide who to listen to.

The conversation about education gathered them around with bubbling enthusiasm. Obviously, education was their top priority. I explained the structure of our school system and the process of becoming a doctor.

"Too many years to be doctor," Lino said.

"There is saying in Sudan," Benson said. "Get education and fight with your mind."

Benson had a large collection of sayings and proverbs. I wished I had a gift for remembering like that. "And you will find good work too," I told him.

Mentioning work brought up a whole new round of questions and concerns.

"I want to work," Benson said.

"What do you want to do?" I asked.

"Any work. Do you know of work near our house?"

I shook my head. "I'm sorry, but I live thirty miles north of here and don't know people or businesses in this area. Joseph said the IRC will help you to find jobs. Focus on school. Once you pass the GED, there are scholarships or grants to help with college."

"Madam Judy," Lino said.

It occurred to me then that they hadn't addressed me as anything yet.

"Please call me Judy. We aren't so formal here."

They smiled but didn't look convinced.

On the way to IRC we stopped by the bank. Each one received eighty dollars a week. They cashed the checks and stuffed the money in their pockets. No wallets. I wondered how many more months they'd receive this assistance.

I was hungry and we had some time to kill. "Do you want to try Mexican food?" A taco shop was just across the street, and I was eager to introduce them to my favorite food.

"No. American."

We walked to McDonald's again. While we ate, I recalled an article that claimed City Heights was one of the most diverse communities in America. Just looking around inside the McDonald's confirmed it to be true. As I pondered that, Alepho said, "We think Americans are beautiful people."

"Really?" I was thinking what a motley, mixed-up bunch we must look like to them. From pasty white and splotchy pink to every shade of brown and black imaginable; from short to tall, thin to fat, though not too many thin people here in McDonald's. Couples didn't match each other, and many kids didn't look like the parents they were with. Lots of variety and still the three Sudanese men stood out. Tall, thin, darker than anyone else, plus their perfect posture gave them a regal bearing. Not to mention, they were dressed more formally than anyone else. "Why do you think Americans are beautiful?"

"Americans very smooth."

"I think many Americans are too fat," I said. "It's not healthy."

"I want to be fat," Alepho declared. "In Sudan there is a competition. The men drink milk for a month and the fattest man wins the prettiest, most clever girl to marry."

Lino held up his well-muscled arm and pointed. "You see the muscles."

I did. Only long hours in a gym would produce that enviable definition.

"Look ugly," he concluded.

"Americans like to see the muscles," I said, thinking that in an odd way showing them some of our magazines with underfed models might actually be a good thing for their self-esteem. "I think the Sudanese are beautiful people."

BLIND DATE

Alepho

Our roommates Daniel and James had become acquainted with life in the US. They said we had to pay for everything. I didn't understand. I thought the house and the things in it belonged to all of us, just like the camp. "Food, water, rent, and electricity too," they said. "In America, you gotta get moving."

Excitement left me. How would I pay for these things? I wanted to get moving, but where does a person go to look for a job? I saw signs for all kinds of food, discount stores, and places to get quick money, but I had not seen any signs that said JOBS.

Most importantly, I needed to complete my education in America. I'd had that goal since I was a child in my village and saw a white streak make its way across the sky.

"What is that?" I'd asked my father.

"Alepho, that's the big bird."

"Where does it come from?"

My father pointed west. "Far away, where the sun sets, there is a huge lake. Only the big bird can cross it. On the other side of that lake is another land where white people live. They use magic power to control the big bird."

"How do they get magic power?"

"They go to school. They have education."

I was only four, but that story stuck with me. I wanted that magic power, too.

The next year a new kind of learning came to our village. My father sold many cows to send my brother Yier, the oldest son of his first wife, to a place called school.

Yier went away for a season to study. When he returned from the university he looked different. The men of our village either wore nothing or the traditional *jalabiyas,* long sand-colored shirts that nearly reached the ground. Yier had a short blue shirt and a separate garment that covered each leg, which he called pants.

All of us village children, maybe fifty together, gathered around Yier. He told us stories we'd never heard before, stories not told in our village. He removed a flat white thing, like a big leaf, from his bag. He asked each child his or her name and scratched the white thing with a small stick that made marks. "Come back tomorrow," he instructed us.

We gathered early the next morning. Yier held up the white sheet with the marks and spoke each of our names in the exact order we had given them the day before. When he called, "Alepho," I couldn't even answer. How did he get our names from the white thing? My brother had become a wizard.

"How did you become a wizard?" I asked.

"School," he said. "That is where I learned to read and write. It doesn't make me a wizard, but it is magical."

I wanted that magic power to fly the big bird and know things like a wizard. But my chance to go to school did not come. War came instead.

Now, here I was in America where people had the magic. I had to find a way to get my education.

• • •

In the evenings, we gathered in the main room of the apartment to watch the television. *BBC World News* was our favorite. A local news show came on after that with news about the weather in San Diego. A man talked so fast that I couldn't understand him, but at the end he always shouted the station name in a funny way. I liked that part. Some shows were about animals, and even though I grew up with lots of animals, educational shows about them—with someone explaining what they ate, how they hunted, and where they lived—interested me. I realized that television was a place to begin my education.

One afternoon I discovered television shows about American culture. I looked forward each day to *Blind Date* and *The 5th Wheel*, which explained two ways to meet girls in America.

In *Blind Date,* the guy stepped out of a nice vehicle, dressed well, and used proper English to impress the lady. It seemed that before I met a girl I needed a car, fancy clothes, and to work on my English skills.

Sometimes the dates did not go well. A beep sounded when they spoke, and their mouths went blurry, as though magic had shut off their words.

"They are saying curse words," James explained.

Those dates were called "Dates from Hell."

When the dates went well and the lady and man got together, they called them "Hot Zones."

The 5th Wheel was more complicated. Two men and two ladies met each other and all went out together. One more man or one more woman joined them. At the end of the show each person voted on who they would like to go on a date with.

Everyone said that America was a diverse country, but I didn't understand at first that they meant the cultures were diverse also. Now I saw there was more than one way to meet a girl in America. Both of these cultures were different from Dinka culture. When approaching a Dinka girl you did not reveal your true personality the first time you met. You went with manners. Some of the people on the American dating shows were so blunt. Only after you had known a Dinka girl for some time could you reveal your true personality like that. The people on TV revealed their true personality on the first date.

I fell between two worlds. Because I'd left my village when I was so young I only knew a little about my own culture, and I didn't know *anything* about American culture. Now that I was here, I needed to understand how American people lived.

What I saw on TV was the American life—so, if I wanted to be an American, I needed to learn these things.

SUN VALLEY

Judy

In early September, Paul and I flew to Boise for a writing conference in Sun Valley. Soon after I'd begun working on my novel, Paul had started a medical thriller and joined my weekly writers group.

It was late morning and at least a hundred degrees outside by the time we started out in a rental car. The air-conditioning ran full blast. Although Idaho wasn't the official "Big Sky Country," these vistas stretched for fifty miles or more. It was gorgeous.

Yet, as I gazed out the window, I wasn't contemplating the writer's conference or even the beauty of the surrounding terrain. All I could envision were little boys walking across something this hot, this barren, and this immense. Thousands like them had made that journey, but it was Benson, Lino, and Alepho who were on my mind. Their stories varied in detail, but each had lost everything a child needs. What kind of impact did that have on a person? When did they realize that they weren't going home? They'd told me so much about the sounds, the smells, the guns, and the deprivation, but nothing about their confusion and terror. I thought I had grasped it intellectually, but I couldn't feel it. It was too foreign from anything in my own reality.

"What's that glassy-eyed stare?" Paul asked. "You look like you're writing a whole chapter in your head."

"Well, not exactly."

"Is there something distracting you from finishing your book?"

"No, I'm just thinking."

"I'm not supposed to say anything, right?"

I smiled. "Not a word."

"I know what it is."

I shook my head. He probably did. Thirty years of marriage rendered private thoughts elusive. "You're right. This last couple of weeks have given me a lot to think about."

"You told me not to let you get distracted from your novel."

"I know. I'll finish it. But you'll understand when you meet them."

He turned to me. "I already understand. But you've helped people before, like your SDSU students, and still wrote."

"I know," I said and touched my fingers to the heated glass of the window.

"This is different, isn't it?"

"Yes, it's different."

"How?"

Some of the students I'd helped were refugees, but mostly adults like Joseph, established, with their own lives and families. Already involved in their communities, enough so they took on projects to help their communities even further. I only assisted them with those projects, not their lives. "It's hard to put into words. But I guess you could say they are different because I see a huge potential in them that is at great risk here in the US."

He leaned back in the seat, straightened his arms against the steering wheel, and looked over at me. "You keep telling me how smart and well educated they are. How they have strong values and are disciplined. Maybe you're underestimating them."

I pondered that for a moment. "That's interesting—I'd been thinking everyone else was underestimating them. The articles and TV shows all talk about how they were coming from the Stone Age. So insulting. They're much more complex than that. Their situation may have been Stone Age, but they have substantial education. When I bring up politics or what's going on in the world, they're often more informed than I am. You might be right, I could be underestimating *them*, but I don't think I'm underestimating how challenging it's going to be for them here. They'll be lucky to start at minimum wage jobs, so they definitely have to work full time. I'm just afraid they'll fall into that trap of sacrificing themselves for their kids like most immigrants do. They're still kids themselves. I'd hate to see them not be able to get that education they really want."

"Sounds like an opportunity to make a positive difference in someone's life. Isn't that what you always wanted to do?"

"Can I make a difference?"

"Now who's underestimating?"

"My novel might make a difference too. Besides, I've always wanted to finish something. I get distracted too easily. That's my problem."

He gave me a familiar grin. "I know. I was one of those distractions."

He was. We'd married when I was nineteen and he was twenty-one. I had quit college in my second year to work while he went to medical school. "But I'm thirty years older now. I said I would finish the book. I'm going to focus on finishing the book."

HARD CULTURE

Alepho

Sometime after I'd arrived in Kakuma camp, my friend Santino told me, "If a girl sees you cooking that will be a shame on you. Only women do cooking."

My mother and sisters cooked for my father and us boys, but that was in the village. No one had ever said that my father and brothers weren't allowed to cook. I'd been cooking or finding my own food since I left home.

"Why can't I cook?"

"You will be considered greedy. No girl will want to marry or engage you either."

From then on, we cooked together near our huts where women or girls wouldn't see us. Yet, I had felt overwhelmed by the hard culture of my people. Since I'd been in America, I'd read about men who were the best cooks in the world. How could that be?

Santino had also told me, "Wherever you go or live, Alepho, remember not to forget your culture."

It had been difficult as a young boy in the camp to stick to and value my Dinka traditions. I'd left my village young and did not learn much about our ways. By the time I reached America, I had been wandering by myself for almost thirteen years, without parental teaching and care. There was no one to teach me my own traditions.

Cultural things were rare in the refugee camp where so many people of different backgrounds were stranded together. And, when one is destitute, life itself becomes a jewel. Just being alive meant more to us than the type of cloth we wore or the way we cooked.

After being accepted to go to the US, we had weighed the pros and cons of going to a place we knew little about. Was it better than remaining in that desolate refugee camp in Kenya? Many called Kakuma home. It provided safety for tens of thousands.

Once I decided to go to America, I received three days of orientation. In the beginning when they taught us the basics like using a toilet or stove, I thought those were the most difficult things to learn and that's why they showed us those things first. I thought I knew what to expect. But I suppose nobody really learns about a country in three days.

America was not the melting pot of people where nobody did anything and machines did all the work like we'd been told in the camp. We'd believed that human work would be with the mind, not physical labor, which was why Americans were fatter and bigger, a status in my country and in the camp. Fatness meant wealth and prestige.

Other information we'd been given in the camp was also clearly wrong. Pillows were just soft things to sleep on. No matter how many pillows you owned, you wouldn't have your life's support in your hands.

We liked Judy, but I resented that our sponsor was skinny,

not as skinny as us, but she was not fat, just a person of average status and power. She said she didn't know how we could sign up for school or find a job. Joseph said to be patient and that the IRC would help. I felt unlucky in some ways.

Then there were the cards. Joseph said I needed a medical card to take care of my stomach pain. That card would come in September. And of course, the green card. So important to have a green card. In the refugee camp we had our ration card for food every sixteen days, and without it we could not get food. Now I needed a green card to support my life.

A green card was also the pathway to citizenship. I'd been an alien since age ten when I'd crossed into Kenya. When I received my green card, I'd no longer be an alien. I would transform into a man in my new world. Recognized as a citizen of a country. The green card was so important. I had to have it. Period.

NO-HITTER

Judy

The Sunday morning that we returned from Idaho, Shannan, a close friend, called. "Wanna go to the game?"

"Love to." Shannan often invited me to join her at Padres baseball games. Cliff and Paul were already going to the same game, but as we only had two season tickets, I usually stayed home. "Just tell me what time to be at your house."

"I can't go. Just wondered if you could use the tickets."

Shannan had four season tickets in the club section. Big, wide chairs right behind home plate, plenty of shade, servers who brought food, and bathrooms that never had lines.

I didn't hesitate. "Love to have the tickets," I told her. "I know three people who've never been to a baseball game, or a stadium for that matter."

I called Benson, Alepho, and Lino's house to see if they'd like to go. They did. When I arrived, Benson, Lino, and Alepho came out from the bedroom where the ironing board was set up. With their freshly pressed T-shirts and brand-new hats they'd be the best-dressed fans in the stadium.

"I like your baseball caps," I said.

They smiled.

We said goodbye to their friends. I wished I had ten tickets and a van.

Benson got in the front, as usual. He was the oldest. He handed me some folded papers. "These are for you," he said. "We want to work on our English."

I partially unfolded one but decided against it. I wanted to read them when I had adequate time. "Thank you, I'm eager to read them." I put them in my purse.

We headed north. I'd only gone a few blocks when a man stepped out into the middle of the street pushing two can-filled grocery carts. I slammed on the brakes. Even on this hottest of summer days he wore layer upon layer of clothes that had soiled into one brownish color. A dappled mutt trailed behind him.

"Why does he have a dog?" Lino asked.

"Probably for company and to keep him warm at night."

Benson cocked his head. "Why these people sleep outside?"

"They don't have a home."

"How does this happen in America?" Alepho asked.

He asked the tough questions. That particular man looked old enough to be a Vietnam vet, but I wasn't going to bring up post-traumatic stress disorder or being emotionally damaged by war.

Before I had an answer, Alepho said, "I gave a man two dollars. He said, 'Thank you, thank you' many, many times."

A creepy feeling came over me that this could be the fate of some of the Lost Boys. "That was nice of you," I told him, swooping down the freeway into Mission Valley. When they saw the stadium loom into view, they chattered in Dinka. I'd been rescued from the subject of the homeless in America.

Inside the stadium we headed for the food concession stand. Benson and Lino only wanted sodas. I couldn't seem to get Benson to try American food. I wondered what he ate at home; hopefully his diet wasn't all Coca-Cola. Alepho was up for that traditional hot dog I'd told them about. Food in hand, we started through the crowd.

We'd never been in such a crowded place. Benson, Lino, and Alepho were the tallest and darkest people anywhere in sight. I barely reached their shoulders, and they trailed behind me. People stared. I slowed down to walk beside them several times, but they slowed too, and we ended up in the same awkward formation.

I stepped onto the steep escalator that rose to our section. Halfway up I sensed that no one was following and looked back. Benson stood at the bottom, eyes riveted on the rising stairs. Of course, they'd never ridden an escalator. "Just step on," I yelled down. Benson poised his foot over the marching steps and finally chose one. Leaping aboard, he grabbed the rail to steady himself. Lino and Alepho watched and then followed in the same manner, juggling sodas and laughing, while trying to stay upright for the ride.

Suffering even more stares, we circled around through the inner hallway until we reached our section. At the doorway a view of the entire field and stadium opened like that first glimpse from the rim of the Grand Canyon. The stadium was full—more like a football crowd than a baseball one. This was a big game because the Padres were playing the Arizona Diamondbacks and their towering star, Randy Johnson, was pitching.

"Wow," Lino said, his mouth gaping.

I pointed to the only empty seats in our section and shouted over the noise of the crowd. "We sit just down there. Those empty seats."

As I descended the stairs, I noticed the contrast between the diverse crowd we'd just left in the rest of the stadium and the sea of light hair and white skin in this club section. Not one black person or even a person of any color. I'd been here many times. Why hadn't I noticed before today? Did they see it? Did they feel out of place?

Our four seats were on the aisle. With their usual courtesy, the guys insisted I go in first. Alepho sat to my immediate left, then Benson, and Lino on the aisle. To my right was a season-ticket holder—a middle-aged gentleman who was there every time Shannan and I came. He was a real baseball fan who knew every rule and player, eagerly answered our most inane questions about baseball, and loved to chitchat with Shannan, who usually sat beside him.

Down on the field three men dressed as fat friars—the Padres' mascot—raced around the field. The crowd roared.

"Hi," I said, like we were long-lost friends. He didn't respond. Maybe he couldn't hear me over the noise.

The race on the field ended—the friar in the hula print had won—and the crowd quieted.

Being weak on the subtleties of baseball, I hoped that if I had questions from my guests the man beside me could help. I tried again. "Nice day for a big game." I was also excited to introduce him to people from another continent, hoping he could help me to show them the game he loved so much.

Again, no acknowledgment, except that he was careful not to put his elbow on our shared armrest. When Shannan was sitting there, he was usually leaning in.

Thankfully, Alepho appeared absorbed in his food, balancing the cardboard box on his lap, ripping open the little condiment envelopes like mysterious treasures.

"How do you like the hot dog?" I asked.

"Dog is good." He spread the tiny green squares of sweet

pickle relish on the next bite. What did that taste like for the first time?

"Are your headaches getting better?"

"I have headache," he said.

One of the things I found most difficult in our stilted communications was their use of verb tenses. Had things occurred in the past and stopped or were they still occurring?

"You mean now?"

"Yes." Alepho rubbed his forehead.

"The headaches haven't stopped?"

He looked a little impatient with me but I wanted to understand.

"Yes."

I had to quit asking negative questions. Yes could mean no. His answer was probably technically correct, if one assumed that the laws of mathematics applied to linguistics.

More confused than ever, I offered Alepho two Excedrin, and he took them with his Coke. *That oughta do it.*

The players came out onto the field and started tossing the ball around to each other.

"May we see your house?" Alepho asked.

"Of course, I'd love that. Perhaps next week. You can swim."

I'd just made another commitment. Oh well, I needed one day off from writing.

"Swim at your house?"

"Yes, I have a pool."

"Pool?"

"Like the one near the library."

"Lino and Benson swim. I do not know how."

He'd mentioned that before. That horrible scene of swimming the Gilo River came to mind again. How had Alepho made it across unable to swim? So many missing pieces to the puzzle. So many questions that it felt wrong to ask. And uncaring not to ask.

The crowd rose. "Stand up," I said. "Take off your hats and put your right hand on your heart. This is our national anthem."

A singer on the field did a slow, dramatic rendition of "The Star-Spangled Banner." I doubted they'd heard it before. They looked serious and respectful. *How moving it must be to hear the national anthem of one's newly adopted country for the first time.*

We sat back down. I pointed to field level to show them where Paul and Cliff were sitting and then attempted a brief explanation of the game of baseball, hoping that once they saw it in action it would be self-evident.

The man next to me, usually so talkative, acted as though we weren't there. I'd begun to sense that he was perturbed by our presence and decided to test my theory before passing judgment. "Who do you think we'll put in as pitcher?"

He hesitated, but instead of answering he swiveled away from me toward his wife and grabbed another handful of peanuts. Sure, I wasn't making great baseball talk, but normally he'd strike up a friendly conversation. He may have thought the "I didn't hear you" technique was benign, but it lit a fire in my belly. I'd never experienced anything quite so rude for having done nothing in the first place.

The game started. Our pitcher was good. No hits. Every Diamondback struck out.

I leaned across Alepho so Benson and Lino could hear. "Randy Johnson pitches next for the other team. He's nearly seven feet tall."

"Like Dinka man," Benson said. "Dinka are the tallest tribe in Africa. My mother was seven feet. Taller than our father."

Interesting. These three were tall, but nowhere near seven feet. Closer to six.

Randy Johnson came to the mound and flung balls toward our hitters at over a hundred miles an hour.

Alepho said, "We're short. Not enough food in the camp for growing boys. The little children born in the camp have rickets. Their legs do not grow straight and their teeth do not come in."

I wondered if his lapful of food had provoked him to share that information.

The crowd roared every time Randy Johnson pitched. One strike, two strikes, then three, and the first batter was out. Second batter out, third batter out, and the Diamondbacks came up again.

I leaned over frequently, trying to explain what was happening in the game, which wasn't much. It would have been easier to sit in the middle of them but by then I had reservations about changing seats with Alepho and sticking him beside the unfriendly man.

More innings went by. At the seventh-inning stretch, Cliff and Paul, who were sitting in our regular seats, came by to say hello. Paul met the guys for the first time.

By the eighth inning, it was clearly a no-hit pitchers' duel. Exciting stuff for a packed stadium of seasoned baseball fans. However, me explaining various scenarios of what would happen if the ball ever *was* hit had surely cured Benson, Lino, and Alepho of wanting to watch baseball forever.

The game dragged into extra innings. I turned to the man beside me again and nearly shouted, "Think they'll keep Johnson in the whole game?" No response. Were there really people like this in the year 2001 in Southern California? I felt like the invisible woman, yet I knew it wasn't me he was ignoring.

DILING

Alepho

I was excited to go to the stadium that we had seen from the freeway. The parking lot was bigger than the one at the store with so many cars, like when all the Dinka from the whole Bahr al-Ghazal region brought their cows together at the camp. There were cows as far as you could see.

We walked through so many people and waited in line for food. Judy said that hot dogs were traditional stadium food, so I told her I would try one. When in Rome, do as the Romans do. Benson and Lino knew the saying too, but they did not want the hot dog, just sodas.

The stairs up to the stadium rose out of the ground and moved up. Judy stepped on and rode. She called to us to come. Benson followed first. Once I got my balance, the ride up was nice. We walked through a dark tunnel with people going all directions. I noticed some people staring at us, but we didn't look different. There were white people, brown people, black people, people of all colors.

Judy stopped at a big door and we could see into the center of the stadium. It was even more enormous than it had looked from the freeway. Thousands and thousands of people in a circle that soared up into the sky, higher than any tree. Below, a green field covered the bottom.

We walked down some steps and Judy told us where to sit. I opened my hot dog and the sauces. The hot dog tasted good but the green sauce with little cubes tasted too sweet.

The game began, but I could not understand what was going on. Was this entertainment in America? Where were the soccer players? Everyone was shouting, and I had no idea why they were shouting. A person ran. They shouted. I asked Benson in Dinka, "That person just ran over there, is that why everyone is shouting?"

Benson said, "Remember that game the adults called *diling*? They hit that round small object with a long thin stick to try and make it hit the target. Except in this American *diling* you hit the ball and then you have to run."

I didn't know the rules of *diling* but I had seen the adults play it.

When it became hot, I wanted to leave. These people were eating and drinking and having a good time. I wanted to have a good time. Why couldn't I have a good time like them? I felt out of place, but I held myself. I didn't want to say that I wanted to go home because I would ruin the whole thing for everyone. Benson seemed to understand what was going on. He was light about it and having a good time. Lino looked confused like me.

The stadium was big. Too big. I was uncomfortable. Judy kept explaining things. I nodded my head, because that's what people do in America to show they understand. But really, I did not understand. They never hit the ball with that stick except one time when a guy hit the ball and it went so high it landed in the crowd. A small boy caught it. It seemed so easy to hit the ball with that wood stick. Why did they keep missing the ball? If they threw it to me, I would hit it.

I'd learned in my journeys that there was a certain code for how everything worked in each country and culture. When you didn't know the code, everything fell apart. I'd learned a lot already about American culture that I could teach the people back in the camp. Still, there was so much more I didn't yet know.

BASEBALL BIGOT

Judy

I hoped my guests hadn't noticed that the man next to me wouldn't acknowledge us. Like everyone else, I'd been slighted or ignored in social situations before, but this barricade of prejudgment was something that I'd never encountered and couldn't charm away. I wanted to call him out on his rude behavior, but these were Shannan's season tickets. I had to be respectful of that. Better to forget him. He was the one who was missing out on meeting some extraordinary young men.

Alepho, Benson, and Lino looked tired, weren't interested in more food, and even though too gracious and polite to show it, I knew they must be bored. I'd had enough of the chilly aura coming off my stone-faced seatmate. "I think we should go pretty soon to beat the traffic. Do you want anything before we leave? It's almost dinnertime and we could pick up some hot dogs on the way out. You won't have to cook tonight."

"Don't eat dog," Lino said.

Oh my God. Did Alepho eat his hot dog just to please me?

"Oh, I'm sorry. I should have explained. They're not made from dog. That's just what they call them. They're made from beef or pork." Maybe they didn't eat pork either. "There are hamburgers and tacos too. Those are beef."

"Then why that man have a dog?"

The homeless man. No wonder they kept asking me why Americans had so many pets. Oh no, he'd suspected it was for the same reason the Dinka had cattle.

"He's not farming the dog. That's his pet. He likes his dog. The dog keeps him warm at night. We don't eat dogs."

He didn't appear convinced.

Benson held up the popcorn box that was still nearly full. "We have enough food."

"Okay," I said. "I think we should go."

I tried to see if Cliff and Paul were still in their seats, outlasting us, but I couldn't spot them.

On the way home in the car Lino said from the back seat, "Nine years. Not enough food. Days with no food."

Nine years. Their whole adolescence.

"We get food every two weeks," Benson said. "It is not enough. The last three days we have nothing."

"Starvation days," Alepho added. "Sometimes no water. On ration day, we stand in long line. Police beat us with sticks and yell, 'Stand in sun.' I fall down sometimes."

They talked all at once. An outpouring of the details I'd been curious about but I was too afraid to ask. No self-pity, not even that much emotion in their voices, as though they were talking about a walk across town. It left me speechless. What words could be appropriate in response? They persisted and repeated things to make sure I heard them. They described some background to the situation, who was fighting whom, where, when, and over what. Similar to what I'd read on the internet. That background made their details more meaningful, but I wished I was hearing from each of them individually; I didn't want to miss a word. From the basic level of information they were sharing with me, it was clear they had already realized that most Americans had no idea what was happening in Sudan.

As they spoke, I thought about that man who'd been in the seat next to me. Sure, he was subtle, didn't do or say anything, a sort of benign racism, I supposed. Benign for me, perhaps, but definitely not for them. I imagined Alepho being interviewed for a job or Benson applying to college or Lino setting up a bank account. Most people weren't like that man, but even a few would be too many. Encounters with someone of his ilk would bar them from opportunities, smother their enthusiasm and confidence.

My grip tightened on the steering wheel. My fears and concerns about making a commitment shrank and felt petty in the face of my anger. If I cared, I couldn't just stew and scream, I had to do something tangible. My outrage had to become a call to action. Finishing my book could wait. I had to do everything I could to help them get jobs and work on their education—anything I could do to prevent them from being thwarted in their efforts. They needed an advocate. That was something I could do.

A huge learning curve lay ahead for all of us. I'd make mistakes, some worse than visiting too many museums or going to a thirteen-inning no-hitter and asking them to eat *dog,* but I had to try. They deserved every bit of the time and energy it took. I'd call Joseph Jok first thing in the morning and let him know that I'd decided.

I looked over at Benson and in the rearview at the others. "Would you like me to be your mentor?"

They didn't answer or look at me. I'd been gone for almost two weeks. I'd been no help when they'd asked to sign up for school. I hadn't exactly shined as a mentor so far, so not wanting me was understandable.

In the mirror, I saw them exchange glances.

Benson wasn't smiling. He always smiled. What was he thinking?

He looked me right in the eyes and said, "We thought you were our sponsor."

"Never mind that question. I am. Yes, of course, I am." *What was a sponsor?*

PART TWO

SEPTEMBER 3, 2001–FEBRUARY 6, 2002

MANIAC DEPRESSION

Alepho

Three weeks in America and I still had so much to learn. Most days James and Daniel attended GED classes or went to work. Since Lino, Benson, and I had just arrived and had time, TV shows were a good way to learn about our new country. We gathered in the main room and watched.

One day a commercial came on and in it a goat spoke English. Lino sat up and said, "Wow, these American people are so educated even their goats speak English."

I laughed at first and then realized he wasn't kidding. "Lino, you know the African goats. Goats don't talk."

"African goats are stupid. That's why they don't talk."

"An animal is an animal. There's no way they can talk."

Lino made his voice aggressive. "Why are you arguing with me? You just saw the goat talk. What's wrong with you?"

Was he that angry about a goat? "You know that's not true.

They make things look real in videos and on television even if they aren't true."

"What's not true? Did you see a goat talk?"

"Yes, I saw him," I said. "But common sense. There's no way a goat can talk."

Lino stood. "You're arguing with me for no reason. You know what, you're stupid, too. Don't even try to talk to me." He stomped into our bedroom.

In Kakuma, Benson and I had seen more movie videos than Lino. We had begun to realize that movies showed things that weren't real. But some boys took them seriously, especially the martial arts stories. Boys acted out the fighting moves they'd seen, and it sometimes became crazy in the camp. I understood that Lino wasn't just angry about a goat and whether it talked. Making a life in America, which was so different from our life in Africa, made us all nervous and worried. I felt removed from people here and those anxieties easily became anger.

Lino was still in the bedroom when *The Jerry Spring Show* came on. We'd seen it before. Jerry Springer was some kind of a mediator. My father had been a mediator. He traveled to other villages to settle disputes. Each time he traveled, he took one son with him. My older brothers argued over the honor of who would be next, but arguing was wasted. My father always chose. Each time a son returned from a trip, he held himself proudly, as if he'd been named chief.

When my father said, "Alepho, tomorrow you will come with me," I was only five.

At daybreak we walked several hours to a village larger than ours. The elders had gathered in a circle under a huge tree, awaiting my father's arrival.

"Sit beside me," my father said. "Listen carefully."

I sat straight and tall, proud to be the son of the man so respected by this village.

The elder who had summoned my father said, "Ajok speared and killed Mamer's cow."

"Ajok," my father asked, "why did you spear Mamer's cow?"

"Mamer doesn't control his cow. She got loose and ate my crops again."

My father addressed Mamer. "Please explain why you do not control your cow."

"She's a very clever cow. She escapes every fence. But she is not aggressive. Ajok did not need to spear her."

My father paused. They both had a good story. How would my father decide who should be punished?

My father said to Ajok, "You must repay Mamer with one of your cows."

Ajok did not protest, but his face did not look happy.

"Mamer," my father said. "You should control your cows. They destroyed Ajok's crops. You will repay Ajok with a goat."

At this, Ajok looked pleased.

Everyone else nodded. No one argued with my father's solution. The dispute was settled.

On the way back to our village, my father explained, "It's important to listen respectfully to all sides of a disagreement, even disputes between a man and a woman."

"Yes," I replied. "But shouldn't Ajok's cow be killed too, so they both lose a cow?"

"No," my father said. "My decision does not involve another animal's death. Why should an innocent animal die because of a dispute between Ajok and Mamer? Imagine if his son had killed a calf. Should the son be killed? No one or their animal should be killed. Revenge is a never-ending cycle that must be avoided.

If someone loses something due to another's action, then a debt must be repaid. A cow or a goat, but never revenge."

"What if he'd killed a person?"

"If it is a serious offense, then the penalty will be many cows. The compromise must be fair and settle the issue permanently."

Jerry Springer did his mediation in a different style. First people shared their problems with talk, but if someone felt frustrated they slapped the other person to make their point. When that happened, the audience clapped and cheered and a big guy came onstage to stop the fighting. I'd never seen people clap for fighting. Maybe this was how they did it in America.

Still, I wondered why people came to solve their problems in front of other people. Had they been forced to go on the show because of what they had done?

People came to my father and presented their cases, but my father took them aside and they mediated under the big tamarind tree. Sometimes, if it was a difficult case, others wanted to hear, but they had to gather on the edge and remain quiet. On Jerry Springer's show, they had a large audience that clapped and shouted, and the cameras showed their personal business to the whole world.

After a commercial, Jerry Springer came back on and introduced a girl who had been with more than one guy. She had a baby. Both guys came on the show. Jerry had this amazing test that could determine the father. After each person told their story, Jerry said, "Okay, now we'll be right back with the results." The people clapped and were louder than ever.

I'd learned to survive on my own in the real world since I was seven. I could avoid bombs and bullets, sense danger in animals and strangers, find food when there was nothing, and smell water a mile away. This world was different. I spoke the language well enough, but the rules were strange.

Watching dating shows had made me realize what I needed to approach a woman: a car, money, and better English. I'd requested books from Judy so that when I dated a girl I understood the culture. I didn't want to make a mistake and have to go on *The Jerry Springer Show* and get slapped.

The longer I lived in my new country, the less I knew about this "new world," as they called it. Things did not quite make sense. I had food and a safe place to live, but small things gave me anxiety. Where I came from we depended on one another. Here everyone seemed to be his own boss.

Lino still hadn't come from his room when Jerry Springer came back to announce the results. The man who discovered that he was the father did not look happy. That was strange.

The show ended. A man came on the TV and asked serious questions.

"Are you feeling sad or depressed?

"Are you anxious?

"Are you worried about the future?

"Are you feeling isolated and alone?"

I felt those things. How did the people on television know what I suffered from? I hadn't told anyone I had anxieties.

The man on TV said I might be suffering from maniac depression. He said I needed their special treatment, Zoloft. It would help ease my discomforts, pains, and anxiety.

I looked over. Benson wasn't paying attention to the TV. It was as though the man was speaking directly to me. Everyone knew all about me now. My anxiety heightened more. If a man on TV could know how I felt, how could I be so sure goats didn't talk?

DIEUDONNE

Judy

I called Sharon at the IRC. "Joseph said to call you about becoming a mentor. But first, please explain something to me. What is a sponsor?"

"That's a different program for people who want to privately sponsor a refugee by providing financial and cultural adaptation support. The Lost Boys came through the IRC, so they don't have private sponsors."

"Okay, I see. That's big. I'm thinking about being a mentor. What does that involve?"

"Perfect timing. The class for prospective mentors is tonight."

"Tonight?"

"I know you've already met with them several times, but we like our mentors to take this class as a basic introduction."

Cooking dinner and helping Cliff with homework were my priorities in the evenings. I'd thought I could keep my mentoring to daytime activities. What had I committed to in a rush of outrage and passion?

Sharon added, "There won't be another class for a month."

I wouldn't go back on my word. "I'll be there."

I'd been a student advisor in the Community Economic Development program at San Diego State University for several years. I emailed my student from the prior year, Dieudonne, who had emigrated from Gabon. He'd been through all this. He replied in an email:

> Oh Judy! Amazing news! In my humble opinion you are already off on a good start because of your nature.

My nature? A soccer mom who'd lived in one city her entire sheltered life? Who'd spent nearly twenty years in the insular computer business world? Yes, the last twelve years of parenting had rounded my edges, given me a less self-involved perspective. But I wasn't a teacher, nurse, or social worker by nature, not particularly patient, I'd never lived in another country, and, unintentionally, I mostly associated with people who came from backgrounds similar to my own. Dieudonne, as was *his* nature—and his name, "gift from God"—was being kind.

His email continued.

> My little experience has taught me that kids, just like the rest of us, have different likes and dislikes, and it is not always easy to reach a consensus. Sometimes you will have to exercise your rule (firmly, but always with a zest of love and care), in an impartial way. It is fine to satisfy their needs, but it is more important to show them how to be considerate of other people's needs, respect authority, as well as learn to compromise.
>
> Showing interest in their history and experiences

will certainly help you relate to them better. Always have a number of suggestions regarding group activities and set some type of democratic system in determining what will take place. You might be frustrated at times with things like time and punctuality. Patience and coaching are the keys. Keep in touch.

Dieudonne's words rang true to me. I saved his email to read again. He'd shared valuable advice. Don't spoil them. Acculturate. Teach them our ways. Be fair and patient.

His reminder that they were still young was appreciated. They were so tall, mature, polite, and had survived so much—it was easy to forget that two of them were still teens.

Since I was sitting at the computer, I emailed a fellow writer friend, Roslyn Carrington. She grew up in Trinidad, a multicultural country, and had been to the US many times. From her writing and friendship, I knew she'd have insights. I wrote: *I'm concerned about how the boys will do here in America.*

She responded: *Don't worry, those boys'll do just fine. They expect little. They don't have BMW values. They just want food, shelter, education, and a right to exist.*

I'd been ready to plug them into the same thing I hoped for our son: a fulfilling career, home, and family. The American dream. But my dreams were not necessarily their dreams. Beyond survival and education, I didn't know their dreams. If someone dropped me in Sudan, could I be satisfied pursuing their culture's goals and dreams?

"You should write about this," Roslyn said. "At least a short story."

A story was emerging, I couldn't deny it, but shelved the idea. I already had one unfinished novel and had begun laborious research on a second. My writing was resembling the incomplete knitting projects in my closet.

I shut down the computer and called Paul. "Will you be home tonight to help Cliff with homework? I have a mentoring class at IRC."

"Sure." He sounded hesitant.

"I'll leave dinner in the fridge." He wasn't a cook. That seemed to satisfy him.

"No walk today," I said to our two Labradors, Casey and Vader, who'd been patiently waiting for me to stand up, their noses pushed against the glass door beside my computer station. I rushed out the other way to the garage, and then the store, picked up Cliff, prepared an easy dinner, and hit the road to fight the afternoon traffic in time to make it to the class.

THAT THING CALLED THE LAW

Alepho

Lino and I were in the front room enjoying the TV one afternoon when Majok, a Lost Boy who also lived in San Diego, came to our apartment.

He held out a strip of paper. "I got a ticket."

It looked like an airplane ticket. "Where are you going?"

"I'm not going anywhere. A policeman gave me the ticket."

"Why did he give it to you?" That was nice of him. The police in Kenya gave us beatings in the ration lines, but they didn't give us airline tickets.

"For jaywalking."

"Not for flying? What's jaywalking?"

"He said I am not supposed to cross the street."

"You need a ticket to cross the street?"

"No," Majok said. "The ticket means I have to go to court and pay money. I asked the policeman, 'If am I supposed to stay on one side of the street, how am I going to get on the other side to catch the bus to work? I have to go to work. I refuse to accept this ticket.' The policeman said, 'Sorry, sir, but you are breaking the law.'"

Why hadn't Judy told us anything about crossing streets? I did not want trouble from the police.

Majok said, "Everything here is governed by the law."

In our village, they did not have this thing called the law. People did what they were supposed to do. If there were problems, my father was our mediator. After the troops ran us out of our village and we made it to the camp, there were committees to settle the disputes when people fought over food or water. Kakuma had a small jail for more serious crimes, like stabbing someone, or the police took them to the Kenyan prison in Lodwar.

Lino asked, "If this is how people do things, then why is it said that America is the land of the free?"

I didn't feel free. Since I'd seen that commercial on TV about depression, I'd been attentive wherever I went. I looked behind and all around, wondering if everyone knew everything about me. Now I wasn't sure about crossing the street. This news about the law struck me as odd. How could I learn all the laws?

Another thing puzzled me. If everything was governed by the law, why did we pay bribes? Each month IRC gave us money to pay rent for our apartment. In Kenya the word "rent" meant a bribe. You paid money to someone to get something. So it shocked me that we had to pay money in America to live in our home. In our village, our parents built our hut. In the refugee camp, we built our hut, we lived there, and it was ours. The idea of paying rent was crazy for us. I assumed this was a temporary situation, which was why we paid the bribe until they found us our own place. All of it surprised me. We thought bribery only happened in Africa.

Benson came from the bedroom. I asked, "Why do we have to pay money for our house?"

Benson said, "It's because you have to prove you are a genuine person. You must prove you have a good character. They are testing us to see if we are sincere people, truthful and in good conduct."

I reluctantly agreed with my brother, but it felt very strange to pay. Now we had to learn more laws about crossing the streets here. "Judy takes us places to show us her country, but it is more important that she teach us about the laws."

"We will ask her," Benson said.

"She is nice," I told Benson. I wanted to see what he thought.

"Yes."

We both agreed that Judy was nice. But my previous experiences had taught me to be always on guard. I questioned people's motives and intentions. Just because something appeared good did not necessarily mean it was good all the time.

Benson warned me, "Do not speak anything negative toward Judy nor any other human being in this country. Can't you see they are testing our characters? You must behave yourself."

I understood what Benson was saying, but uncertainty and questions swamped my mind. Why was Judy helping us? What did she want? I needed to find school, work, a car, and a wife. Would she keep helping us? Was her direction the right and good thing?

Benson advised me. "Relax. She will show us where to go and what to do."

Lino said, "Some people here don't have manners. Someone bumped into me the other day. Then after, he said, 'Excuse me.' Why is that? Do you have an answer for me?"

"I am just like you," I said. "We are here to learn."

We often advised each other. "Do not react when people do strange things." Our favorite line was, "Be careful of how you behave, you are in a strange land."

FISHING LESSONS

Judy

When I arrived for the mentoring introduction, a dozen or so people were already seated around the conference table in the IRC classroom. I took the only empty chair. Except for one woman who was thirty at most, the other eight volunteers looked to be college age. I felt like a parent sitting in on a class.

We introduced ourselves in turn. Undergraduates. Law school students. Graduate students. Many worked as well. Young women and men. Interesting. Where I lived and volunteered it was almost all women. This was good to see.

My contemporaries often whined that this generation of young Americans was materialistic, spoiled, and self-centered. Yet here, altruistic eagerness surrounded me and no one was even near my age. We had more time and resources than college kids to help others. Many of our parents were first-generation immigrants. So much for the idealistic love generation and our communes and kibbutzim. What had taken me so long to do something like this?

When the introductions were done, Sharon, who was closer to my age, thanked everyone for attending and shared a little of her background in the Peace Corps. Then she said, "Now I'd like you to close your eyes, please." She read a first-person account by a refugee forced to flee their home due to war. The danger, the terror, and the unknown future were made more poignant by listening in darkness.

When she was done, I opened my eyes and avoided glancing at other glistening eyes.

"The refugee application process is rigorous," Sharon said. "It typically takes several years. The refugees who get to be resettled in other countries have been in camps the longest, some of them for generations. The average is seventeen years. Those who come here are in the most dire or dangerous situations with no hope of returning home. By the end of 2000, there were nearly forty million refugees in the world. The US takes in about forty thousand a year. That's more than all the other countries combined. So you can see, refugees who get to come here are very lucky."

Lucky, I'd say so. One in a thousand chance.

"IRC provides basics like housing, English, job training, etc. We want the mentors to focus on socialization and acculturation."

We'd tried new food together, that was acculturation. I needed to think up more opportunities along those lines.

"Ease into activities," Sharon said. "Do the small things first."

Oh my. I guessed that meant don't drag them through the library, beach, park, and museums all in one day, like I might have done with my visiting relatives. Definitely not to the world's longest baseball game and attempt to force-feed them mysterious meats. Egad, I did need work on my mentoring skills.

Sharon passed around a handout: "Triangle of Self-Actualization" by Abraham Maslow. The levels of human motivation. It resembled the nutrition triangle put out by the FDA, with five horizontal levels of multiple colors. I vaguely remembered it from my one college psychology course in the 1970s.

"Very applicable with refugees," Sharon said. "Maslow theorized that one could not move to a higher level until the prior level was satisfied. The first level, the triangle base, is physiological needs. Like food and water. Until a person has enough to eat and drink, that's all one would be concerned with."

I'd never experienced not being able to satisfy my thirst or hunger, but it sounded logical that that would be my only concern in such a situation. For the Lost Boys, just getting enough food and water had been a daily struggle. I wondered what kind of impact being stuck at the bottom level for the last fourteen years would have on a person, especially as a child and teen.

"The second level is safety and security. Home. A sanctuary. A safe place."

Like not being shot at or having lions attack you. They hadn't had much of level two, either. Even Kakuma hadn't been safe. A refugee camp couldn't feel like home.

"The third level is social. A sense of belonging."

Since they'd been together, they must have felt like they belonged, but perhaps not on a larger scale, having been displaced from home and living in someone else's country.

"Once a person has food, shelter, family and friends, they can advance to the fourth level, which is ego. Self-esteem."

I'd never thought of those things occurring sequentially, but rather simultaneously, as they did in my life. If I understood correctly, working on their self-esteem had not been a large concern to them, if one at all. That was bound to affect them eventually. In what way remained to be seen. They'd been so preoccupied with survival that issues of self-worth might overwhelm them at first. A sure risk for insecurity and depression.

The information was fascinating and insightful, although worrisome in terms of Benson, Lino, and Alepho. It also made me wonder about us middle- and upper-class Americans. We seldom worried about food, except eating too much, and that was not what Maslow had been referring to. Most of us had homes and safety and friends and family. That could mean we were entirely focused on that fourth level: ego. Our efforts to make ourselves seem strong, smart, rich, beautiful, or young were our own kind of survival skill. Perhaps advancing directly to the fourth level, when the mind was originally engineered for the challenges of basic survival, was why Prozac and Zoloft, both antidepressants, were two of the biggest-selling drugs in America.

"The pinnacle of the triangle," Sharon said, "is the fifth level. Self-actualization. A strong and deeply felt belief that as a person one has value in the world. Contentment with who one is rather than what one has. Secure in one's beliefs. Not needing ego boosts from external factors. Having that sense of well-being that does not depend on the approval of others is commonly called happiness."

Happiness, hard to define, yet obvious when present. Most of us struggled our entire lives to achieve it, perhaps what had brought some of us to a mentoring class that night.

That happiness pinnacle was only one level up for most of us. For a refugee starting at the bottom, a much longer climb.

"Let's move on," Sharon said. "I'd like to leave you with an African proverb." She wrote on the chalkboard, *Give a man a fish and you'll feed him for a day. Teach him to fish and you'll feed him for a lifetime.*

I'd heard that proverb years earlier, but now it took on more meaning. That saying would be my guide.

I waited until everyone had left and went to Sharon. "Thank you for encouraging me to come tonight," I told her.

She laughed. "I forced you."

"You did, and now I know why. You gave me a much better idea of what the refugees face and what my role will be. I'll be honest, it's more involved than I thought, but I'm even more determined to help them succeed. Can't imagine not helping them now."

"You are welcome to call me anytime."

• • •

On the way home, I thought about their metaphorical fishing lessons. The start had to be a job. And soon. What job though?

Some of the Sudanese refugees who had arrived earlier worked in factories, making circuit boards for a few dollars over minimum wage. They remained temporary employees, however, and were frequently laid off and rehired as the high-tech sector struggled. The workplaces were far away, out of reach of the bus, and the employers didn't provide benefits. Medical insurance would soon become an important issue. Alepho and Lino would have Medi-Cal for another year or so, until they were twenty-one, but Benson would lose his coverage in eight months. They didn't have family to fall back on if one of them got sick. Even Americans didn't have that kind of money.

Hotels would have been the ideal job, something they were immediately capable of doing. Daniel and James managed that work. Yet the occupancy rate had been so low this summer they hadn't provided enough hours to their existing employees. Tourist season was just about over. That situation was bound to worsen.

We didn't have much manufacturing in San Diego, mostly high-tech. Taxi drivers needed driver's licenses and they wouldn't have those for a while. Fast food should be a possibility, but their

English wasn't clear enough yet to take orders over a counter, much less an intercom. Their English was fairly good—their vocabulary as extensive as many Americans'—they just weren't used to *our* accents. Nor us theirs.

I ticked off cook, waiter, construction, gardening … The boys were bright, strong, and eager to work. Surely someone would hire them.

GOOD SAMARITAN

Alepho

Daniel was standing at the stove when I entered our kitchen. I picked up a clear package that was lying on the counter. "What is this?" I asked. The IRC put food in our kitchen but we didn't understand most of it. "It says spaghetti. Looks like worms but they are so straight and long."

Daniel already knew how to use the stove and he was making asida from flour and water like we had in the camp. We liked to eat *sukumawiki,* big green leaves that were our favorite vegetable in Kenya, with asida, but the IRC people didn't seem to understand us when we asked for that.

"They grow them on huge farms," Daniel said.

"They farm worms?" I'd eaten worms on my journey, but they were white or some were dark, almost black. None of them were so straight. We had to find them in the dirt, or the short curved ones were inside trees. I wasn't on my journey anymore. Why would I eat worms?

Daniel handed me a cup. "These are small and not straight,

like our worms." The cup was white and felt empty. On the side it said CUP NOODLES in red letters.

"Open it," Daniel said.

I pulled back the top. "You are right. These are small like our worms. Americans are just like Chinese. They eat everything."

American food came in boxes and cans. In Kakuma camp we got olive oil in cans, and when the oil was gone we cut the cans and flattened them to make shingles for our roofs. Here, we already had a fancy roof. What would we do with all the empty cans? Coke cans were already filling our kitchen.

I didn't have an appetite for American food yet. I didn't know what was good or how to prepare it.

Hunger was with me most of the time, but it wasn't a problem. I was familiar with hunger from our journey. In the camp, there had never been enough food. The first day a person goes without food brings headaches. If still no food is found on the second and third days, the headaches become intense. After that, the headaches fade away and the body aches. It recognizes it's going into starvation mode and readjusts itself. By day four, I would feel numb. When I did get food after so many days, my body shook, sweat covered my skin, and my blood began to flow again. We'd warm water to put on ourselves to calm the shakes. After eating, we'd become tired and fall asleep.

Being a refugee is something that many people cannot understand. Refugee life isn't so pleasant. We lived five of us together. The little ration we received we collected together and cooked as a meal once a day. Though we had appetite, there wasn't enough to eat for young, growing boys with tender bones and body. Nutritional diseases were rampant in the camp. Children died from marasmus, kwashiorkor, anemia, and beriberi. Rickets was the worst with young boys—almost every boy was bowlegged. It was a hardship for all boys to go to school with an empty stomach. Remember, an empty stomach cannot carry the healthy mind. Many times I felt as though I was being devoured by wild animals.

In order to survive, people had to subdue their pain and desires and live on faith. We could not stretch out our ration for fifteen days, and black days came every two weeks when there was nothing left to eat in the three days' time before receiving rations again. All we could do was keep busy by reading or gathering around and sharing stories to forget the hunger.

The longest I went without food was on the journey right after I found my brother Benson. We'd been separated by war for five years. I did not even think he was still alive. There was a brief time of peace in our lives, and we were happy to be together at last. But not long after our joyous reunion, we heard bombs coming from the nearby town. Survivors straggled in. They said we had to flee. Food was distributed for the journey, three cups of corn and two cups of beans to each person. We were about to receive ours when a shrill whistling broke the peace.

"Lie down, lie down," a man shouted. "This is the way to survive."

I threw myself down. A bomb exploded. The ground shook. Dust filled the air like a storm cloud. I couldn't see a thing; only screams and moans reached my ears.

When the cloud cleared, dead people lay all around. People who still lived got up and ran in all directions. They didn't know where to go.

I jumped to my feet and ran with the screaming crowd. We fled toward the Lotuko hills for shelter. Bombs exploded behind us. We'd almost reached the hills when a *tut-tut-tut* came from the bushes. Bullets! People scattered in all directions. A man went down in front of me. *Tut-tut-tut* whistled all around. An ambush. More people fell. I stopped. Shaking overtook me. *Lie down. Lie down.* I'd heard that so many times. *That is the way to survive.* I fell to the ground and crawled into some long grass where women were crouched. I hid with them as explosions and guns thundered around us.

The shooting stopped. The women who were still alive fled in a crouching run. Something told me to remain hidden in that grass, even though I was surrounded by dead bodies.

Soldiers moved in. They went from body to body, checking to see who was still alive. Each time they found a live person a shot rang out. I hid my blanket under my body. I trembled inside but kept my eyes closed in a relaxed way and let my mouth fall open. I made myself like a dead person and waited.

Footsteps approached. A boot poked my side. I didn't breathe. A toe went under my belly and flipped me. I let my arms fall crooked and my legs twist like a dead person. He'd kill me if he thought I was alive, but he wouldn't waste a bullet on a boy that was already dead.

The soldier grunted and went on to the next person, ignoring my blanket wrapped in the dirty old cloth. I lay perfectly still. When I could no longer hear the soldiers, I opened my eyes to be sure they were gone.

I picked up my blanket and ran back to where we'd come from, looking for Benson or anyone else. Where was he? Was he alive, or was my brother's body back there in the grass? How would I find him again?

I found a few survivors huddled in a circle. I couldn't see anyone I knew. I hung to the side of them. Women cried; children cried. In the middle of all that pain and sorrow, a blind child stumbled on a land mine and died in a thousand pieces. Fear built inside me like an earthquake. My body shook. I'd never seen so much dying.

An elder took charge of the group. "We must move on.

Control yourselves. No talking. No crying. No whining that I am hungry, I am thirsty. No noise whatsoever."

We settled our fear. We had to. I followed like a sleepwalker in total confusion. Why was our government hunting and killing families—women and children who had done nothing but live? Why were they shooting at me? I'd had many desperate days, but this was the most unforgettable. That morning our family had all been together. Now I was completely alone again, just like the first days after I'd fled my village.

• • •

I walked for three days in that large group. I knew no one. Most children had parents who helped them with the walking and gave them any little bit of food or water they found. I had no food, no water, and no family. I'd already been starved to a stick, barely able to shuffle my feet along the dusty road. Weakness overtook me. Each step became a huge effort that needed all my focus. I couldn't keep up with these strangers.

Ahead, a huge mango tree spread its branches. I went into its shade and collapsed on the ground. This was it. I couldn't go farther.

I looked up. Mangoes grew from a nearby tree, but my arms were too weak to even raise up; I could never climb for those mangoes. I'd come close to dying before, but even then, I'd had hope of finding someone or something. In this mess, adults couldn't even help themselves. They weren't going to help a strange boy.

I rolled to my side. Smoke curled up into the leaves from the other side of the tree. Long legs and dark boots came into my view. Someone else was in this place. A man sat near where I'd fallen. He looked at me, and his look told me that he realized I was about to die.

His wife was preparing grain in a small can. When it was cooked, she brought the food to the long-legged man.

He said, "Bring another spoon."

"This is too small," she said. "There is no way you can share it with that boy."

They argued. Their angry words passed over me like a dream. The man said, "If that kid dies, you will be responsible. It won't change my life to share this little bit of food."

The wife sobbed. "My five children all died. Why? Why did this kid survive and not my children? Why?"

She threw her utensils down and stomped away.

The man gave her an understanding look and said to me, "Share this grain with me."

He held out his spoon and gave me small bites. My body shook, and I sweated. After a bit, I felt better. I wasn't going to die. Not today.

The man who had saved my life packed up his things and moved on with his wife. I rested there in the shade, looking up through the leaves and small green fruit until afternoon, when I had the strength to get up and move on, too.

Before that day, I'd begun to think that all humans were bad, but that man changed my thinking. Now, remembering those events, I also know that his wife suffered, like me. She wasn't greedy, but she was hurt by the loss of her children. That experience made me see people in a new way. I could see that whether adult or child, man or woman, rich or poor—war changed people.

My journey to America had brought me to an unknown world, where people flew on planes, rode buses and motorbikes, and went to a place called Disneyland. Everything smelled differently, even the air. I might as well have been on the moon.

Exposure to the unknown had its advantages and disadvantages. Coming to a new world was exciting. Who doesn't like new things? I met interesting human beings with knowledge and understanding about life and the universe. I experienced things I'd never imagined.

A big disadvantage was that I was lost again. I had to cope with being farther away from family. In the refugee camp, we'd never received news about our home, where war still raged. Part of me wanted to forget those hopes that my family might still be alive and move on with my life. I wanted to be humble and do my best to make a new life for myself in my new land, with my new culture and new language.

Here, we had a card that bought food and we knew how to go to the store, but they said the card was only good for three months and then we needed a job. How did we get a job?

People helped us. They donated food, clothes, dishes, and towels and offered guidance. That never happened in the camp.

We were grateful to America because they'd brought us from that most desperate situation. Here we could get our education. Make our life. We appreciated everything. When so much of your life has been just barely surviving, you become grateful for anything.

When my feet touched America, at times I felt I was dreaming. Since the attack on my village, there'd been moments that I could not distinguish between dreaming and reality. I'd lived that violent life while awake; now in America, when I shut my eyes, the displacement, unceasing fierce journey, loss, confusion, sickness, starvation, wild animals, bombs, and those soldiers with bloodshot eyes, eager to fire their guns—it all came to me again when I slept. I woke with my heart pounding my ribs, sometimes lying on the floor where I'd fallen from the bed.

Even small things made me uncomfortable or gave me anxieties. Like not knowing the food. So, we drank sodas and ate chips.

Headaches kept me from reading and learning. My stomach gave me pain. This suffering wasn't as bad as no food, but it kept me from working on my new life. I couldn't solve everything as soon as I wanted, but I could learn about food.

Daniel brought the pot of asida to the table in front of the couch. We gathered around and in turn dipped our fingers into the gooey warm dough like we had in the camp and on our journey.

I said to Benson, "We will ask Judy to show us about the American food."

ANTS DISTURBED IN THEIR NEST

Judy

I settled onto the couch with the stack of writing that Benson had handed me in the car on the way to the game. I opened up Benson's first.

> The life of the Dinka changed according to the seasons. We harvested in the autumn and planted at the end of the summer or the middle of spring. When heavy rains came, the brooks filled with water, and the young men took the cattle to graze at the cattle camp, a huge grassy area where all of the villages collected their cows. When the sun shone again, the sky was clear except for the smoke soaring from the village cooks and an outpouring of tiny winged termites. Marabou storks, swallows, glossy starlings, shoebill herons, and the egrets that walk with cows flew in to reap the termite blooming. Indolent birds perched at the tops of the heglig and

acacia trees, and ground hornbills waddled lazily along the prairie, howling.

Benson's distinctive voice sprang from the pages. His lush descriptions of a village life still so dear to him sounded just like the young man I was getting to know in person. He'd once told me how his mom made termite soup in enough detail that if I'd had the ingredients I could have cooked it myself. He was seven when he left home. How does such a young boy remember those things? I imagined that during the terrifying nights and sweltering days of his journey, with no loving parents to rescue him, those were the memories that kept him alive. Yearning for those old times must have etched them into his mind.

His writing voice differed from his speaking voice only in its degree of richness. English was his fourth language after Dinka, Swahili, and some Arabic. Writing gave him the luxury of time to express himself in English. All the young men sprinkled uncommon words into their simple English that often seemed incongruent with their language skills. Perhaps they'd read them or learned them from their Kenyan teachers. I never used the word "indolent" myself, although I knew its meaning. But I had no idea what a heglig tree was, and had never thought of termites blooming, yet that was exactly what they appeared to do when they took flight.

I read Benson's account of life in the village again and then picked up the page Alepho had written.

The name Lost Boys came to be when our village was attacked by fierce Arab horsemen. We, little boys, spewed out of the blazing village like a colony of ants disturbed in their nest. We ran in different directions, not knowing where we were going. We gathered some fruits for our breakfast and lunch. We, little boys, were so messy, all chaos and cries filling the dark, fiercely lightless night.

I put the pages down. The intensity of his words stunned me. And surprised me. He was so quiet, usually, and reserved when he spoke. These words were on fire. I read on.

Young grown-up boys who survived that disastrous attack directed us. We trekked a thousand miles. I could tell how some of my friends disappeared, wild animals devoured them; an ogre snatched another, and his last cry echoed in the darkness.

I can't forget the deprivation from my home. My lovely village, Juol, full of palm and coconut trees, faded in a way that I can't understand.

I wondered what he meant by an ogre. Perhaps some human monster the boys had encountered as they fled from the wars. It wasn't hard to believe that some people behaved monstrously with these children; they did here.

Alepho had been five and still living in his village when Benson disappeared. Benson had been at his sister's house two hours north when her village was attacked. Two years later, Alepho fled during another attack on his village. Reading Alepho's experience as a seven-year-old in his vivid poetic words was nothing like reading the news stories. While reports saddened me, they were too soon forgotten. Knowing Alepho and Benson, and hearing of their loss and the journey forced on them, I didn't even realize I'd stopped breathing. When I finally did take a breath and let it out, I knew I couldn't read Alepho's words again. Not right now. I would need to save them to read another time.

That had happened in 1989, the year Cliff was born and the Berlin Wall came down. Europe was moving on from its dark past, but a genocide that would kill two million and displace five million was just getting started—yet it wasn't even in the news. I wanted to know more. I often heard about Muslims killing Christians, Arabs killing blacks. They'd been living side by side for a thousand years. Why now?

I got up from the couch, grabbed an empty bag, and went outside. Casey and Vader followed me into the orange grove. Even though Cliff was twelve, I still worried about him crossing streets or walking to the store after school. Imagining him in a situation similar to the Lost Boys was too painful. Impossible.

As a mother, I couldn't stop thinking about their mother. She'd had no choice but to send her sons out into the night in the midst of a battle. They didn't know if she was alive to this day. She couldn't know if they'd survived.

I filled the bag with Valencia oranges. What a different world we were fortunate to live in.

SAINT LUKE'S

Judy

Earlier in the week I'd suggested to the guys that we go to the zoo on Sunday, since Paul and Cliff would be at a baseball game. When I arrived to pick them up, Benson said, "There is a meeting at the church. A professor has returned from Sudan. He has videos. Do you want to come with us?"

That sounded interesting. I'd heard about the church several blocks south of the IRC offices where a group of Sudanese had become members. The zoo would always be there. They were teaching me flexibility.

We were the first to arrive at the church. As we waited, Alepho looked irritated, frequently checking his watch, which someone had donated, and asking where everyone was. One month, and he'd become just like an American.

I'd planned to get us all lunch at the zoo, and clearly there was no possibility of food here. A headache was coming on. I popped two Excedrin. Alepho saw the pills. "I have headache."

He always did. God, I understood how he felt. I'd struggled with them for years. They'd robbed me of joy and productivity so many days. I had to find the cause and a solution for him.

I handed him two Excedrin. "Many boys have headaches," he said.

"You mean other Lost Boys have headaches?"

"Yes, many."

Weird. Perhaps they were dehydrated or still not eating enough food. They were all still so thin. "Have you eaten anything yet today?"

"No," he said.

I gave him a scolding look.

He smiled. "Eating makes my headache worse."

It didn't sound like our headaches were from the same cause.

People began to straggle into the basement, mostly young Sudanese men—Lost Boys, I assumed. Each one came directly up to me, hand extended, and introduced himself. What a nice custom. Going right up to the person you do *not* know and saying hello. Especially when someone like me was such an obvious outsider. I wondered if the same thing would happen if I took one of them to a meeting in my neighborhood. Actually, I didn't wonder. A few would greet them, but most would not. The baseball game had proved that.

The basement had filled with thirty or more Lost Boys, all of whom had politely greeted me, when Dr. Jok of Loyola University arrived and introduced himself. He'd just returned from Sudan and had a video and news to share. We took seats on folding chairs behind banquet tables.

I didn't have to look around the room to know I was the only white person there. This was a first for me. Although they'd made every effort to welcome me, the feeling was still awkward. I felt like an interloper.

The video began. A soldier in a smartly tailored, camouflage uniform, orange beret, and mirrored sunglasses was being interviewed by Dr. Jok, who was both the cameraman and interviewer.

Benson, who was seated beside me, explained. "That is captain of SPLA."

The man was dashing, like a Hollywood mercenary, with his bodyguard standing behind him, holding a large automatic gun of some kind.

"He is rebel fighting to save the Dinka villages in the south."

"What language is he speaking?" I whispered.

"Arabic."

"Can you understand him?"

Benson smiled. "Yes. He say he has been shot two times in the chest."

Damn. He didn't just look the part, he *lived* the part. Medical treatment in the field couldn't be that great and he'd survived twice.

The interview went on for twenty minutes. I didn't want to interrupt Benson, who was listening intently, to get a translation. They were all eager for news from back home.

The video switched to a village, and then out to a cattle camp. The *60 Minutes* clip had just shown brief glimpses of their homeland. This was one of the reasons I had wanted to come.

The land was rich, with rusty-colored earth, beautiful—just like they had described—and flat like our Great Plains, with lush green grasses and occasional acacia trees of that distinctive African variety that has a flat top and spreading limbs. I pictured a giraffe reaching a long black tongue up into their thorny branches. There were no giraffes in the video, or any other wildlife for that matter, only the colorful Dinka cattle with their magnificent horns, which they used to fight off lions.

The camera panned to a large grass-roof structure that was

supported by sturdy poles and open on all sides. Benson leaned over. "That is where the old people and the girls rest. The camp can move where the grass is good and they build a new one." I heard longing in his voice.

The young men in the film were tall, slender, and well nourished. They moved unhurriedly and gracefully, holding a stick and singing to their cows as they drifted among them. Their shirts were as long as dresses and some had a sarong tied over one shoulder. In the center of the camp, where the girls and younger boys milked the cows and did other chores, the boys wore nothing and the girls were bare-breasted and wore short, flaring skirts.

"These are the girls," Benson said. "Girls not married. Women are married. They wear dress. Only the girls can milk cows. Not women. Men can milk cow if there are no girls. My father had ninety cow."

Lots of rules about who could and couldn't milk. Given that Benson left his village at seven years old, how much he knew about his culture amazed me. Although he was never boastful, in keeping with the Dinka tradition of modesty, I sensed a deep pride in his people and his country.

He pointed out the teens standing around. "The young people from many villages go to cattle camp to tend the cows and sometimes that is where they meet the person they will marry."

No wonder the mood was so cheery. Laughter and talking rang out over the ever-present mooing of the herd.

"I did not go to cattle camp," Benson said with a definite sadness in his voice. "I left before that time."

I felt for his loss. What an ideal environment for teens. Working together in a structured situation with plenty of social contact and teamwork, all thrown together, much like our college years.

The video shifted from the cattle camp to scenes of schools and hospitals that had been demolished in the war.

"They always bomb these things the most," Benson said. "They don't build them anymore because the government bomb them. Kids go to school under the trees now."

Throughout the video presentation, more people arrived. Women in brightly colored long dresses and matching head wraps. Some had babies and young children and brought food they placed in the kitchen behind the hall. A little boy nearby kept staring at me from behind his mother's skirts. I smiled and waved. He smiled and ducked back behind his mom.

The video skipped to another village with a celebration in progress. "A bull is killed," said Benson.

"What is a cow worth?" I whispered.

"You can buy a big bull for seven thousand shillings. That is one hundred dollar US. To buy a wife costs seventy-five cows."

Seventy-five cows. Substantial dent in the family net worth. Nice to hear their culture placed such a high value on women.

"Do people hope for a baby girl or a baby boy?" I asked, wanting to hear how valued girls were.

"Either one is good if it is healthy. Many of the babies die."

"Yes, just healthy, of course." Nice that both genders were valued.

In the celebrating village, the huts were large and circular with red mud-brick walls and roofs made of fronds or grass, laid in impossibly tight, neat, symmetrical patterns. The huts seemed to be clustered into smaller compounds within the village, and in the background tidy rows of corn and some kind of grain grew.

Benson anticipated my question. "These are sorghum, millet, and wheat."

I asked about the huts clustered in groups behind walls.

"Each wife has a hut," Benson said. "If a man's brother dies, then he must take that man's wife."

"Just like the Old Testament. How many wives can a man have?"

"He can have many wives if he is rich with cows. My father had five wives."

Five wives meant a lot of children growing up together. What a wonderful childhood he'd lost.

"I don't understand," I said. "Isn't the war going on there, too?"

"This village very remote. No war there now. But the Sudan government give the northern tribes guns. They come on horses and steal the cattle and shoot people."

In spite of my progressively worsening headache and the video going on nearly three hours, Benson's narration and excitement at seeing his old homeland made time fly by.

Alepho, who sat across the aisle, was quiet throughout. Headache or homesickness, I couldn't tell. They'd been on the run or in a desolate refugee camp for fourteen years and now, for the first time, were watching the life they'd lost forever.

Excited chatter had erupted occasionally throughout the video, but for most of the people now gathered in that windowless basement, I suspected that seeing what they'd left behind was a profoundly painful experience. It left me stunned.

Dr. Jok went to the front for a Q&A. I expected the audience to erupt with questions about what they'd just seen but heard nothing. I looked around the room. Everyone wore serious expressions. Even the children were silent.

*

BIG GUN BATTLE

Alepho

In the evenings, news came on the TV and anyone who was home gathered to watch. The news reported about car accidents and crimes. Sometimes the criminals had drugs and the police had caught them. They also reported the traffic and the weather. I liked the way they showed the map and could tell us how the weather would be several days ahead.

What we were most eager to hear was information about the situation in Sudan. We never did.

One evening, when the news had a story about dogs who could jump up and catch a flying round thing they called a Frisbee, James said, "In my class at IRC today they said you can find anything on the computer."

I had been wanting to learn to use the computer Judy had brought us.

"The computers know everything," James said. "Even when I spelled my own name wrong it corrected it for me. You can find jobs in the computer, even people. Maybe we can find news about Sudan."

I'd like to find news about what was happening back in Sudan. Could I even find my family through computers? I liked this idea of a machine that knew everything, yet it did not altogether make sense to me.

I asked Benson, "How did people come up with something like this computer? How was it created? I am not sure about it."

"Don't be hasty," Benson said. "Take time to understand before we jump to concluding about things."

That led to a discussion among us. "This place is really strange."

"It might have been better to stay in camp."

"How can someone stay in the camp? That was the worst place."

I said, "There was no hope in a refugee camp. Here we have hope for our future. We must learn new ways."

We turned off the TV and Benson and I went to our room.

I liked to read in bed. I read for a while, but my eyes grew tired. I closed the book.

Boom!

My heart leapt like a rabbit.

"What was that?" Benson jumped from the bed.

Boom! Boom!

"What is it?"

"I don't know."

Boom! Boom! Boom! Explosions. Coming faster. We looked at each other. We knew those sounds.

I slid under the blanket and covered my head. "Those are big guns."

"It sounds like it's in the next town."

The gun sound grew louder. No time between explosions. A

raging battle. A shrill sound whistled before one exploded. "Did you hear that?"

"Sounds like bombings. War."

"Should we go under the bed?"

"That won't help if a bomb hits the house."

We were on the second floor. If a bomb hit the house we'd fall through the floor. "Should we go downstairs?"

Benson didn't answer.

I stayed under the covers. "What will we do if the house is destroyed? There are no refugee camps in America. People just sleep on the street."

"I don't know."

We stayed under the blankets. After about fifteen minutes the battle grew more fierce, with louder explosions that came closer together. Suddenly it stopped.

"It's over," I said.

"Maybe for tonight," Benson said.

I didn't sleep that night.

STORIES

Judy

"The stories you wrote are wonderful," I told the guys the next day as we got into my car. "The writing was very good." It was true, and I assumed that's what they were most eager to hear.

Benson climbed into the front, Alepho and Lino the back. They buckled their belts. They looked depressed. "Ready for your class today?"

"My writing is not good," Alepho said.

"Good writing is storytelling. Not perfect grammar. Your stories were powerful."

No response.

"Keep writing. It's a good way to practice English."

"We have more," Benson said.

From his pocket he pulled lined sheets, covered front and back in small writing.

"You *do* like to write, don't you?"

"Yes," Alepho said.

An idea came to me. "I was just thinking …" Stop. Don't

finish that thought out loud. Don't get them caught up in your writing pipe dreams.

"We don't understand American food," Alepho said. "Can you take us shopping and teach us to cook?"

I was happy that he'd asked about food. The empty red Coke cans still metastasizing in their kitchen concerned me. They only seemed to eat once a day, at least when they were with me, and were still as thin as the day they'd arrived. Finding jobs was priority number one, but they couldn't work without energy.

"How about tomorrow after class?" I'd picked up a large bottle of multiple vitamins on my way and handed it to Benson. "These are for all of you. Take one a day."

Benson shook the bottle.

"They are vitamin pills," I said.

"Like Tums? In the camp if there was no food, we stood in line at the clinic and said our stomach hurt so they would give us Tums."

"That was smart. But these are different and better to take with food."

"They didn't always have Tums and they would tell us to go away."

I started the car.

"Our cousin Benjamin is coming," Benson said. "He called from Nairobi. He's going to Brussels and then America. He will be here on September eleven."

"That's tomorrow, Tuesday."

"He was small boy with a huge belly. He is very, very tall now. He talk a lot too. He tell many, many stories. He is the most black of all of us."

The most black? I wondered what that meant to them. Was it a positive thing in their culture? "I look forward to meeting him."

"You can be his mentor."

Alepho saved me from responding. "The Lost Girls are coming too."

"Really, that's great. When?"

"We don't know when," Alepho said. "But when they come, you could be their mentor, too. You would be good at that."

Girls might be interesting. "Thank you. I will think about that." Yet, a houseful of young girls in *their* neighborhood sounded overwhelming.

Alepho's voice turned more solemn. "I think it will be difficult here for the girls."

We agreed on that. I wondered what his reasons for thinking that were. Perhaps something I didn't know about their culture. I didn't want to disparage their neighborhood here but it certainly wasn't where I'd locate a household of girls, or anyone for that matter. I nodded in agreement.

Lino showed me a shirt and backpack. "You have machine?"

The shirt had a small tear that could be easily repaired. The nylon backpack was ripped near the binding. Not something I could fix. "I have a sewing machine. We can give it a try when you come to my house."

We hadn't planned a specific time yet for them to visit our home. Their classes at IRC kept them busy most days. This week was job preparedness. How to fill out an application. Do an interview. Becoming comfortable with looking into someone's eyes when you spoke to them. I could see that their habit of looking down would take time to break.

As I pulled out of the parking lot, Benson asked, "Did you see shooting in the television?"

"Shooting? What shooting?"

"Guns. Lots of shooting. Big guns."

"Here? In your neighborhood? Are you sure?"

They talked all at once. "Yes. Big battle. Guns. Bombs. It go a long time."

No wonder they seemed so sad today. This wasn't the safest or quietest neighborhood in San Diego. It made the news frequently for its crime and gangs. But a gun battle? Surprising that they hadn't mentioned that when I first arrived. Were they that accustomed to violence? "What did you do?"

"I stay in bed," Alepho said. "Go under the covers. Very big guns."

If anyone was familiar with gun sounds, they were. I didn't doubt what he said. The news had been covering the busting up of a large drug cartel that worked both sides of the border. Big guns could only be SWAT or really serious drug dealers with those custom-made automatic weapons I'd seen in movies. I had begun to think this area was more interesting than dangerous. How naive was I?

"Very, very bad," Alepho said in a resigned tone.

That stunned me into silence. They'd come all the way here only to be thrown into another kind of war zone. There had to be a way to move them to a safer neighborhood.

A few blocks from their house, I topped the rise and waited at the traffic light. Mission Valley lay below. Malls, secured apartment complexes, condos. Too bad they couldn't afford the rent to live there.

Qualcomm Stadium came into view. A thought popped into my head. "What time did you hear the guns?"

"It was about nine-thirty," Alepho said.

Relief flooded through me. A fireworks show after the game. "That wasn't guns. You heard fireworks."

"Fireworks? What is fireworks?"

"Fireworks. Little rockets that explode and make pretty lights. After the baseball game last night, they had a celebration and shot fireworks."

"Like the Chinese," Lino said.

"Yes, a big party, not a battle. You may hear it again. Don't worry."

"We don't want more war," Alepho said.

"I know you don't. But you're in America now. You'll never hear a real gun battle or experience war again."

SEPTEMBER 11, 2001

Judy

My car careening, sluggish foot seeking the brake, not fast enough, not hard enough. The steering wheel doesn't work. I'll crash ...

The crash never came. A slamming heart awakened me. Drenched sheets. Nothing more than a nightmare. No way to sleep again.

I'd been driving over thirty years and never had a car nightmare. Was PTSD contagious?

Paul's side of the bed was empty. He must have had an early surgery.

Even though the big gun battle had ended up being only fireworks, I wanted some way for Benson, Lino, and Alepho to move out of their neighborhood. Their priority was education. They kept asking about school, but their financial support would end soon and it wasn't clear they understood the ramifications of that. Work had to be the first step. Job-preparedness training all this week at IRC would give them some skills and allow me time for research and exploration on my own. Next week, we could look for work in earnest.

Their hearts were set on a college education. They deserved it. Too often, first-generation immigrants sacrificed themselves for the benefit of the next. Their childhoods had already been sacrificed to something not of their doing. Dues paid.

Still young, unmarried, no kids, they should go for their dreams. Maybe they didn't have BMW values, like Roslyn said, but ten years from now they might. Toyota values anyway. They came to America to get educated. It wouldn't be free, as they'd been told or assumed, but it was possible. That's what counted.

How to make it possible was the puzzle. I didn't question their abilities. If overcoming adversity were a sport, they'd be X Games champions. I did question my aspirations for them. Some minorities still found it difficult to achieve *the dream*.

Money or lack of it stood in their way. They couldn't go to high school at their ages, so they needed their GEDs to get into a community college while supporting themselves at minimum wage and adjusting to a foreign culture and language. A lot to juggle. Laundry was still a challenge.

Dare I think of my book idea again? Their stories were amazing. I'd had no idea that was happening to tens of thousands of little boys in the 1980s while I went about my work, driving my car to a grocery store or Macy's, never thinking about hunger, much less thirst. If they were willing to tell their stories, people needed to hear them. With one incomplete book, it felt flaky and irresponsible for me to start another. Not to mention going down my well-trodden path of too many diversions to really do something well.

Writing wasn't easy for me. Once the idea for my first book had come to me, a year went by before a word hit the page. I wrote in the closet that next year. Rumors that I was an alcoholic or having an affair were preferable to declaring, "I'm writing a book," and having to admit later that I never finished it.

Books demanded immense amounts of time. They impacted family and friends. Chances of financial benefit were minuscule. Every writer knew that. However, even if this book was never published, the stories would be theirs, something that memorialized all those years of hardship. After all, they didn't have photos.

The phone rang. Paul's car phone on the caller ID. "Turn on the news. There's a plane crash or something in New York."

I ran downstairs and turned on the TV in time to see an airliner plunge into one of the World Trade Center towers. The other tower was already a huge plume of black smoke. Two jets crashing into both the World Trade Center towers on the same morning couldn't be an accident. Who? Why?

I woke up Cliff. He loved the World Trade Center towers, knew all their facts and figures, and had models and pictures of them in his room. I dreaded his reaction but wanted to be with him when he saw the news.

From the couch we watched together in disbelief and horror as the first tower crumbled into an ash cloud. Then the second. "I'm going to call Dad," I said. "I'm sure he'll want to talk to you." I dialed over and over. "The lines are jammed."

How would Benson, Alepho, and Lino react to this? This time it wasn't just fireworks. Just yesterday I'd promised that things like this never happened in America.

"Oh God," I said. "Benjamin is leaving Brussels today. They all came through New York."

"What will happen to him?" Cliff asked.

"I'm sure he'll be safe. I'll call Joseph when the office opens." Benjamin could not have arrived on a worse day. I'd call Alepho, Lino, and Benson too. I hoped they weren't in complete panic mode.

Cliff and I watched replay after replay of the jets obliterating the towers, people fleeing, falling, jumping to their deaths to escape the pain of burning jet fuel, and the awful ash cloud. Two jets had to be intentional. Where had this evil come from? It could be a Timothy McVeigh–type, product of some hate-incubating cult, pissed off we'd killed McVeigh, or that they had to pay taxes, or that their guns might be taken away. What if the perpetrators were from outside, like the group that failed to bring down the towers the first time? Question was: How would we react? Would war come to America?

AMERICA ATTACKED

Alepho

I awoke early and lay in bed. This was America. No need to jump up and stand at the water tap for hours with my jerry can or line up before daylight to get rations. Food and water were only a few steps away in the kitchen. Our own TV was on in the main room.

What a long journey it had been to reach here. We'd left so many people behind. The friends we'd made on the trek. Our communities in the camp: Sudanese, Rwandan, Somalian, Zairian, Congolese. Many countries were at war at that time, many people displaced from their homeland. Only a very lucky few, like us, were taken to the United States.

Benson and Lino still slept. Setting our feet on the American land was a blessing. I had no words to describe my feelings. My life would be an amazing experience. I'd go to school. Education would allow me to help those left behind and help me in my life here. My hopes were as high as the peak of Mount Kilimanjaro.

I pulled up the blanket, warm and safe, dreaming of my future.

James shouted from the main room. "America has been bombed!"

Bombed? More bombs? No!

James turned up the TV. Something *was* happening. I swirled out of bed and jumped to my feet. Still in my pajamas, I went to the front room.

James stood akimbo, staring at the TV. I'd seen that look of terror too many times before in my life. "What happened?"

James motioned to me with his eyes to look at the screen. A plane flew into a tall building and made a fiery explosion. Debris flew everywhere like birds scared off a fruit tree.

"That's not a bomb. It's a plane crash. The pilot ran into the building."

"Watch," James said.

The screen showed that a second plane hit another building beside the one with a huge smoke plume rising into the sky. Another fiery explosion. That glued my feet to the carpet in wordless utter shock. The enormity of what I saw threw me back into my old world.

"Two planes don't crash like that," James said.

The screen switched to a man giving the news. My English comprehension was shallow. The newsman confused me. I'd flown into New York just three weeks earlier. That could have been us. I didn't know about the twin towers then. Even if two planes hit buildings, couldn't it still be a fault in the planes? *Please, not an attack.*

They kept playing the video over. Crowds of panicked people fled down the street, through buildings so jumbled together they could all catch fire.

"Look up there," James said, "above the explosion. People are jumping out of the building."

"Could soldiers inside be pushing them out?" When my older

brother Yier was at the university, northern troops set the black students' dorm on fire. Yier and his two friends jumped from the window and were the only students who survived, even though the soldiers shot at them. But that was from the second floor. This was too high. These people could not survive.

"They are jumping to escape the fire," James said.

Shock stopped my breathing. Would I jump from that high to escape fire?

Daniel, Benson, and Lino came into the room. "*Ya ngo yin de?*" they asked. What is going on?

"America has been attacked," James said.

"No way," Daniel said. "No one would attack America."

He was right. Who would attack America?

The five of us stood in a circle, trying to understand the news, but the reporters didn't seem to know what had happened either, or who had done it, or if it was an attack. The awful images of people fleeing with smoke and dust covering their skin reminded me of how we'd often fled from cross fire and bombs in our homeland. They had the same look on their faces.

Judy said the explosions we'd heard the night before were just fireworks. This wasn't fireworks. This was war. Was there no safe haven on earth? My skin blistered with fear.

"Evil has followed us," James said. "We brought bad luck. Our government is angry at America for bringing us here."

Could he be right? No one had ever attacked America before, but now it was attacked right after we came here. If evil had visited this land so far away, we could never outrun it. I would not have left Africa if I'd known it was going to follow me here, too. I would have faced it there. I'd seen what evil did to innocent people; it devoured everyone so quickly. I didn't want to bring this to America.

Lino shook his head and headed into our bedroom. Daniel, Benson, and I sat on the couch, each of us silent in our thoughts. James still stood, his legs spread and hands on his hips, a military man. James had been forced to be a soldier as a child.

What about Benjamin? "Benjamin. He is coming today. Did he fly to New York like we did?"

Benson hung his head. "I don't know."

How could we know? We would just have to wait.

I turned back to the television. The news reporters were talking when the screen changed to a building falling down in a huge crash of white dust.

We looked at each other. No words came from our mouths. For so long South Sudan's population had suffered under the regime of the North. Sudan hosted terrorist groups. Osama bin Laden had been there for four years recruiting and training. Now they had come after us to destroy us once and for all.

"This is our fault," I said. "This is the biggest mistake of our lives that we have brought this here to America."

We were so sick of war in our native land. By sheer luck we were alive and here in the United States, the safest place on earth. But maybe it wasn't as safe here as we thought. Would danger always lurk? Peace would be only the moments in between, when no danger took place. I'd always be looking over my shoulder with a sharp eye. In Sudan, I'd learned how to avoid war. Here in America I didn't know where it might come from. I had to be alert for war all the time.

DANGEROUS PLACE

Judy

The day after the attack on the World Trade Center our country was paralyzed. Planes still weren't flying. We were glued to the news as the search for the attackers began. The world had our back.

Like first awakening from a nightmare, I was dazed and suspended. Nothing but eating, brushing my teeth, and trying to sleep seemed appropriate.

Joseph had told me not to worry about Benjamin. He was with a group of Lost Boys. Their plane had been diverted. He'd know more in days to come.

I'd called the apartment and spoken with Alepho. He'd said they were sorry for the attack on America. If it had caused him more angst than that, he didn't reveal it on the phone.

Alepho had asked to visit our home more than once. I'd been hesitant, concerned about their perception of our relatively large suburban home after they'd lived in a mud hut with a tin-can roof and no water or electricity for nine years, and now they were in a dingy apartment in City Heights. Even though they'd been too busy to visit, my slowness to invite them was beginning to feel rude. A day at our house seemed more fitting than a park or some other public place, which everyone was avoiding.

I picked them up at their apartment. As usual, Benson in front, Alepho and Lino in the back.

"Any more news about Benjamin?" I asked.

"We did not hear," Benson said. He handed me folded papers. More writing than ever this time. "Thank you, Benson, I really look forward to reading these." I tucked them into the side of my purse for later.

We headed north on Interstate 5. The car was quiet, full of people in a state of shock, including me. "I live about thirty miles from here," I said to lighten the mood. "So we'll get to be on the freeway for a much longer time than we have before." I thought that might even excite them.

No response. No chatter about *Rush Hour*, Jackie Chan. Guess they were feeling the way we all were about the disaster in New York. I wanted to know, but the moment seemed inappropriate to ask. No words came to me.

Few cars were on the roads. People were hunkered down. We passed homes, condo complexes, and business centers. About halfway there, as the freeway veered toward the coast, I said, "You'll see the ocean soon." I thought that would get an *ooh* or *ahh*, but it went by without comment.

"Now we're leaving the city," I said.

The guys were quiet. New York and its potential consequences must have triggered some awful memories and emotions. Talk about it or not talk about it? I'd wait for them to bring it up.

We came to an area with sprawling gated communities that had recently recontoured the rolling hills where I used to ride my horse. I exited the freeway. Paul and I had relocated north of the city twenty years earlier to enjoy a rural lifestyle and find a place where I could keep a horse. That meant a forty-minute commute for both of us. I'd quit working when Cliff was born, but Paul still drove it, sometimes more than once a day if there was an emergency at the hospital. He said the refuge from the city was worth the trip. With new housing developments spreading far to the north of us, the area was no longer as rural as it once had been. Quiet horse trails had been consumed by homes and streets.

A few pockets of older neighborhoods retained that country feeling, and we drove through one on the winding, shrub- and tree-lined road to our house in silence until Benson turned to me. He looked worried when he asked, "Why do you live in a dangerous place?"

"Dangerous? No, not at all." Especially compared to their neighborhood. "Really, it's very safe here." After their night of fireworks and planes flying into skyscrapers, I'd hoped this would be a peaceful day in the country for them.

"Too much low bush. Animals can hide and you can't see them."

"Oh, animals. I thought you meant people."

"Soldiers, too."

"We don't have soldiers or dangerous animals here. No lions or leopards. Oh, except for rattlesnakes. Just watch where you walk. They're not aggressive unless you step on one."

"Oh. That is good."

I didn't want to mention the mountain lion that hung around. Few people had seen it. Not the kind they were familiar with anyway. In fact, it wasn't technically a lion, just a big cat in the cougar or puma family, about one fifth the size of an African lion.

"Are there bears?" Alepho asked from the back seat. "We don't have bears in Africa. I read there are bears in America."

"Yes, there are bears in America but they live way up north."

Benson said, "I did not know there is forest here. It look like Africa."

I thought they might be pleasantly surprised and relieved not all of America was cemented over. I felt the same way at times, when I stayed too long in the city. "Actually most of America looks like this. Large mountains with forest and huge deserts."

Benson pointed a long finger toward the hills. "Very beautiful here. It look like Sudan with all the trees."

Benson's description altered my image of Sudan. I needed to find a book with more information. Barnes & Noble hadn't had one. Maybe the downtown library.

The road straightened and we passed through our one-block-long town. Small, older tile-roof, Spanish style buildings housed banks and real estate offices now. The bookstore, toy store, and market had closed up, unable to pay the increasing rents.

"Is this your village?" Benson asked.

"Yes, this is the village center." I pointed. "That's the school where Cliff is right now. That's the library."

We passed a golf course, went around a reservoir, and up the hill to our house. We'd built in the middle of an old orange orchard. At the entrance to our long driveway, Casey and Vader, our two Labs, greeted us. They knew my car coming up the hill. They pursued us all the way into the garage.

As the dogs circled the car and bounced up to look in the windows, I recalled that Alepho had said he'd been bitten and was wary of dogs. "Don't worry. The dogs are just happy to see us. I can lock them up if you like."

"No, it is okay," he said.

The guys got out. Casey, the yellow female, ran straight up to

Alepho. That figured. She was overly friendly and had boundary issues. Alepho didn't flinch.

"Outside, Casey," I commanded.

To my surprise, she ran out of the garage.

Alepho looked stunned. "You talk to your dog?"

"Well, yes."

He shook his head. "He understand you?"

"The yellow one is a she. She understands a lot, but she doesn't often obey."

Benson reached out to touch the black Lab, Vader, who ducked and ran out of the garage.

"It's okay, he's just shy." I didn't want to mention that he'd been rescued from a bad childhood, though probably not nearly as bad as theirs.

We entered the house straight from the garage and headed toward the kitchen. Benson looked down a side hallway. "Does another family live there?"

"No, that's Cliff's room."

Benson pointed up the staircase. "Does another family live up there?"

"That's our room up there. This is one house. For just one family."

He looked perplexed. "Then where is the family?"

"Paul is at work. Cliff is at school, but he'll be home at three."

"Where is the family in the photo?"

Oh, he meant the twenty-five of us in the driveway for my dad's eightieth birthday. No wonder he looked confused and disappointed.

"I'm sorry, Benson, those were cousins and relatives who were visiting. I'll be sure you meet them soon. Each family has its own house. Just the three of us live in this one."

"Only three." His eyes widened. "Why?"

"American culture. Each family lives separately. It's just me here today."

"You are alone?"

"Only in the daytime. I like it. Come on in."

I'd wondered how they would interpret my lifestyle but hadn't anticipated *him* feeling sad for *me*.

We entered the open area that housed the kitchen and family room. "Have a seat," I said. "Sit anywhere you like."

"Your house is nice," Alepho said. "How much does it cost?"

I'd rather share details of my sex life than give him the answer to that. "We get a loan from the bank to buy a house so actually the bank owns it mostly."

"Do you pay rent?"

"No. We pay the bank."

"How much does that cost?"

"It depends on the price of the house. They can be a few hundred thousand or millions."

Alepho took a chair at the kitchen table. "Is your family safe?" he asked.

Safe? "Yes, they are fine."

"Does anyone live in New York?"

Newspapers were spread out across the tabletop, every page covered with photos of New York. "My brother once lived in New York, but he is here now. They're all here."

I gathered the newspapers into a pile. "I'm sorry this happened so soon after you arrived in America."

Alepho's eyebrows furrowed as they often did. "Will Americans blame Lost Boys for the attack?"

"Oh my, no. Why would they do that?"

JUDY'S HOUSE

Alepho

The night after the attack in New York, a friend of our uncle Ajak Awer who had a phone called us from Uganda. "Uncle Ajak Awer needs your help," he said. "He's stranded in Kampala. He came here to Kampala to make some money for the families, and there is nothing here for him. He can't get home. He needs to get back to the kids in Pageri."

Pageri was back in southern Sudan. Uncle Ajak needed six hundred American dollars.

The news saddened us. Our uncle had stood up for us in hard times. He'd supported us during the war. He'd inspired me to go to school and get my education. We couldn't just leave him in Kampala. His children and those of his dead brother depended on him for food.

We were in America. Maybe people thought we were rich now, but how could we ever collect six hundred dollars?

"Our sponsor seems rich," I told Benson. "Her car is new. We could ask her."

• • •

Judy came to take us to her house. Every time I saw Judy she wore different clothes. How many clothes did she have? The women in Africa wore dresses. Judy never wore dresses, always pants like men do. African women braided their hair so that it was neat and close to the head. Judy's hair was always loose, and the wind blew it everywhere like dead grass.

I didn't feel well, but I went with Benson and Lino to Judy's house. I'd always thought my headaches were due to lack of food in the camp. Now in the US, there was a lot of food. At first when I ate the American food, the feeling of a full belly was good. Then it became bloated and a problem.

Back in the camp, I did not consider that there was something wrong with me. My headaches had been going on for years, but everyone suffered with them there. They made me tired all the time. It didn't matter how long I rested or slept. I really couldn't do much.

Now with all the food in America, my headaches had grown worse, my stomach hurt too, and I just wanted to sleep like a lizard in the sun.

I'd expressed to Diar, the IRC caseworker, my awful stomach pain. I didn't tell him that I had this problem for years in the refugee camps because those things were normal there. You bear your own suffering silently.

Diar took me to a clinic with a Chinese doctor and also the Catholic Charities clinic. They didn't find anything wrong. "Your stomach is going through adjustment." That sounded right. Since I'd just arrived, every part of me required adjustment.

Driving to Judy's house I asked myself: *Why should I suffer this much when our sponsor's husband is a doctor? I'm sure he can find out what is wrong with my head and stomach.*

Asking Judy would be a hard task. A sense of embarrassment came over me. Where I came from, a man expressed his problem to another man, not a woman. I was new and didn't know the cultural etiquette.

The area where Judy lived was farms with more space than the crowded area where we lived. Kakuma camp had been crowded too. I thought maybe I'd like to live here one day. I wondered if it would be boring out here by myself. I couldn't see any other houses around, just trees. Did she get lonely with no cars or businesses like in the city where more things happened? It was nice but isolated, hiding out here alone.

Judy's dogs chased our car to her house. She had told us there were no dangerous wild animals in her area, so why did she keep dogs? We kept dogs to scare away lions and hyenas and strangers.

When I got out of the car, the dog the color of a lion ran up to me. Judy talked to it. It understood her and ran outside. The black dog went to Judy. She rubbed its body and hugged it like a human. Then she kissed the dog.

"She kissed the dog," I said to Benson in Dinka.

The black dog ran over to Benson but when he tried to touch it like Judy, it ran away.

"The white people must be very loving," I said. "Look how they love their animals and the animals love them."

Judy's house was big and smelled different from our house. Why didn't our house smell fresh and clean like this? After Kakuma, where we'd lived in mud huts with flattened tin-can roofs, our apartment in San Diego was the best home we'd ever seen. Now I saw that Judy's house was the best.

"One day I will own a house like this," I said. "How much does it cost?"

I didn't understand Judy's answer but when she said thousands, that made me forget about it. I didn't even have my job yet.

Often, when Judy explained things to us, we didn't know what was the right thing to say. We just said, "Oh. Oh. Yeah." And nodded our heads like Americans. When we asked Judy a question and she gave us an explanation, then we didn't have more to say.

I sat at Judy's table. My head hurt and my stomach felt like I'd drank bad water but I knew the water in America wasn't bad. I expressed to Benson how embarrassed I was to ask Judy about my personal problems.

Benson said, "First inquire what is culturally acceptable before you plunge into a raging water."

In the Dinka culture, "plunging into raging water" was an expression for someone who is full of follies, someone who does not read the situation carefully. A person who acts spurred by instancy. After hearing Benson's advice, I decided not to ask Judy about my headaches and stomachaches.

BOTOX

Judy

Alepho's brooding gaze didn't leave the stack of newspapers with the burning towers.

"The attack in New York wasn't your fault," I said.

His eyebrows knitted. "They are angry at America for bringing the Lost Boys."

I didn't want to say *it had nothing to do with you*; that sounded belittling. But ... really? "We don't know who did it yet. Could be an American. No one will blame you."

Lino held up his torn backpack. "Where is sewing machine?"

I led him to the spare bedroom, opened up the cabinet, and lifted out my Sears sewing machine. Twenty-nine years earlier my mother had given it to me as a wedding gift. For a dizzying moment, I thought of how much she would have liked to meet these three young men. Living through the Depression, a war, and a peripatetic life not of her own choosing had given her a big heart for the underdog. Unfortunately, she'd passed away in 1984. I missed sharing things like this with her.

"I know this machine," Lino said. "Just like one in Kakuma."

"Really? Wow. You had one like this? That's interesting." I opened the supply drawer. "Help yourself to whatever you need." He took out the seam ripper and set to work taking apart the backpack.

In the kitchen, Alepho was looking through a research book on Native American medicine.

"Alephonsion sounds Spanish," I said.

"That name was given to me in the camp."

"What's your Dinka name?"

"Awer. Sounds like 'aware' in English."

"Oh, I like that. What does it mean?"

"It means like a window where the light comes through."

"You're so aware of things. How prophetic. That means—"

"I know what prophetic means."

Alepho's intensity could put me off balance. I was about to make apologies for assuming he didn't know what "prophetic" meant when he smiled. His smiles were rare and restrained. He had one darkened front tooth, as though it had been broken and bled. Perhaps he was self-conscious. I'd have to ask Joseph if dental care was covered.

He found a newsmagazine and settled onto the couch.

I'd had plans for us today—swimming, taking a walk, and having lunch on the lawn. Within minutes, however, they'd each become occupied on their own, not adhering to my agenda. My purpose had been to give them a nice easy day and they were relaxing. I wasn't. Why did I feel like I had to organize them?

After a while Benson came into the kitchen from the living room where I'd set him up to copy his music tapes. "My tape is dubbing now."

Alepho asked Benson a question. A discussion ensued in Dinka that I couldn't understand but somehow seemed like Benson was giving advice. Or orders.

I went to the kitchen, waited until they were through and asked, "Would you guys like to go in the orchard? Pick some oranges?"

"I will be here," Benson said.

"Okay. Alepho, would you like to come?"

Alepho and I crossed the lawn, bags in hand, dogs at our heels. The orchard was awash in the sweet pungency of spoiled citrus. Decaying fruit squished underfoot. The branches sagged and the ground was littered with one of our best crops ever.

From trees still laden with ripened fruit, we picked juicy Valencias. Alepho reached easily into the upper branches and his bag quickly filled.

"You will be rich," he said.

Rich from farming? I wished. The orchard was a lovely money pit. The fruit would be left on the ground this year because the price of oranges was so low it wouldn't pay for the pickers, never mind the water bills. "No, it's not like that."

"May we take another bag for the Bols?" he asked.

The Bols, a Sudanese family with some pretty young daughters, lived downstairs from him. "Yes, of course. We can pick all you want."

I couldn't bear to tell him that all of this would rot. Standing beside someone who had once nearly starved, and was now surrounded by trees dripping with potential food, "waste" took on a whole new meaning.

A squirrel darted by and disappeared in the undergrowth.

"What is that?" Alepho asked.

"Ground squirrel."

"So small. Our squirrels are bigger than your cats."

"That big?"

"Yes." He looked a little offended. I'd meant to show how impressed I was, instead it must have sounded like I doubted him. I did wonder about some of the things he and the others said. Not that I thought they were lying. But, for instance, that their mother was seven feet tall. The Dinka are tall, but they'd left home at such a young age. I also thought my mother was tall when I was young and she was only four foot ten. Did they even measure or think in terms of feet? We had so many language issues between us. Our life experiences had been very different. Our perceptions must be, too.

"What other animals lived near your home?" I asked, trying to lighten things up.

"These wild cow, antelope, gazelles, zebra." He stopped. A homesick look came over him.

"Did you ever see elephants?"

"Yes, they are dangerous. They come into our village sometimes."

"Wow. You're kidding."

"No, it is the truth." He looked offended.

"I'm sorry. It's a common saying that really means 'I'm surprised.'"

I picked up an orange from the ground that still looked good.

"A man brought me a baby monkey who lost his mother. I gave him milk."

I wondered if he saw the irony in that. On his journey, had he hoped someone would take him in like he had done for the monkey?

"The monkey picked up the cup just like people do. Monkeys imitate people."

"Yes, I've heard that. Amazing."

"The big monkeys got mad that he came to my house. They like to steal our corn. Just one monkey goes in the field so we don't see him. Just like people do, he ties a vine around his body and puts the cobs of corn in that vine. Very clever."

"Really clever." Sounded too clever to believe. "How about giraffe? They're so beautiful."

"My father hunt giraffe."

"Do people know it's illegal to kill giraffe and those other large animals?"

He gave me a kind look, but with an expression that said, *You don't get it.* "The country is in war. There are no laws."

That shut me up. My Western conscience, concerned with endangered animals, had not grasped the reality of the situation. Of course a country at war was a place with no laws.

"The animals are gone," he said. "They left because of the war."

Alepho became quiet but seemed comfortable with the silence. I wanted to be. There were a thousand questions I wanted answers to, but I'd learned from Cliff that asking them was probably the least effective way of getting answers. When Cliff and I were alone in the car, he was the one who often initiated filling the void, and that had led to some of our best conversations.

Alepho picked until the bags were all full. I reached out to carry a couple, but he resisted and insisted on carrying them all. As we walked back to the house, he said, "My mother loved Benson more than me."

What? That was out of the blue. He'd survived a genocide. And that was the thing that bothered him? So revealing and personal. So universally human. As the oldest child, I remembered feeling the same way when my little sister came along.

"Oh, Alepho, mothers love all their children."

"Benson was always helpful to my mother."

Was that why he insisted on carrying all of the oranges? "I'm a mother. I can say that I'm sure she loved you just the same."

He looked the other way and didn't say anything.

Back in the house, Lino was still sewing and Benson was

dubbing more tapes. Alepho put the oranges on the counter and picked up the newsmagazine and resumed reading.

As I prepared lunch—butternut squash soup and turkey sandwiches—Alepho brought the magazine over. It was opened to a page with a photo of a needle inserted above a woman's eyebrow. "Very bad poison," he said. "Why they want to put this in their faces?"

If he knew that poison was being injected, he'd read the article and also knew it was to treat wrinkles. His observations often probed well below the surface, and yet seemed in the spirit of acceptance and a willingness to adapt. It probably wasn't intentional, but he tended to corner me with questions that required embarrassing answers, like explaining SlimFast to someone who'd not had enough food. Now Botox. I had to be honest though. "They do it to look young," I said. "Cure wrinkles."

"You do that?"

Did he see my wrinkles and wonder why they weren't cured? Or did he not see them and think I'd been using Botox? "I haven't done that. I'm afraid of the poison."

He furrowed his brow and crinkled his forehead. "We don't like to cure the wrinkles." He pointed to his face. "The elders like these because you can see their feelings."

I smiled. Good point. "Americans care a lot about looking young."

"I see that. My uncle need money to take care of his family."

"Your uncle?"

"Yes. His friend called from Kampala. My uncle need money to get back to the family in Pageri."

"Kampala. That's Uganda, right?" I took the soup bowls down from the cabinet and set them on the counter to fill. "How much does he need?"

"Too much."

"Where's Pageri?"

"Southern Sudan. That's where the kids are. They need food."

Wasn't war there too? So complex. I'd ask another time. "How much is too much?"

"Six hundred dollars."

I turned the magazine page to avoid being asked what it cost to be wrinkle-free for a couple of months.

"I need a job," he added.

Jobs. A week earlier, before the attack, his prospects had looked dismal. Who would be hiring now? Particularly a young man with no job skills from a country with a Middle Eastern–sounding name? If he did find a job, it would take months to accumulate six hundred dollars.

Benson had shared with me how their uncle had helped them so much. Now he was caring for their orphaned nieces and nephews. Of course, Benson and Alepho would be eager to repay his kindness to them. I wanted to help this guy, and I'd never even met him.

With planes crashing into the towers, the whole world was on hold. Not quite real. I wanted my family around me more than anything, more than ever.

That must be so true for them. Was this how they'd felt for fifteen years?

Six hundred dollars wouldn't change my life but it might save their uncle and his family.

That meant breaking my vow: *Teach them to fish.* I'd been so sure that eliminating money from the equation was the right thing. But the right thing no longer felt so clear-cut. If I gave money to help their uncle, why wouldn't I do the same for all of them three months from now when their refugee assistance ran out? Even if I explained that it was only this one time to get their uncle out of his dire situation, would the underlying message be:

My sponsor can easily solve problems with money if she chooses to? That notion was hard to defeat while sitting in the kitchen of our home they thought large enough to house several families. I'd been struggling to keep Cliff from thinking that money came easily and that it could solve all problems. He saw it all around him. That was one reason I'd gotten involved in the first place.

I needed more time to think it over. "Let's have lunch!"

SEEDS OF LOVE

Alepho

Judy took me to the trees. I'd seen the fruit of lime trees in Sudan, but I'd never seen oranges. They were bigger. The day was warm, but cool in the shade, like under the mango trees in my village. White blossoms sweetened the air. Ripe fruit, turning fuzzy, squished under my feet. Didn't they harvest their crops in America?

I wanted to ask Judy to help us get our uncle out of Uganda. I was afraid. It was too much money. A friend had been sick for a long time in the camp. We sold our shirts and a pan. We grew okra where water leaked from the water tap. It needed to be protected from thieves until harvest and then we sold it. We saved for a year like that to get six hundred shillings for our friend's treatment. In America, six hundred shillings was only six dollars. Saving six hundred American dollars would take a hundred years in Kakuma camp.

Judy picked an orange and peeled it. She divided the sections and offered me one. The juice squirted in my mouth and ran down my chin. It wasn't sweet like a mango. She offered me more but I declined and she threw the rest onto the ground. "Here's a bag," she said. "You twist the fruit like this until the stem breaks."

So that was how they harvested. In our village at harvest time everyone went to the fields. That was the happiest and most content time of the year. My mother roasted the corn on top of the firewood and peeled back the husk. The kernels burst between my teeth, shooting sweetness into my mouth. Food, milk, and grain were plentiful everywhere.

How sweet my childhood had been. My memories so precious. Planting season was my favorite time. Everything became green. The air was alive with the buzz of bees and insects. A type of tall grass called dog tail grew at that time. We kids trudged through it, looking for the rare double dog tail. We plucked those for good luck. When I returned to our house, my mother treated me to my greatest desire: clotted cow's milk, which was fresh milk mixed with soured milk.

My family were cattle keepers and farmers. Farmers had to be smart. My mother placed the healthiest seeds under the fire. The smoke acted as a preservative. She kept those special seeds safe for the next planting season. Even when we ran out of food, those seeds were never touched. She'd say, "If you want to have a good harvest don't eat your seeds."

Without those times, those loving seeds from my family, I don't know how I could have continued living, considering all the things that I'd experienced and seen. Like corn seeds, every child needs a healthy, loving life with their parents.

I filled my bag and asked Judy if I could pick another bag of oranges for the Bols, who lived downstairs from our apartment. She approved my request.

I carried the bags of oranges back into Judy's house. She brought a lot of food to the table and invited us to sit down. She showed us the proper tools to use for eating.

Judy was helpful, teaching us cultural ways. Even though I'd grown up in a traditional village with a traditional way of life, I'd always felt like I didn't fit in. I wanted to fit in in America. Benson learned the cultures and followed the rules. In our village, he always helped our mother. I did what I wanted, and my mother often scolded me, saying that I went against our people's ways. She loved Benson more for that reason.

Since I'd left our village in war when I was seven, I'd been taking a bit of culture here and a bit there from different places, but I never felt a part of anywhere. I didn't like being told the proper way to dress, or to speak, or do things. How did they know? I had to find out those things for myself.

At IRC they were training us to look in people's eyes when we talked. I told Benson that when I walked down the street in America and looked at a person coming toward me, many times that person gave me a look like, *Why are you looking at us?* They looked angry, like I shouldn't be there.

Benson said, "Don't look at people. You have to look away."

Benson was wise. He had a way of reading things and going in the right direction. I liked to try things like a blind man, needing to touch and get his hand burned to learn.

I decided I shouldn't look at strangers here. I didn't have bad intentions, but some people seemed to perceive they were not good. People didn't understand what was going on inside me. I lived life more in my head than in the world.

The food Judy shared with us tasted good, but how could I enjoy it? I felt shameful being comfortable in America when our brothers were still in the camp, Benjamin was lost, and our uncle's kids were suffering.

I needed to find a way to help him. America wasn't like Kakuma. I couldn't grow okra; we didn't even have an outside place and crops wouldn't grow in the apartment. San Diego was a city. I needed to work. But where did one go to find a job? Who did we ask?

I wanted to ask Judy if I could harvest the oranges and sell them. During the traditional Dinka ceremony when a boy becomes a man, he recites his grandfathers' names back twenty generations. My people had been farmers all that time. I hadn't learned yet, but I could be a farmer. But I didn't have money to buy the oranges so it didn't feel proper to ask Judy for her family's crops.

CLASSIFIEDS

Judy

At the table, Benson lifted his fork. "What is this called?"

Until today, we'd only eaten together at fast-food places, nothing yet that required tableware. I wanted them to feel comfortable when they encountered that situation.

"That's a fork, this is a spoon, and the table is set like this with the fork on the left and the spoon and knife on the right." Such formalities must have sounded fussy to someone who'd been eating cornmeal with his fingers for fourteen years. They picked up each utensil, repeated the name and practiced the placement with a sincere desire to learn.

Use of the spoon came naturally and the squash soup was gone right away. Then the turkey sandwiches. When I brought out a plate of sliced papaya, Benson said, "Very common fruit in Africa," and it disappeared like the rest. Such a pleasure to see them eat like the young men they were.

"In the camp," Benson said, "we queued up at four in the morning to get rations."

Lino said, "When the water pipe broke, we didn't have water for three days."

Presence of food often brought out stories of their time in the camp. Benson was the storyteller and shared a lot of details. His perpetually smiling eyes and cheerful tone made it strange hearing about hardships. From Lino, on the other hand, I heard outrage, a sense that what he'd been through wasn't right. Alepho was quiet with a far-off stare, like he'd seen and experienced things he didn't want to talk about.

"The grain wasn't ground," Benson added rather flatly. "One needed money to grind it."

"Cooking took hours," Lino added, "or it gave a serious stomachache. That took a lot of firewood. People were robbed collecting firewood."

Listening to them relay conditions in the camp reminded me of their uncle's predicament. If a refugee camp was that bad, how were his children surviving in the middle of a war?

Yet, how could I know if the whole story wasn't made up to get money out of Americans? I couldn't imagine these earnest young men scamming me, but the so-called friend of their uncle, some desperate guy in Africa, might be trying to get six hundred dollars out of some naive guys in America.

"So," I asked, "once you get jobs and save up, how will you get the money to your uncle?"

"We will wire it to Uganda."

That didn't sound secure.

"We must find jobs," Lino said.

"Yes, that's a really good first step. What kind of work interests you?"

"Any work is good," Benson said. "I need forty hours."

Forty hours. Of course. James and Daniel's situation at the

hotel with only one or two days a week had made a big impression on them, had them worried. "Yes, we'll look for full time."

I pulled out the classified section of the newspaper. Even though I'd worked most of my adult life, I'd never searched the classifieds for a job. I'd never even filled out an application. One day after school when I was fifteen, my friend Stephanie and I decided we wanted to work. She stopped into a convalescent home, first business outside the school grounds, and got a job helping distribute food to the patients. I went a few more blocks down the street into a grocery store. Even though I was underage, my job in the deli started that afternoon and lasted three years. During college, my dad "asked" one of his tenants, a start-up computer company, if they could use some help. That was my second job, and I ended up staying with that company for nineteen years. Connections sure helped. I hadn't known or appreciated how lucky I'd been.

Things were different now. "Let's see what's in the paper." I read out loud, "Accountant, auto mechanic, clerical, construction. Construction, that might work."

"I like to build houses," Lino said. "I build in Kakuma."

Interesting idea. Talented with his hands and excellent in math, helpful skills in that industry. I called on a few ads under construction. "Does he have welding experience?" "We could use an estimator." "Got a backhoe opening." All wanted experience. Many two years. Nothing for day laborers.

"Okay. I'll make calls later about that," I said. I read on. "Customer service, dancer, dental ..." I skipped hotels, too unreliable now that tourist season was over; we were in a recession, and not to mention the whole unknown impact of the World Trade Center attacks. Three janitor positions wanted experience. Ads under general labor required driver's licenses or specific skills. I moved up to restaurants. Bartenders, experienced line cook, hostess, sushi maker. They probably didn't advertise for dishwashers—too expensive—maybe they just took walk-ins. I'd originally thought that taking the boys around to places and filling out applications would be the way to go. Worked for me forty years earlier. But there were many reasons to expect rejections these days, and how many rejections would it take before their confidence would be in the toilet?

Toward the end of the alphabet, past the jobs that held the most promise, I realized this was just as big of a mistake with the three of them looking over my shoulder. I closed the paper.

Alepho said, "I could pick your oranges and sell them?"

That sounded so simple, so logical, so right. Just not possible. "I'd be happy to let you have them, but I think selling them would be a problem. No one is buying. When is that job-training class at IRC?"

"Job preparedness," Benson corrected me, "is next week."

"The week after you finish the class, we'll look again. By then there'll be more jobs."

Hopefully. There had to be something three smart, strong, English-speaking young men who were eager to work could do.

"Want to swim?" They'd said they wanted to go in my pool so outside a local drugstore, on an end-of-the-season special, I'd bought the last three men's size medium swimming trunks for a dollar each. They were all red, the only choice. "Here you go. Get changed. We'll work on jobs in two weeks." After they'd finished the class. After I'd done my homework. And hopefully when the country had resumed a more normal life.

At first touch, they complained the eighty-degree water was too cold but soon our pool had never looked so full as it did with three six-foot men splashing around. Their slender dark bodies glided through water as elegantly and gracefully as they did on land. Even though Alepho claimed he couldn't swim, he moved like a dolphin in the shallow end. They tried to climb aboard flimsy blow-up rafts, and when I brought out a pair of fins they fought over them like siblings. Fortunately, I had three face masks. They spent a lot of time below the surface looking at everything.

I sat down in a lounge chair and reveled in the joyfulness bursting from the pool. With all that they'd been through in their lives, and all that had happened in the last few days, a delight at being able to give them this moment came over me. Moisture pooled in my eyes. I went in the house for my camera. And a tissue. Three young guys wouldn't understand tears. It'd spoil the moment for sure.

I took lots of pictures. They loved getting the photos the next time we met. Always a copy for each of them.

School would be out soon and I needed to go pick up Cliff. They were having so much fun, I didn't want to make them get out. But leaving did not feel right somehow. Did I still picture them as those five- and six-year-olds in the video? Alepho said he couldn't swim. He was doing fine. They were young men now who had crossed rivers with crocodiles while being shot at. They could take care of each other.

"Hey, guys," I said. "Going to pick up Cliff. Towels are on the lounge chairs. Be sure to shut the door so the cats don't get out."

THE MEDIATION

Alepho

After we ate the food, Judy showed us how to look in the newspaper for jobs. There were so many, I didn't know which one I wanted. How did I get the job? It was there in the paper, but then what did I do?

Everywhere I looked, I saw the news that shocked America and shook the world. The attack on New York grieved me. Some said that North Sudan was involved in the plot to attack America. Others said the attackers might have been citizens of America like the ones who blew up a building in Oklahoma. That idea of an enemy from within sent greater fears into my soul. It'd been my own government that had sent the militias that had attacked our villages.

What would happen now that America had been attacked? I couldn't be at peace with anything that led to war or destruction of human lives. Why couldn't the world use dialogue to solve every disagreement, from individuals to countries? They could find a good mediator, like my father, and bring lasting peace. Maybe we were sworn enemies or simply hated one another, but there had to be a common ground where resolution could happen.

My father had been a mediator up until his death. A respected man in the Bahr al-Ghazal region for knowing how to find that common ground. That day he took me with him to solve the dispute over the killed cow, everyone had nodded in agreement. No one argued with my father's solution. But the talking went on. Their voices grew aggressive, they used big words like "racism," "religious discrimination," "resources," and "oil," which I didn't understand. The discussion grew louder and louder. I became eager to leave.

One man rose and walked toward another in an aggressive way. My father stood and raised his arms. "We must depart in order to reach home before dark."

The men quieted. The villagers gave my father a bag of grain and thanked him for his services as a peacemaker.

On the way back to our village, my father asked, "Did you learn anything today?"

I didn't know the right answer.

"What did you see happen?" my father asked.

"You stopped the fight."

"Yes, that's right. Did you see how important it is to listen respectfully to all sides of a disagreement? Blame and revenge should always be avoided. They are a never-ending cycle that causes worse conflict and harm. The goal is a compromise that settles the issue permanently. Both parties must feel like they have won."

As I walked, listening to my father's wise words, I stepped around an acacia thorn as long as my finger.

"Alepho, stop," my father said. "Pick it up and throw it to the side of the trail. We must be sensitive to the ones who follow us and might not see the danger."

We walked on and he continued to instruct me. "Do not step on bugs. Everything around us means something, and it matters. If you are big and strong, you must take care to not harm those who are smaller and weaker."

He told me never to pluck flowers. "If you don't need it, you don't have to play with it. They are there for us to see."

He cautioned me about dangers. "A warthog may be small, but he can be as dangerous as the lion. Beware what you eat; it too can take a life."

"Father," I asked, "why were the men still angry after the dispute was settled?"

"They are worried and angry about other things."

"What things?"

My father stopped in the middle of the trail. "This is important," he said. "Listen carefully to me and obey my instructions. If anything ever happens, you must run and hide in the bush until I come for you."

"Why, Father? What will happen?"

"Danger may come to our area. Just follow my instructions. You see, a child must be guided from fire until death."

He walked on, and I followed behind. I didn't understand then what he was telling me. I had imagined it meant that he'd guide me away from the fires that sometimes swept over our valley. I'd listened and tried my best to understand, but I was only five then, the youngest of all his sons. Still, I was the fortunate one receiving my father's wisdom gifts, and I didn't want to lose a single one. How could I have known then that he was warning me about the attacks that were about to come and change our lives forever?

The feelings of those times surrounded me now after the attacks in New York. What would happen next? Would fighting begin? Could war come to America?

THE GILO

Judy

"Do you have much homework?" I asked Cliff in the car on the way home from school.

"Only a little," he said.

Oh good, he'd have plenty of time to visit with the guys before I took them home. He liked to procrastinate doing his homework anyway.

We entered the house through the garage. The sewing machine whirred. Lino had gotten out of the pool and was back at his project. He showed me his backpack. I couldn't see where it'd been repaired. He must have taken the whole thing apart and put it back together. "Lino, this is outstanding. Where did you learn to sew like this?"

He straightened and a proud smile spread across his face. "In Kakuma camp I take sewing class for one year."

Great skill, but not a job possibility anymore in Southern California. Most clothing manufacturing took place in Mexico these days, or in the sweatshops in Los Angeles that had made the news lately for keeping Asian women as slaves. A used sewing machine would be nice for him to have in the apartment though. That could be a reality.

In the kitchen, Alepho surfed the web. I'd shown him how to access my computer. Benson came in from copying tapes just as Cliff came from the garage. I had been limiting my volunteering time to the day, so they hadn't seen Cliff since he'd started school. They greeted Cliff and shared some tentative guy hugs.

Cliff convinced Alepho to go outside for some basketball. They were back soon—September was our hottest month, and that garage courtyard baked. They washed the asphalt off their blackened hands, leaving the sink a gray mess. Alepho cleaned it up with a sponge. How thoughtful. I'd noticed their apartment was always clean, except for the towering pile of Coke cans. Beds made, dishes put away.

"Let's play pool," Cliff said.

"No," Alepho said. "I went swimming one time."

"The other kind," Cliff said and beckoned him outside.

Alepho refused to move. His eyebrows knit with a determined look. They'd been that way most of the day, a sort of squint that looked like I felt when I had a headache. He looked perturbed that Cliff had ignored him. A brief standoff ensued.

Cliff shrugged and headed out to the pool table on the covered patio. Alepho watched him through the French doors. As soon as he saw the colorful balls roll around, he was out the door as well.

I watched from the kitchen. Cliff, cue stick in hand, showed off his shots, going from one to the other in rapid-fire sequence with his mouth moving just as fast. He could use some work on his teaching skills, but his pool game wasn't bad.

Alepho stood rigidly, observing with a skeptical look, brows still pinched together.

Cliff stopped shooting and handed Alepho the cue stick. His first shot missed the ball. Cliff picked up another cue stick and showed him how to hold it. Alepho tried a few awkward shots.

Seeing them interact made me smile. I'd wanted Cliff to meet people who had grown up without all the comforts and privileges he'd always enjoyed, to see firsthand that those things shouldn't be taken for granted, and to break down the feelings of entitlement that came from good fortune.

I hadn't given race much thought. We had a few African American friends, but maybe these were the first black people near his own age Cliff had interacted with personally, other than at places like McDonald's.

Although growing up my family had little money and we'd lived in a small trailer park, my childhood hadn't been that different from Cliff's. San Diego in the 1950s, especially in the beach towns, was white. I don't recall seeing a black person other than on TV.

Snippets of my family life came to mind. Sunday dinners at my grandmother's house had been a tradition. My grandfather had died in Philadelphia during the Depression, and his sons, including my father at age fourteen, fled to California on foot and by hopping freight trains, to pick fruit and send money home to their mother and younger siblings.

Many years later my grandmother married my step-grandfather, Frank, who had a little shop where he repaired broken televisions. When we went for Sunday dinner, Frank was distant if he even bothered to acknowledge us kids at all. My mother excused his behavior by saying he just wasn't used to children.

Frank always finished eating first and immediately left the table for his chair in front of the television.

Sunday nights meant *Lassie,* my favorite, and afterward *The*

Ed Sullivan Show, which bored me, so I'd play with the toys from the trunk my grandmother kept for us.

When the show featured black entertainers, which was increasingly more often, Frank would jump out of his chair and yell at the television. Shaking his fist, he'd let words fly in his gravelly smoker's voice, hurling them at the screen like stones.

My mother would cover my ears and hustle me away, leaving my two-year-old sister, Tamara, crying on the floor. In the back bedroom, I received a lecture.

Those experiences confused me at first. Black people came on television, my cranky grandfather exploded, and I was taken away from my toys and into a back room like I'd done something wrong.

Eventually the essence of my mother's message came through. Frank was the one misbehaving. And I knew I didn't want to be anything like the person who despised children, put my mom into a tizzy, and was bigoted to boot.

Cliff took up the cue stick again and made an impressive bank shot. He teetered on adolescence. My friends, experienced with older teens, warned me that the entry into teenageness was not necessarily a gradual thing. The suddenness could shock both parent and child.

Cliff and Alepho took a few more shots, but the pool lesson never evolved into an actual game, and the two came inside.

Alepho paced around the family room. Maybe it was time to get on the road to their apartment before the traffic got too heavy.

Alepho stopped in front of the television and the twenty or so videotapes stacked on top caught his attention. "What's this?" he asked, pointing to the *60 Minutes* segment about the Lost Boys.

I should have put that in a drawer; he didn't miss a thing. Too late. "That's a documentary. A news show about you guys."

He pulled it out of the pile. "I want to see it."

Would they know people in some of those awful scenes? "It's kind of long," I lied. "You sure you want to watch that?"

"We want to see it."

Benson and Lino came over. The three of them tried to figure out where to stick the tape in. I gave in and helped them.

Cliff gave me a *Really, Mom?* look and said, "I have homework." Even homework beat watching an emotional story in their presence. I eyed the tissue box.

The four of us sat on the couch. The tape began with scenes in the camp and their villages. They leaned forward, excited, talking all at once, pointing and saying, "I know this guy," "That's like our house," and, "Dinka cows!"

"Lino's father had the best bull," Benson added. They all agreed and explained how the bull, black and white, was the most prized color.

The thought crossed my mind that this would be a good place to stop the tape. I knew what was coming. I had the remote in my hand. Oh, whoops, sorry the tape broke. But I couldn't do that. If they could live it, I could watch it with them.

As I knew it would, the scene switched to tanks crashing through mud huts, explosions, grass roofs bursting into flames, and people fleeing for their lives. They sat back. A quiet as thick as fog descended on the room. I had an urge to escape like Cliff. But whatever I felt, they had to feel exponentially worse. Was watching this the wrong thing to do? A PTSD trigger?

The video skipped to the crossing of the Gilo River, where boys were shot by soldiers or eaten by crocodiles. Lino said, "I was stuck in the grass on the Sudan bank after I crossed from Ethiopia. I watch two thousand people die in that river." I wanted to ask how he got across in the first place. He'd only been five. The question caught in my throat.

Original footage from 1992 showed tens of thousands of desperate stick-figure children streaming into Kakuma camp in Kenya. I looked over at the three young men intensely focused on the TV screen. Did they wonder who had filmed this yet hadn't done anything to help? I did. I also wondered why I hadn't seen this on the evening news when it was happening.

During the scenes from the camp, they pointed out old friends, but didn't mention Peter, their brother who was stuck there. Would he ever be able to join them here? The New York attacks might impact refugee resettlement.

The last portion of the video showed Lost Boys exploring their new home in America. One boy turned on a noisy vacuum cleaner and the other boys fled its path. Another opened a can with a manual can opener and declared it an "amazing machine." Benson and Lino laughed out loud. Alepho was quiet.

When the credits rolled, I let out a sigh of relief. The first time I'd seen the video, I'd been wiping tears. With Cliff, I'd mostly been looking for his reaction, hoping he'd get excited about meeting them.

Sitting beside the survivors, my practical side wanted to say to them, "Put all that behind you. You're in America now, life will be different. Don't think about those horrible things happening in other parts of the world that you can't control."

Be like us.

I knew they never could.

"Time to head home?"

They agreed.

In the car, Alepho was quiet and looked as though he still had a headache. "Are you feeling okay?" I asked.

"I have headache, and my stomach is not good."

I asked a few questions but he seemed hesitant to speak

more about it. I'd try another day when we were alone. Chronic headaches or stomach problems in a nineteen-year-old did not make sense to me, especially now that he was eating regularly. I'd ask Joseph about what could be done. "Next time we all get together," I said, "let's go to the grocery store and you can learn about American food." Good nutrition would benefit all of them.

That evening, as soon as Cliff was in bed and Paul was working in his home office, I pulled out the pages the boys had given me and settled on the couch. I'd seen the documentaries and read news stories, but I wanted to know more about their individual experiences. I began with Alepho's writing.

CLAY CAKES

Alepho

In the car on the way back to our apartment Judy asked me if I was sick. I shared my suffering with her. That led her to ask a series of questions that made me regret giving her truthful answers about my condition. I felt an invasion and sweated my embarrassment.

In the refugee camp, when we had stomach pains from no food, we went to the clinic. At first they gave us a Tums, but then they shooed us away after that. As a solution, we went to the stream outside camp and collected clay. Clay neutralized acid. We'd bring a whole chunk for each person and make mud cakes that we put on the ledge of our hut. We could eat some whenever we wanted. Our giant candy. It tasted good and the elders said it had vitamins.

One day an elder told us, "You're eating too much mud. The little particles of sand will get into your appendix and it will burst. If it bursts, you'll die."

We stopped eating mud for a while, but went back to it later when the pains returned.

In a place like the refugee camp there was no room for complainers; you had to find your own solutions.

CORNFLAKES

Judy

I read the writing that Alepho had given me. Then I read it again.

I couldn't stop thinking of their mother. First, she lost Benson. A year later, her husband. A year after that, Alepho. No wonder Alepho thought his mother favored Benson. He'd watched her grieve for her lost son the last two years Alepho had been with her. More grieving when her husband was killed. With just keeping their family alive under such horrible circumstances, she couldn't have had the time or energy to satisfy the emotional needs of a young boy.

It explained why Alepho couldn't forget what he perceived as favoritism. As a mother, I wanted for him to understand her anger, her fear, and her certain love for him. But for him to believe he was loved, it needed to come from his own mother. Was there even a possibility of finding her in Sudan, where there were no phones, no mail service, and in the middle of an ongoing war? The odds were stacked against us.

• • •

On the way back to their apartment we'd discussed our next steps.

"American food and cooking," they'd said.

The next time we got together, I took them shopping and talked to them about getting the best value, dollars per ounce, budgeting their available money, etc.

At their apartment, we unloaded the groceries from the car. "Have you heard anything from Benjamin?" I asked.

"No," they responded. "Joseph said the group went to Canada when they couldn't land in New York and should be here any day." It'd been almost two weeks since they'd left Africa. How much longer?

"Please," Lino said, "may I have photo with the cornflakes? I want to send it to my friends."

He posed at the bottom of their stairs and held the cereal box in front of him as though it were a trophy. I took his photo. Alepho selected a package of catfish and stood in front of my car. I took his photo. Grinning, Benson held up two bulging bags of groceries. I took his photo, too.

Photographing these smiling and laughing boys, who'd been deprived for so long of things I found common—and mostly took for granted—was such a privilege. So, I'd come to realize, was being able to just walk into a store and buy food. I'd never complain about a long grocery line again.

These weren't things I'd anticipated when I'd first met them and had doubted whether I had the time for them at all. They deserved whatever time I had to give. Not only because they'd been through things no child should even know about, but they were trying so hard to make a new life and they had so many challenges ahead. They'd need the kind of support every child did.

Going up the stairs with the rest of the groceries, Alepho whispered to me, "I will keep my photo here. I don't like to show that we have so much now."

READY TO EAT

Alepho

I'd never seen so much food as I saw in America. A person could just walk into a restaurant and ask for whatever they wanted to eat. Or go into a store. Or it was in our kitchen just a few steps away.

Until war changed everything, food was everywhere in Sudan also, but you had to find it, pick it, grow it, catch it, or kill it. Then you had to prepare it. In America it was ready to eat.

When I was on my journey, food was sometimes nowhere to be found. We survived on leaves or tubers. I became an expert rat catcher. I'd find their paths in the grass and create a little tunnel with my feet. When one came through, I grabbed it by the back of the neck and squeezed. They cried and died easily. A problem came when I trapped two at once and had to grab them by their tails, and they'd bite me. We'd put them right on the fire and watched them carefully until the fur had burned off and they were cooked. Then we divided them into pieces among us. They tasted like the dark meat of birds or chickens. There was never enough; rats only teased our hunger.

Often, we needed to find new ways to get food. When we were in Torit town, the rebel soldiers organized us into groups each day to work or look for food. I liked to climb the *lang* tree and take its sweet fruit, even though its thorns grabbed me. If too many got me at once, someone had to come get me out. I figured out a way to brush against the thorns in the right direction, like a serpent gliding through. Once at the top, I'd shake the tree and everyone on the ground gathered the fruit.

My cousin Joseph—who I had found along the way—and I became expert mango-tree climbers. We collected the fruit and sold it in the market. Business was good until the rains came and the river flooded the mango-tree area.

The adults said, "No one can pick mangoes when the river covers the ground. Too dangerous. Fire ants stranded up in the trees are very angry. If you climb they'll bite you, and you'll fall and break your leg or arm or even die."

Hunger had us again.

"Come," Joseph said. "I know how we can get some mangoes." We waded to the base of a big mango tree. He showed me a tin can.

"Are you going to catch ants in that?" His plan didn't seem like a good one.

"No."

"What's the can for?"

"Pee in it."

"What?"

"Pee in the can."

I peed.

"Now splash that pee all over your legs and arms."

"What?"

"The fire ants will run away from you. Watch."

Joseph peed and spread the urine all over his body and climbed the tree. I didn't know how he figured that out, but he was right. The fire ants ran away. We picked mangoes, and we were the only ones selling them in the market, so we made more money than before. With that money we bought grain and corn.

In Palataka, a boy's camp in the middle of Sudan where Joseph and I were forced to go by the soldiers, there had been no rations. Five thousand boys constantly searched for their own food. There was never enough. Boys became unruly. To calm things, the soldiers began a small distribution of dried corn, though not nearly enough. Bigger boys stole from smaller ones. We ate together in circles to enforce fair shares. Each boy took a pinch of food when his turn came. If one boy became greedy, the others grabbed his hand. Our stomachs burned from the emptiness, our heads ached, and our bones stuck out. The soldiers didn't protect anyone. Groups formed for protection.

Sometimes we were given no food. When we weren't working, we searched in faraway places for something to eat, anything to eat. We ate grasshoppers, leaves, and fruits. The most delicious was a dark fruit called *kunyuk* that grew in very large trees. *Kunyuk* was a tricky tree: it didn't want its fruit stolen. The branches looked sturdy, but when we climbed out on them they broke. So did the legs and necks and arms of many boys.

If we found a hive, we smoked the bees out to get the honey. That was a great treat, but the smoking needed cleverness or the whole tree and hive burned down.

If no food at all was to be found, we stole yam leaves from the local people. On lucky days we found a whole yam or a cassava. We had to be cautious because the locals had guns and they used them.

Hunger made our eyes able to detect new things. We observed birds eating unfamiliar fruits, or a rabbit nibbling leaves, and that way we knew they were safe. Some boys became so hungry and weak they ate things they didn't know: strange leaves, ugly roots, or fruits we'd never eaten before. Some died from that. I was careful to eat only what I knew to be safe.

In America, food was always right there and ready to eat. I knew it was safe, but I had to learn to adapt to new tastes. My stomach was giving me pains. It wasn't learning about the new foods as fast as I wanted it to.

WAR

Alepho

The video of Sudan that we had seen at the church brought back both good and bad memories. I began to think more about war and all its consequences. When our village had been peaceful, people had looked after everyone's children and helped each other out. War changed that. Desperation made people hateful and angry. I even saw adults take food from children.

After the attacks on New York happened, our moods changed. In the apartment, we spoke of war in terms of politics and our opinions, but down in our guts we knew it was just blood, destruction, and death. We'd been exposed to violence in our homeland. We knew the danger it posed to a good way of life. The thing called war destroyed prosperity and took from people the potential to become what they wanted. It robbed people of life and destroyed everything they'd built. War meant the end of the world for somebody—a child, a mother, or a father. It meant loss and deprivation without logical reason.

It seemed like the fight was always between two leaders. If two dogs wanted to fight, why not put them in a cage and let them have it out with each other instead of including every other dog on earth? Yet, it never worked that way.

We had received the news from IRC that our cousin Benjamin was on his way in September, but we didn't know what day. Then we found out that he'd been coming to the US on the day it was attacked. What were the odds of such a thing happening? We thought we'd outrun our past. Our past was mimicking itself right before our eyes, as though it had slipped forward, gone ahead of us, and waited for us in ambush.

I called a friend who was still in the Kakuma Refugee Camp. "My friend," I said, "America is different than what they told us. It is different from our jungles in Africa, but it is also a jungle and requires new sets of survival skills in order to make it out here."

He reminded me of how important it was to go to school.

Going to school in America had been my dream. Now, so many other things distracted me from that goal. Life here was not clear to me. Daniel and James were desperate to find jobs to work every day. They said the first three months are free. Our rent was paid for. I still thought the food stamp card was just an extra thing until we got our green cards that could buy anything. I was eager for my green card to buy things and send them back to the refugee camp.

IRC gave us classes to prepare for working. Judy seemed worried and talked a lot about jobs.

I had trouble learning and using my survival skills in America because my head hurt all of the time and I didn't know why. I had food now, but that food gave my stomach a problem.

Attacks on New York, jobs, rent, and sickness distracted me, but I could not forget my goal to get my education. I had to keep that first in my vision. My father had faced lions. I could do this.

LUNCH WITH FRIDA

Judy

Sharon from IRC invited me to lunch. She'd been in the Peace Corps and had worked in San Diego with refugees. I gladly accepted; I needed all the insights and advice I could get to help Alepho, Benson, and Lino. Sharon's advice would be helpful.

We met at a Mexican restaurant in a transitioning area that lay between the roughness of City Heights to the east, where Benson, Alepho, and Lino lived, and the artsy upscale atmosphere of Hillcrest to the west. Patrons were an eclectic crowd when judged by any measure: race, age, style, or sexual orientation. Unlike east of here—with its standard uniform of jeans baggy enough to fit two people, paired with oversized basketball shirts—identity in this area was expressed through punctured and adorned body parts and a vast array of skin art. If anyone could stand out in such a diverse crowd, I felt like I did with the blond hair, chinos, a T-shirt, and a blazer. An SUV-driving soccer mom who didn't fit into either world.

Inside, the café's rustic atmosphere simulated a Puerta Vallarta hideaway and created a charming oasis from the center-city streets. Plants dripped from Talavera ceramics hung on terra-cotta colored walls, fountains burbled to classical Spanish guitar music, and every inch of wall space was covered with Frida Kahlo's self-portraits.

Sharon, in her midthirties with chin-length brown hair and large, warm bluish-green eyes, was easy to talk to, smart, fun, and quick to laugh. We chitchatted about lighter subjects through a lunch of enchiladas with the best mole sauce I'd ever had.

"I didn't realize," I said, "how little I knew about refugees, their finances, health care, education, and, oh man, job-hunting. I thought I'd have that one nailed, but I haven't done it in years. Things have changed. I feel like the newcomer."

She laughed and sipped her iced tea.

"Don't get me wrong," I added. "Your mentoring class was really valuable. I made those mistakes you warned us about. You know, running them around to too many activities in one day, like I was taking a class of second graders on a field trip. I totally wore them out and I'm sure they were dreading my next visit."

"Don't worry." She laughed. "They're young. It's a special time."

"I know. Speaking of a special time, they're so eager to start school. That's my next project, looking into that."

Sharon gave me a questioning smile.

"I know, I know," I said. "Jobs first. I get it. But in the meantime, I have found it's best if we do fewer activities and focus on the things they really need. I'm learning to hang loose. Or you could say, they are teaching me."

"Enjoy it now." Her tone became serious. "Things start to change. We call that first month or so after they arrive the honeymoon period. Soon the realities set in. Rent, bills, not driving, driving. You can imagine how it is for refugees. It's tough for Americans."

"Oh, yeah," I said, quite sure that I had a pretty good grasp of the challenges ahead.

"Holds true for mentors too. You know: getting acquainted, doing the tourist stuff. It's all fun in the beginning."

I was just beginning to feel confident and comfortable with the mentoring thing. "So what you're saying is from this point on it's a test to see whether I have staying power?"

She smiled. "There's no *formal* test, but I guess you could put it that way."

"I'm not sure who has the most to learn. Me or them."

NEW KIND OF LEARNING

Alepho

In Dinkaland, mothers taught girls to cook and take care of the home and children. Boys learned to be warriors, care for cattle, farm, hunt, and defend the village.

When my father sold many of his precious cows to send Yier, the oldest son of his first wife, to a place called school, not everyone in the village agreed. They said, "Deng, this goes against our traditions."

My father listened politely since he was a gentle man with a quiet spirit who didn't anger easily. After they spoke, he said, "Tomorrow's future will belong to those who can read and write. The people who possess such power will hold magic in their hands. They will be the strong who survive."

Yier went away for a season to study. When he returned, he had magic power like a wizard. I wanted that too.

Not everyone felt that way. Even after they'd seen Yier's magic power, many in our village strongly disagreed with my father. "Deng," they cried, "you are a visionless man. Who would dare send his own children to a place far away? We don't want our sons going to this school. It goes against our traditional way of life." They thought my father had gone out of his right mind.

Yier took me aside once. "Alepho, our father has a heart for his children's futures. But his heart is not only for his own family. His heart is for our people and all of humanity. Your time for school will come, too."

My brother Benson, two years older than me, was seven then. I asked Benson, "Do you want to go to school?"

"Yes, I want to go when I'm older."

"I will go when you go." I didn't want to wait long or miss my opportunity.

The next season, my father sold more cows and sent another son from his first wife to school. The elders continued their protests. "These children leaving the village for education will speak strange languages and lose their principles and values. They will become useless rascals—city boys, who have no respect for elders and culture."

My father ignored them and gathered more cows. Another son was about to have a chance, but my father's second wife said, "No, I won't allow my son to get his education."

Our mother was the third wife.

I asked Benson, "Do you think our mother will allow us to go to school?"

"I don't know," Benson said. "My time has not yet come."

"Father told me danger may come. Are you worried about the danger?"

Benson gave me a serious look. "You must obey what our father has told you."

"What is the danger? What is coming?"

"Our father is wise. Always follow his instructions."

"I will," I said, still not understanding this danger. "But don't forget, when you go to school, be sure to take me." I'd miss Benson if he went away without me, and I didn't want to miss my opportunity to read and write like a wizard.

BUS INTERVIEW

Judy

James, the guys' roommate, called me on Friday afternoon. He'd never called before.

"The hotel only give two days of work," James said. "I go in every store, every restaurant. Always the same. No jobs, no jobs."

Planes were still grounded. Things were only going to get worse, especially for the local tourist industry. "Did you fill out applications for them to have on hand when they are hiring again?"

"I fill out some. But they will not call. Others say not even application available now. I go all the way to downtown. No job."

"Okay." I wasn't prepared for this. The attacks had postponed everything, including my research and good intentions of helping them find employment. Unfortunately, their needs couldn't wait. "Have you looked in the paper?"

"I look. I call. There is one place. They say to come on Monday at ten. It is where they clean the buses."

"Oh, that sounds good," I lied.

"Can you take me there?"

James had a bus pass and had traveled all over San Diego County. He'd passed his GED, was learning to drive, and had applied to college—all on his own. He was the most independent and capable of the Lost Boys I'd met. His request caught me off guard. Technically, I was a mentor for Benson, Alepho, and Lino—and apparently Benjamin too, when he arrived—but it seemed like James and Daniel didn't have mentors at all. I didn't mind helping them out if I could. "I'd be glad to take you, but doesn't the bus go there?"

Silence. Then I understood his request. *Will you, American lady, go there with me?*

• • •

Monday morning, I dropped Cliff at school and went straight to their apartment. Alepho, Benson, and Lino were on the couch, glued to the news on the TV. I'd had it on all weekend myself. There was only one story. It impacted everyone, and everyone wanted answers. None had come yet.

I gave each of them an envelope of the photos from the day at our house. "Anything new on the news?"

"Very bad," Alepho said in a heavy, knowing voice.

"I know. I'm sorry."

"It's not your fault."

He took things so literally. "I mean I'm sorry it happened so soon after you guys arrived."

I didn't want them to think that they'd come all the way here for nothing, that they'd never be free of terror. I couldn't think of reassuring words except "things like this don't happen in America," and I'd already made that false promise after the fireworks. Besides, who was I to tell them anything? They knew more about terror than I ever would.

"Who do you think did it?" I asked, not sure why I brought it up, but it was the question we'd all been asking the last few days.

"There are Lost Boys in New York."

"I hope they're safe."

"They are angry that the Lost Boys have come here."

Not again. Hadn't listening to the news the last few days made them realize they had nothing to do with it? "Oh God, no," I said. "No one is angry about you. We're glad you're here. If they are angry at us, it's more likely because they don't like Bush or Ariel Sharon or that we backed out of the UN conference two weeks ago. You haven't brought this down on America."

"Thank you," Benson said unconvincingly.

A silent pause. There were many pauses in our conversations, and I was learning to be comfortable with them, even when they happened on the phone.

A commercial for dog food came on the TV. "Are we going to the zoo?" Benson asked.

"Sure, of course."

"Can Benjamin come too?"

"Yes, of course."

"You will be his mentor?"

I'd meant to call Joseph about that but hadn't gotten around to it. "Yes, I will, if he wants me to."

"Let's go to the zoo when Benjamin gets here so he can go too." The truth was I was concerned about going to the zoo or any public place right now due to warnings on the news, and maybe just because everyone else was.

The commercials ended and the news came back on. Another rerun of the World Trade Center collapse played. The whole country was transfixed, in shock, or numb, and in a holding pattern. The only thing that was clear was that things in our country would never be the same.

Alepho was quiet and rubbing his forehead. "How are your headaches?" I asked.

"All the time."

"Did you eat breakfast?"

"The tea makes my stomach hurt and then I don't eat."

Then don't drink tea! "Tea on an empty stomach makes me feel sick too. Have you tried the cereal we bought in the store?"

"Yes."

I'd steered them from the sweet varieties in the colorful boxes and we'd selected cornflakes and raisin bran. "Did you like it?"

"No. Too sweet."

I'd have to share that with Cliff. He thought raisin bran was inedible because it wasn't sweet enough.

"Joseph said I have a parasite."

"Really?" A frightening thought. Were they contagious?

"Joseph said he will take me to a tropical medicine doctor at the university."

I hoped that was soon. This could help the other guys who probably also had some foreign creatures making a life in their guts, or who knew where else.

They had so many challenges. Including many within, from nightmarish creatures to memories of war. It had to be hard to get the motivation and the energy for jobs, school, and all the learning about their new country.

"Where is James?" I asked.

"He is preparing."

I had arrived plenty early because I enjoyed spending time with them. But I wanted to turn the TV off. Enough of that for now.

Would war always be present? The boys sitting beside me had had their lives and loved ones devastated by war. I hadn't, yet much of my life had been molded by the aftereffects of war. My grandfather was an angry, reclusive eccentric as a result of his experience in WWI. My father wouldn't say much about his own experience in the service except for an often-told story, with inappropriate laughter, about his boat blowing up.

I'd been born during the Korean War, and the Cold War had punctuated my elementary school Mondays with noon air-raid sirens, just ten years after Little Man and Fat Boy had obliterated Hiroshima and Nagasaki. In school we studied strontium-90 fallout, and at home we knew which neighbors had bomb shelters.

The Vietnam conflict sputtered to life in my middle school years and raged during high school. Friends went away and didn't come back. The Berlin Wall finally came down the year Cliff was born, heralding the end of the Cold War, hugely symbolic for anyone who spent kindergarten diving under a desk during bombing drills.

After the brief Gulf War, we'd had a decade of relative peace. I'd had high hopes for this new millennium and for Cliff's lifetime to be a peaceful one. But here we were, just a year into the new century, and our ability to transcend violence seemed to be on shaky ground again.

James came from the bedroom ready and dressed in his best pants and favorite shirt. That was the problem. The shirt. He loved it. I assumed so anyway, since he wore it frequently. An aloha style, brightly colored, mostly green, short-sleeve silk-type print worn outside the pants. At first glance the design was abstract, but a closer look revealed martial arts characters performing a variety of moves. The real clincher was the gray-and-black life-size machine gun that ran diagonally across the front from shoulder to hip. Not appropriate for a job interview. Even a job cleaning buses.

"You look very nice," I said. "But that's your best shirt. Maybe you should save it for going out."

"I like this shirt."

"A long-sleeved shirt is more appropriate for interviews."

"You see, Judy, I don't like long sleeves."

If this had been Benson, he would have immediately run and changed. In fact, he would have read the job-preparedness manual and had on the long-sleeved shirt *and* a tie in the first place.

"James, we're going for an interview. You really need a plainer shirt, and long sleeves are best."

He grumbled and disappeared into the bedroom, reemerging a few minutes later in a cotton long-sleeved shirt that was still not tucked in. This one had a busy but faded green print and sleeves so short he couldn't button the cuffs.

"We go," he said.

"What happened to the solid shirts I brought over?"

At this point everyone was gathered in the living room, observing our negotiations. This made for a delicate balancing act. James was the oldest, had been a child soldier, and was now a strong leader and role model for the household. I didn't like challenging him in front of everyone, but I didn't want him to blow this interview or others in the future.

"I like this shirt."

"Okay, okay, it's fine. Just tuck it in."

"Tucked in does not look good."

Now he was a fashion expert. If I didn't admire his capabilities, fierce determination, and independence so much, I'd be tempted to walk out and let him go by himself, even after driving all the way down here. "James, if you were a big boss in Sudan and three people came in and applied for a job, one Dinka, one Arab, and one white American. Which one would you hire?"

He laughed. "The Dinka man."

"Okay, what if all three were American but one had on traditional Dinka clothing? Would you hire that one?"

"Yes."

Lino came out of the bedroom with his job-preparedness manual open and his finger on a line. He pushed it into James' face and spoke sharply in Dinka. James looked resigned.

"You see, Judy," Lino said. "It say right here. No green shirts for interview."

It said no black or red ones either. That was a new one for me. "Thank you, Lino." *Especially for the support.*

We departed with James in a peach-tone dress shirt, tucked in, and a belt. The sleeves were too short, but that was true of all the shirts that fit them otherwise. At least they were buttoned.

James and I stood in the lobby of the bus-cleaning business for ten minutes, watching the office staff pass by and completely ignore both of us. When I finally got someone's attention, I first introduced James.

She said to me, "We aren't hiring."

"They told James to come down today and fill out an application."

Still speaking only to me, she said, "You have to have a driver's license to move the buses around the lot for cleaning. Does he have a driver's license?"

Did she think that because he looked different he couldn't speak English? I guided James out the door. A driver's license wouldn't have helped.

We stopped in several other places. A grocery store that was not even giving out applications. A fast-food restaurant where all the workers were Hispanic told us they weren't taking applications. Another hamburger fast-food place where all the workers were young, white males would not take applications for future reference. It was hot, depressing, and demoralizing. We headed back home. Clearly, I needed a better strategy.

LIZARD POOP

Alepho

A few months after I'd fled my village, soldiers took over leading our large group of boys. They loaded us into lorries headed for a town called Torit, where they said they'd won the battle.

When we arrived in Torit, it didn't look like anybody had won. Broken buildings reeked of dead people. Black ash covered everything. Back in my village, ashes had protected grains from weevils, new plant shoots from bugs, and our food from rodents. My mother brewed ashes with water to make spice for soup. Seeing all those ashes made me wonder if my mother was still in the village weaving her baskets and making her soup. I hoped my village hadn't been destroyed like Torit. Seeing burned souls shrouded by ash inside vehicle skeletons made me fear that my own body would soon burn up and disappear forever like a piece of wood.

The lorries left us in that black ash and roared away. People could see that we were just young boys and directed us to the UN aid tent for sacks of dried corn and beans.

"We have no cooking materials," I said.

The aid worker said, "We don't provide cooking utensils."

We formed into groups of twenty or thirty boys and set about trying to feed ourselves. Behind a building we found a large metal barrel as tall as me.

"We need to cut it in half first," my cousin Joseph said.

We scattered and found sharp rocks and an old metal blade. The sawing, hacking, and pounding took several hours but hunger made us determined. Finally, the top came off. Black goo coated the inside.

"That goo is what makes vehicles go," an older boy said. "It's oil."

"It smells sort of nice," I said. The elders had talked about oil when they talked about war. I hadn't understood what it was all about.

We washed out the barrel as best we could, filled it with water from a pump and started a fire from gathered wood. When the water finally boiled, we poured the beans and corn from their large rough brown sacks into the water and watched. The cooking took hours. Once the grain and beans were tender, we laid the sacks around on the ground and poured the contents onto the sacks for eating.

"It smells like the black goo."

Joseph tasted it. "Tastes bad."

No matter the taste, no boy missed his turn for a bite. The beans were so hot they burned my hands and my mouth, but with so many hungry boys, I had to take mine when my turn came. We fed like vultures on a stinking carcass.

Soldiers came by. "You boys clean out that building and you can sleep there." They gave us pails and a few rags and we headed to the building.

"Ew! Ew!" The boys ahead stopped outside the door. I smelled it too. The rebel soldiers had been stranded inside while they fought. Feces, urine, and dirt slimed the floor, like a hundred dogs had been locked inside for a month. All we had were pails of water and a few old rags. Just standing outside made me gag. We had to do as we were told so we held our noses and began.

"I don't like Torit," I told Joseph.

He didn't answer, he just looked at me as though whether I liked someplace or not was only a silly thought.

Inside the building a large dark board covered one wall. "What is this?" I asked.

"Blackboard," said an older boy.

White markings of short lines and patterns looked like someone had made a design.

"What are these?"

"That is writing."

"How do they make it?"

"They make it with chalk."

"What is this chalk?"

"A white stick like dried lizard poop."

"I want to see a chalk."

"The chalk is gone," the boy said. "All of the schools were destroyed by the war."

I looked around the room again. I couldn't believe this dirty old building was a school. Nothing seemed magical here. I ran my finger over one of the markings. The writing went away. Oh no, had I destroyed some magic? I stared at the board. I wanted that magic power to go into me like it had gone into Yier.

GUNNA

Judy

When I spoke with the boys in person or on the phone, our conversations had grown more fluid. I still exaggerated my enunciation and spoke slowly, but I no longer dropped contractions or limited my vocabulary as much as I had in the beginning. I had begun to use words that were unfamiliar to them because they always asked the meaning, especially Alepho, who generally had a dictionary in his pocket. They'd tell me they were getting to know our American accents but when they watched British films it was much easier to understand the English.

I was getting used to their accents too. Through conversations, observations, their writings, and our interactions, I'd learned much more about the Dinka culture as well. My job was to teach them our culture and traditions, but I'd discovered to do that effectively I needed to know something about theirs, because otherwise it wasn't obvious what they needed to learn about ours. An unexpected twist was taking place. I was learning more about my own culture, too.

You don't need to go outside. It's hot." Maybe he'd overheard me admonishing Cliff about not dropping fries in the seat cracks.

"It's okay outside," he said. "No girls there."

"No girls. Are they going to take it or something?"

He didn't move or answer. From the back seat Daniel said, "In our culture we do not eat when there are girls around."

Oh, I was the girl. And women probably didn't eat around them. But I'd had many meals with the others.

Later, Alepho explained to me that James and Daniel were from a different tribe. "They are Dinka, but Dinka Bor. Benson and Lino and I are Dinka Rek. They have some different customs."

I wondered how relaxed James would be on his first dinner date in America, seated across from a young lady, forced to eat in front of her. The thought made me smile, right in front of the boys.

HEAD OF THE CAT

Alepho

The soldiers led us from Torit. They said we were going to a camp with a missionary school. A thousand joyous boys stretched out like a trail of ants headed for Palataka camp, singing and marching, so happy to leave Torit behind.

Our joy had a short life. The rainy season was upon us. Nights were so cold that I shivered until morning. Each day my feet dragged me from one place to another place, like a homeless insect. No dry, warm, safe place to sleep in months. If I talked of going home, everyone said, "No, the war is still there." Palataka was now my hope.

Stories kept me going. If two days of walking lay ahead, I imagined that in an hour people would be waiting with water, porridge, and a bed. Even if the destination was six hours ahead, I pretended just to that tree or that hill, and a beautiful village and school would greet me. The stories I told myself saved me.

After each mountain, no school or village greeted me, just

mountains higher than any I'd seen in my life, and more rain and less food. The view from a tall peak revealed more mountains rolling out before us. We rested on a hilltop. Whispers traveled through the group. "Palataka has chiggers and no food. We're running away tonight."

A few boys disappeared.

"What shall we do?" I asked Joseph.

"Let them go. We're going to Palataka. There's a school and we can find food."

"What about chiggers? They'll go in our skin."

"We've faced lions and snakes. Chiggers are smaller than ants. We can deal with them."

Chiggers or not, Palataka had a school.

At last we climbed a long, steep hill and stopped to rest at the top. A rumble ran through the crowd. "Palataka, Palataka," drifted from mouth to mouth. On a distant plateau, buildings with red roofs clustered together under huge trees with sparkling green leaves. The towns we'd passed had been destroyed and covered in gray ash. Palataka looked alive, like my village before the attack. Tears of joy burst from my eyes. Who cared about chiggers? The closest thing I'd had to a home was only an hour's walk away.

Thousands of boys lined the trail going into Palataka. They watched our exhausted group straggle in and yelled things in languages I couldn't understand. I watched them, swiveling my head back and forth, trying to see every face. I still had hope that my brother Benson could be alive.

We flowed into an area at the center of the buildings that we'd seen from the plateau. Massive fig trees with branches thicker than my body swept close to the ground. We lounged in the python roots, making ourselves comfortable like chiefs.

A tall, uniformed soldier with a shaved head shouted to us

in Dinka. "Welcome to Palataka. Boys from all over southern Sudan are here together. The war has exposed all the people to each other. Your languages and tribes won't separate you. You're no longer Nubian, Dinka, or Nuer. You are the new South Sudan. One people, one cause. We're united as one."

We cheered. The new Sudan. United together. No more war and fighting. Palataka was a dream come true. That night we slept there on the ground, nestled together in the arms of the tree.

"Clean out the buildings," the soldiers ordered the next morning. "Those will be your sleeping quarters."

The stink from the buildings told the usual story. Like Torit, but worse. The rebel soldiers had slimed the floor with every kind of waste. Rats, adding their own fresh waste, scattered to the far corner. We settled into our buildings and looked forward to starting school.

In Palataka camp, the commanders liked to gather all the boys and tell us things. Those tellings were long boring days sitting in the sun. One day, as the commander lectured us about our duty to obey, I was about to nod into a nap when the commander said, "You have a new duty."

Those words snapped me from my daydreaming. "This duty will give you strength and South Sudan strength. It is the only way you will understand these things and have the power to build this new country. More teachers have arrived and you must go to school now."

School. Magic power. I'd fulfill that duty anytime. When could I start?

The following week they lined us up first thing in the morning.

"School begins today."

We paraded through the camp, skipping and chattering like a bunch of excited monkeys.

Joseph went off with the taller boys. My group was mostly from the Nuba Mountains and spoke Arabic. They sat us in rows on the floor. The cement was hard as a rock, but I didn't care, I was in school. Best of all, a blackboard hung on the front wall. I couldn't wait to see a real chalk and for the magic markings to appear on the board.

A man entered and laid his stick on the table. Silence spread over us like fog. He began to speak but it was in Arabic. I didn't understand Arabic.

I asked a Dinka boy near me, "How can we learn if we don't understand Arabic?" The teacher stopped talking and looked straight at me. Oh no. Was speaking not allowed in school? I didn't know that.

The teacher went to the blackboard and made markings with the white chalk. What was it?

More Arabic talking. The teacher tapped the board. "A-B-C."

Some of the students parroted, "A-B-C."

"A-B-C," the teacher repeated, hitting the board harder.

I joined in. "A-B-C."

"What is this A-B-C?" I asked the boy beside me.

"That is English."

"What does it mean?"

"Those are letters."

"They teach us English in Arabic language. I don't understand."

"Just say it over and over. They will ask you the next day. It is a test."

"A-B-C. A-B-C."

I didn't know what we had learned, but I said *A-B-C* in my head for the rest of that day. It became easier to remember and say. Maybe this was the beginning of magic power. The starting was slow.

We learned more over the next few days. The teacher made the letters into a song. By the end of the first week we sang together: "A-B-C-D-E-F-G ..." I just sang with the others, not knowing what it meant but happy to learn. By the time we rose from class each day, the hot sun was straight up in the sky, and my behind was numb. I couldn't wait to return each morning to receive more magic power.

By the end of the month the teacher would point to a boy and instruct him to say the whole alphabet. If he couldn't complete the task, he got a beating with that stick. I feared that stick and learned the whole alphabet.

Math classes began, taught by Mr. Boldit, who never put his stick down. I only spoke Dinka, making it difficult to understand the math taught in Arabic and English. Addition and subtraction made sense to me, but I became lost when we started the many steps of multiplication and division.

I was afraid to look at Mr. Boldit for fear that he would call upon me. One day my turn came anyway.

"Stand, Alepho." He wrote fifty-four and nine on the board. "What is ...?"

I didn't understand the rest of the question, so I couldn't know the answer. Was it better to guess and get it wrong or not answer at all? I'd seen the consequences for other boys. A wrong answer meant a whack on the hand. Mr. Boldit liked his stick. I froze.

"You don't know?"

I waited for my whack. No whack came. He went to the blackboard, picked up a piece of chalk and drew a circle. Relief swept over me. I wasn't getting whacked; he was going to explain it to me.

He drew two triangles at the top of the circle. A few boys chuckled. He added eyes and whiskers. "*Lamonga*. Head of cat."

The whole class broke into laughter.

His lesson was that I was as stupid as a cat. My body heated like I'd been in the hot sun. My humiliation was hilarious to everyone. Ten whacks would have been better.

I left school that day not wanting to ever go back. Of course, I didn't have that choice. This was my new duty.

Mr. Boldit took pleasure in calling on me frequently after that. My hands were whipped so many times they became swollen. Fear of his stick stopped my mind from working. I couldn't think and I didn't learn.

When exam time came, a student said to me, "We know you're not going to pass even if we give you the answers." They called me dumb and stupid. The only happy person was the one who had been last place in class before me.

There was no magic power in school for me anymore.

JU DEE

Judy

One day, while in the area, I decided to stop by the guys' apartment unannounced. Climbing the stairs, it felt strange, dropping in like that, but they'd assured me over and over that it wasn't rude to just come by. Other boys came and went without fanfare. Apparently, the policy was that all guests were always welcomed or invited to any activities—I never knew who might end up joining us for an outing or need a ride—and the host continued with whatever they had been doing. Except for a glass of juice. Guests were always offered juice, served on a tray, and usually a very sweet red or orange variety. I expected them to try new things from my culture. I could at least try theirs. The detours from my plans had often led to delightful experiences and discoveries. Things that needed to get done somehow did anyway. For someone who regimented her life like a German train engineer, the new spontaneity hadn't hurt me a bit.

I stood at the door and knocked. Lino answered, and I was met with a round of hugs and greeted as though they'd been waiting for me. That was before they noticed the photos and albums in my arms. One of my favorite things was to arrive at their apartment with a package of newly developed photos. I always ordered four copies, one for each of us. Besides new photos, I had brought three photo albums. We gathered on the couch and looked through the ones I'd taken when they visited our house.

Benson kept running into the kitchen to tend something on the stove. It smelled delicious.

"What are you cooking?"

"Beef and pasta. Would you like juice?"

"No, I just had some water, but thank you for offering." Daniel was on the computer, surfing websites. "What are you looking up?"

"News from Sudan. I go on Sudan.net. They say that the government drop bombs on a food line in a displacement camp. Eighteen people die from that."

"Why would they bomb a food line?"

"They say SPLA are there and they want to kill them."

"Did that ever happen when you were in a camp?"

"Many time," Alepho interjected emphatically. His brow knit and that serious expression clouded his face like too many bad recollections had just cluttered his mind and he wasn't sure what to do with them all.

"Did you run?"

"No!" they all shouted in unison as though I desperately needed this vital information. "No running."

Benson waved his arms in a halting motion. "You must lie down. The people who run away, they die. Metal cuts off their arms and their legs. Sometimes it cuts off their head. They run anyway because they are scared. Lie down. That is how you survive."

"Metal. What metal?" I had no idea what a bomb was made of or how exactly it killed people.

"All kinds of metal. It is a big can they fill with trash metal. When the bomb explodes, it shoots out pieces everywhere. You must lie down. If you are running that is not good."

"Is there any warning? Can you hear them falling?"

"The little planes go very, very fast, and when you hear them they have already gone by and dropped the bombs. The big ones are the Russian Antonov. You can hear a very big roar but the bombs are falling. You cannot run."

As we glanced through more photos of them swimming in our pool and playing on our lawn, I could only shake my head in disgust at the image of giant cans falling from the sky and shooting out scrap metal that planted itself in torsos, severed limbs and cut off heads. That young boys were as familiar with how to deal with that as Cliff was with using a crosswalk ran chills up my spine.

"Benjamin is coming now," Lino announced.

"Now? You mean here?"

"He come now."

I didn't understand if Benjamin was landing at the airport or about to walk in the door, but it was a relief he'd arrived somewhere. "Do you mean his plane is landing today?"

"He is here. He come now."

Lino was so accustomed to being misunderstood he just repeated the same thing when asked again. I felt pushy asking too many times for clarification and let it rest. We looked through the rest of the pictures until I saw how late it was. I needed to stop by the grocery store before picking up Cliff at school. "I'd better be going."

"You don't want to see Benjamin?"

"Well, I do, of course, but when exactly is he coming?" *Please don't tell me* now. *We really have a different concept of the preciseness of that term. I'm beginning to think it could mean anytime today. Or this week.*

"He walking from IRC."

That was five miles away. I decided to skip the groceries and lingered a bit longer, until I couldn't stay anymore without keeping Cliff waiting on the curb. "I'm sorry I am going to miss him, but I have to go pick up Cliff." As I pulled out of the parking lot, two unmistakably Sudanese young men, one very tall, were walking down the other side of the street. I pulled to the side of the road and rolled down my window.

"Hello," I yelled.

They stopped and eyed me warily.

"Are either of you Benjamin?"

The taller one cocked his head, but was still cautious, like a child offered candy from a stranger. He said nothing. I recalled what Benson had relayed to me. They'd been warned while still in Africa that because American men marry only a single wife, there were many women here who were not married and looking for husbands. They could have guns or knives and kidnap men. No wonder they were so cautious. I shouted, "I know your cousins, Benson, Alepho, and Lino."

The taller one raised his arms into the air. "Oh. Yes." He took sweeping strides across the street with the shorter man trailing behind and came around to my passenger window. "I am Ben-ja-meen." His face lit up with a huge smile that unveiled a dazzling set of perfect white teeth.

"Hi, welcome." I extended my hand to his outstretched one. "I'm a friend, well, mentor, of your cousins."

"Ah, yes, Ju … dee!" He exuberantly pumped my hand. They'd told me that Benjamin was the tallest and the blackest, but they hadn't told me their cousin was probably one of the most striking human beings I'd ever seen. Maybe he wasn't to them, but a photographer wouldn't have been able to find a bad angle on that face.

He smiled. "You are my mentor, yes?"

"Yes." I smiled. "So, you just got here, now, to San Diego?"

"I come right now. You go?"

He still held my hand.

"Yes, sorry, but I must leave and pick up my son from school. I will see you soon, okay? You can tell me about your trip."

He let go of my hand. "Okay. I see you later. Bye, bye, Ju … dee."

ESCAPE

Alepho

I'd been in Palataka camp for two years, and I hated it. Never enough food. Chiggers burrowed in our swollen, infected hands and feet. Boys were sick and dying. Now that school was not for me, Palataka became the worst place I'd been.

One night Joseph came to me. "We have to escape."

My heart pounded. Yes, I wanted out, but if a soldier on guard saw a group of boys just sitting and talking together, he accused them of making a plan to escape and punished them. Every week boys were caught and whipped. Could Joseph be serious? I didn't say anything because I didn't want him to think I was a chicken, but the beatings gave me bad dreams.

"Alepho, listen to me. Older boys, like me and maybe you, will soon be taken to a camp called Gromlee to be trained as soldiers. After that, it's to the front lines for fighting."

My stomach twisted into a knot. Some boys were eager for this. They wanted to have guns, and they wanted to kill. I hated guns and I hated fighting. The boys on the front lines were the ones doing the most dying.

"How do we get past the soldiers?"

"We can do it," Joseph said. "Don't worry. I have a plan."

"Okay, but even if we get out, what about the locals? They'll shoot us."

"That's what the soldiers tell us to scare us. We'll stay away from their areas. We're just boys. I don't think they'll hurt us if we don't bother them."

"Where will we go?"

"We'll go back to Torit," Joseph said.

Back to Torit? I couldn't wait to leave there. But Joseph was right. We had to escape Palataka or we would surely die on the front lines.

PAPER OR PLASTIC

Judy

I stopped by my local grocery store on the way home. Benjamin had finally arrived, what a relief, but that meant another nonexistent job to find.

"Paper or plastic?" the box boy asked.

Oh, my God. They could do *this* job. Why hadn't I thought of it sooner? *Hi, how are you? Would you like paper or plastic? May I help you out to the car?*

"Uh … paper," I told the young man.

A job like this would keep them in contact with people instead of burying them on some graveyard shift in a factory. Those jobs didn't exist, anyway. Precise English was not required, just politeness. They had plenty of that. I rushed home, excited to make some calls.

I debated the best approach. Classified ads had gotten me nowhere. Pounding the street and asking for applications had been unproductive and sometimes humiliating. Time to circumvent the conventional routes. I called a Ralphs grocery store in their area and asked for the manager.

"I'm Bob Sullivan, the assistant manager. May I help you?"

"Yes, great, thank you. I was wondering if you need box boys."

"We call them wrappers now," he said. "We haven't used boxes in quite a while."

"Oh, dating myself."

"We do need them, though. Holiday season coming up."

Bingo. Bob sounded nice.

"Is he over eighteen?" Bob asked.

"Yes."

"Is he in school?"

Dare I mention there are three? No. He probably thought I was calling for my son. This was my opening. I let out my spiel. "I work with the IRC and mentor refugees. He's nineteen now, but as a boy he walked a thousand miles across Sudan and grew up in a refugee camp in Kenya. He speaks English. He'll make a wonderful employee. He's so eager to work if only given a chance."

"I can't promise anything," Bob said.

Did I detect a change in tone? Or was it all in my head?

"Come in and pick up an application. I'd like to meet him."

Hallelujah! A meeting was nearly an interview. But who would *him* be? I couldn't choose between the three of them, or more accurately the five or six.

The only fair option would be whoever answered the phone.

THE TREES DANCED

Alepho

Joseph shook me awake. "Shhh. Be quiet."

I bundled my few things in my blanket, trying not to wake anyone else. The walk from Torit to Palataka with a thousand boys had been terrible. The walk back would be worse with no one to help us.

We snuck out of the building and into the night. I'd never been so scared. The last escapees received forty lashes. I didn't want to consider the consequences of being caught, but I couldn't stop thinking about them either.

We went to the end of the building and waited in the dark.

"Where's the guard?"

"Wait here," Joseph said.

He returned in less than a minute. "He's sleeping."

Holding our breath, we crept past the sleeping guard to an area outside the camp where we met eight other boys. Ten of us altogether. I was the youngest.

We headed north on the same trail we had come on from Torit and soon came to a split in the path. Nothing looked familiar. On our way to Palataka, we'd been an excited horde that wouldn't have noticed a fork in the trail from another direction.

Half the boys pointed to the right. "This path goes to Torit."

Some trees on the left looked familiar to me and it felt like the left fork was the way we'd come. When we had come to Palataka, I had tried to remember the path, in case I needed to find my way back.

I pointed left. "That is the way we came."

No one listened to the youngest boy. We followed the path on the right until dawn. The sun rose and caught the sharp edges of roofs.

"What?"

"That's Palataka."

"No, it's another town."

"No, it's Palataka. See? Those are the school buildings."

"Shhhh," Joseph said. "The guards will hear us."

We'd gone in a big circle and were right back where we'd started. We headed out again, taking the trail I'd suggested the night before. I couldn't say anything, but inside I felt angry. Proud, too, that I'd been right in the first place.

Close to noon we encountered a local man. "I think he's Acholi," Joseph said. "I will speak with him just to be sure we are on the right path."

Joseph went up to the man. "Is this the way to Torit?" Joseph pointed. "Torit?"

The Acholi man shook his head and pointed in another direction.

We set off again. After a while, Joseph stopped. "This man didn't direct us well. Follow me, I know where to go."

That started arguments. Two boys went the way the Acholi man recommended. Eight of us followed Joseph's way up over a hill.

We came to a long valley. The trail disappeared at times. Sharp grass stalks sliced my feet like knives. With no trees to escape the summer sun, my shoulders and back cooked. In the afternoon, we reached a small stream and drank and soaked our heads but I had nothing to carry water.

A steep hill rose out of the valley. We walked without water. My eyes became red and itchy. They burned and drained yellow pus. I couldn't see well. By the time we reached the top of the steep hill, my tongue had dried out like bark. Each breath was a chore. Talking was impossible.

We started down the other side and reached a grove of papaya, banana, and guava trees. The others picked fruit and ate it.

Joseph said, "The elders say don't eat if you don't expect to get water, especially sweet fruits."

Joseph and I didn't eat the fruit even though it would have wet our shriveled mouths and filled our bellies.

We started out again. The boys who had eaten the fruit became dizzy and weak. Some couldn't see. One boy wandered away, refusing to follow us. The rest of us were too exhausted to argue. We needed water soon or we would perish. Dizziness overtook me. I knew in my head that if I sat down to rest, I might not get up again. My body was fighting me. I walked slower and slower, falling behind the others until I could no longer see them. I came to an area with trees. The trees danced and laughed and sparkled their leaves, inviting me to their shade. I leaned against a trunk. My legs quivered. I slid to the ground and the world disappeared.

"Why are you on the ground?"

Who was speaking to me?

"Come on, let's go."

I came to with a jolt. How long had I been there? My eyes wouldn't open. Pus stuck them shut. I had to get up or I'd die. I pried open my eyes enough to see, but they burned like fire. I got to my knees. No one was around. "Hello?" I tried to speak but the words stuck on my dried tongue like in a bad dream. "Hello?"

I crawled to the path. Footprints. I rose and followed them down the trail, stumbling along in full sun. I had to find Joseph and the others. I didn't know how to get to Torit. Nothing looked familiar through my blurry eyes. Was this my day to die and join the boys who had dropped on the road and were now just all those skeletons I'd passed on my journey?

Up ahead, beyond the next hill, I made out a dark area. More trees. If I could just make it to that shade, I could rest again. I pushed on from this tree to that tree, from this hill to that hill, step by step, the only way to survive.

I reached the trees and stopped. Shade cooled my hot body.

"Alepho."

Joseph? I could be hearing things again. I moved farther into the trees.

"Alepho, over here."

Joseph and the rest of the group rested in the shade. "We lost you. I couldn't find you anywhere."

I sank to the ground with relief. We weren't out of trouble, but at least I wasn't in it alone.

"We'll rest a few more minutes," Joseph said. "Then we must go."

Some strength returned. I had to stay with the group no matter what.

We moved on together, weaving and confused as a bunch of drunks.

Down the trail a familiar scent came to me. "Do you smell it?" I mumbled.

"What?" Joseph asked.

"Water. I smell water."

No one argued with me this time. At my direction, we cut across a flat area. The smell of water became stronger. An hour later we reached a wide stream. I crawled into the shallows on my hands and knees. The water washed over my body. I drank like a cow. I'd never been so close to dying.

OH NO. FOUR?

Judy

Benson answered the phone when I called. "Get your best clothes ready. You have your first job interview tomorrow."

The next morning, I awoke at four and wasted an hour trying to go back to sleep. Why couldn't I stop worrying? If I was going to keep mentoring, I better get a grip on my emotional involvement. Benson had an interview. A glimmer of hope. Four more to go.

What happened if they didn't get a job? Or worse, couldn't keep one? I couldn't stop thinking about that. What would they live on? And what about health insurance? They'd been checked for the communicable things, like HIV and TB, but they'd never been to doctors in their lives. They could have other things. Or, they could have caught things here they didn't have immunity against. They needed medical benefits, that was certain. If they didn't feel well, they couldn't work.

Be calm.

I got up anyway, made coffee, and turned on the news.

There'd been predictions of a second wave of attacks. The whole country was on pins and needles and rallied behind New York. Fortunately, nothing new. All those dire forecasts had been so discouraging, I'd lost hope the job market would ever improve. Now Benson had an almost-interview.

Relax.

My own first job had been in a grocery store, in the deli department. I'd pitched in as a "wrapper" occasionally, too. Paid my dues to the Culinary and Bartenders Union without complaint. I made $1.75 an hour, three times as much as babysitting.

Wrappers did more than bag groceries. They directed customers in search of an item. Just about any American teen could find Oreos, Formula 409, or SpaghettiOs. But what logic was in those names for people new to this culture? Froot Loops, for goodness sakes. Would they search produce? There were sixty thousand items in the average grocery store. With the exception of meat, fresh fruit, and vegetables, most had brand names familiar to Americans from advertising. Would customers be patient with some dark-skinned foreigner who hadn't the slightest clue where to find Ragú?

Be calm.

I dropped Cliff at school and headed straight for the Mission Valley Ralphs grocery store.

The store was newly remodeled, large, and quiet. I requested three applications from a woman at the customer-service desk. One Benson could fill out ahead of time at their apartment and two extra copies in case of mistakes. That would leave time to practice for the interview and the job, too, just in case he needed to start right away. I grabbed a few grocery bags. I hoped there were enough food items in their kitchen to practice with. More importantly, I wanted to share tips on customer relations. Lack of knowledge could be compensated for with manners and friendliness. That came naturally for him. *Smile. Ask politely,* "Excuse me, would you like paper or plastic?" *Smile. Work quickly. Smile.* His smiles were irresistible.

I waited around to watch the wrappers in action. None appeared, few customers to help this time of day. I asked a checker if I could speak to Bob Sullivan.

Instead, a Mr. Murphy, the store manager, came to the front. Oh no. Bob had been interested. I might get the "job was filled yesterday" line from this guy.

"Bob said you need a wrapper," I said and added a little about Benson.

He listened with interest and smiled. "Well, where is he?"

"I'll bring him in today."

"Make it after lunch. Before five."

• • •

I knocked on their apartment door. Benson answered dressed in the slacks we'd bought the first day, a shirt, and tie. Perfect.

The ironing board was set up in the living room. Alepho, Lino, and Daniel came from the bedroom. All dressed in their best.

Oh no. Four? Bob asked for one. Damn. I couldn't bring in four. I should have known by now that Benson wouldn't have gone with me alone. Too shameful in his culture to seize an opportunity without offering it to the others. Just as shameful for me to leave anyone back.

"You look great," I said. "But just so you know, if they hire anyone today, it will probably just be one of you, so don't be upset or take it personally. There will be other opportunities. If he offers only one job, how should we choose who takes the job?" I figured the manager would choose, but in case he faced the same dilemma, I wanted to be as democratic as possible.

They looked from one to the other. Daniel needed work the most immediately. He no longer received financial assistance and within a month, because he was twenty-one, he wouldn't have medical benefits. The hotel job didn't offer any; they hadn't even offered work recently.

"How about the oldest?" I suggested. Age seniority seemed to have major priority for them. On the other hand, I was their mentor, not Daniel's. He and James didn't have one.

"That's fine," Benson said.

Even filled out, their applications were mostly blank without a job history to report. That bothered them. We did some practice interviews. I made suggestions for answers to common questions and took photos of them in various combinations to memorialize the day of their first interview.

"Did you eat breakfast?" I asked.

They gave a sheepish response. "No."

"If you get the job, you must eat before work each day. It's very important because your break might not be for four hours. You'll be hungry." They didn't appear panicked. Four hours without eating just didn't rank up there in this crowd.

I was hungry, though. We couldn't go to the interview until afternoon. That left plenty of time for a sit-down lunch at a nice restaurant. A special treat I'd been wanting to give them. Better to go before the interview in case there was nothing to celebrate afterward. They could relax and be served an abundance of food. Growing young men who'd spent most of their lives on survival rations deserved an abundance of food. Someone waiting on them would boost their confidence for the interview, I hoped.

There was an upscale Mexican place with great décor and big booths on the way to Ralphs. Perfect. They could relax in luxury.

The restaurant was crowded. "We only have one large table." We didn't have time to wait. The hostess led us through the restaurant. I tried, but much like the ball game, I couldn't miss the stares. Too many. A few were so obvious I wanted to whip around and stare back.

At the table, I explained the menu, but with the noise and the food names in Spanish, they were still confused.

"Five fajita specials," I told the waitress to make it simple for her and them.

We tried to have a conversation, or I tried, but their voices were so quiet I couldn't hear them. I'd been noticing that all of the Sudanese spoke softly. At first, I'd thought the guys were shy about their English, but some older Sudanese who had been here awhile and spoke perfect English also spoke in quiet voices. So, it had to be a cultural thing, along with their reserved regal presence. I often found myself straightening my posture around them, which left me still about a foot shorter. How did I seem to them? A short, sloppy, loud know-it-all who invaded their space?

Regardless, speaking so softly simply wouldn't work for them in this country. "Be sure to speak up in an interview," I emphasized a few times during lunch. I still overenunciated and avoided contractions. It seemed to help their understanding of what I was saying but I also wondered if it wasn't a bit like my father whose attempts at Spanish were often adding an *o* to the end of English words.

"Are you ready?" I asked outside after lunch.

Alepho sighed.

"Nervous," Daniel said.

He couldn't be more nervous than I was.

THE UNIVERSE WAS WITH US

Alepho

I sat on the couch and watched the news on the television. America was preparing for a bloody war. That gave me a worrisome fear. My heart pumped with adrenaline.

The apartment phone rang. Benson picked it up. "That is good," he said into the phone. "We feel honored when we are with you." He hung up. "Judy says we are to prepare for job interviews tomorrow."

The universe was to be with us that day. I took out the board and ironed my favorite shirt. Did an interview mean we would get a job? I needed a job while I waited for my green card. A few days earlier, I'd stopped in a store on El Cajon Boulevard and put a soda on the counter. I'd seen other people pay with their cards, so I took out my I-94 and gave it to the clerk.

The clerk said, "What am I supposed to do with this?"

I stared back at him with my confident look. "That is to buy a soda."

"That's not a credit card," he said.

What was a credit card? I walked out of the store with a disappointed heart and no soda.

• • •

Judy arrived at our apartment the next morning. We greeted her in our interview clothing.

"Oh. All of you are prepared," she said. She looked surprised. "They might only hire one person."

She said it should be the oldest. That was Daniel. That was fine with us.

She gave us applications. There were only three. She said Daniel could do his at the store. I wished I could do mine at the store. My headache was strong that morning.

In the refugee camp, we had the choice of going to school or making money doing small businesses. During orientation in the refugee camp, they told us that in America we either chose to work or go to school. The choice was ours. I thought James and Daniel wanted to make extra money and that was why they looked for work every day. I wanted to go to school. I told Judy that many times. She seemed more concerned about getting jobs.

I'd probably misinterpreted some things in orientation. I had pretended I understood English well when I attended and that I did not need a translator.

Judy gave us pens and said to follow the example we'd learned in job-preparedness training.

How could I answer the questions about previous jobs, places I'd lived, or the school I went to in the camp? My application looked blank. I said to Judy, "Brianna told us we must fill out the whole form."

"Turn the application over," Judy said. "Fill out the essay section."

Judy was telling us something different than Brianna, our job-preparedness teacher. Some Lost Boys wanted to marry Brianna. She was tall like Dinka girls.

We did some practice interviews. Judy called them common questions and took our photos.

"Did you eat breakfast?" she asked.

"No."

"When you begin work, it's important to have food before you go."

She drove us to Mission Valley.

"Where is the store?" I asked.

"There is time. We will have lunch first at a restaurant."

I did not have an appetite for food; my stomach was not good. But maybe it would help my headache. In camp, when I got food, my headache often left. In America, sometimes the food made my headache greater.

We walked into a large place that was cool and dark. That felt good. A young woman led us through the place. Everyone stopped eating and looked at me as though a giraffe had just walked in. They could see that I had never been to a place like this.

The young woman led us to a table where we each sat in a big chair. She handed us a thin book.

"That's the menu," Judy said. "Just like at Burger King, but it's not on the wall."

I read it but I didn't understand any of it. The names were different than my understanding of American food. I felt ashamed not knowing what to order.

Benson made his choice. "Beef."

"Okay, they have a special today," Judy said. "Fajitas. Kind of like African food."

I agreed to what Judy suggested. I didn't want to appear to not know anything. I didn't like being a newcomer. I wanted to be a sophisticated fellow.

"Put your napkin in your lap," Judy said. "It catches the food and shows good manners."

I took the little square paper from the table and placed it on my lap.

Judy said, "That small napkin is a coaster, it's for your drink." She pointed to a cloth in a roll. "Open that and your utensils are inside. Put the big napkin on your lap, and the little one on the table."

There were many things to learn. Even in the camp, a person needed to follow the traditions, but here there were more tools and things to know.

A man brought a basket with a cloth. Benson looked inside. "It is like *injera*. In Ethiopia they make a large round bread like this one. We use it to take the vegetable and meat."

"Same here," Judy said.

Another man brought us each a huge plate filled with food. We looked at each other. One plate in the middle of the table would be enough for all of us to share. We'd always eaten from one bowl. A few times when we'd saved a few shillings and gone to the Ethiopian section of Kakuma camp to a restaurant, they'd placed a big plate like that in the middle with cooked meat and vegetables and each person took their share with the injera.

"I know it looks like a lot," Judy said. "You don't have to eat it all. Just let me know if you want a doggy bag."

What was a doggy bag?

Judy took up the bread that looked like injera except that it was more like paper. She filled it with food from her plate and folded it, then used her tools to eat it.

I did the same. But when I tried to cut it with the knife, the meat and vegetables squished out. Some people watched me. They could see that my eating skills were not good. I wasn't from this country and didn't know how to follow the traditions. I only ate a few bites. I didn't want to mess up my interview clothes. Worrying made my stomach not willing to accept food. Daniel ate his food. What would Judy think if I did not eat my food? There was enough for the rest of the week.

Judy said, "Okay. It's time to go to the store."

We left. I felt shame for leaving all that food behind. What would they do with it?

I NEED A COKE

Judy

We huddled outside of the restaurant for a last-minute strategy session. "If we're lucky today," I said, "we'll meet the manager. If we're really lucky, he may interview one of you. Just remember that your English is excellent. But sometimes you speak too softly for Americans. Show off your great English. Speak up loudly and clearly so the manager can hear you."

They all nodded.

The five of us filed into Ralphs grocery store. I told a clerk, "We're here to see Mr. Murphy."

After a few minutes, a medium-height dark-haired man, maybe forty, in a white shirt and dark tie came to the front. Not Mr. Murphy. Oh no.

"Hi, I'm Bob Sullivan," he said.

Bob Sullivan, the guy I'd talked to originally on the phone. Even better.

He shook my hand and somehow managed to hide his shock

at four, not one, job applicants. Without missing a beat, he extended his hand to Benson and introduced himself. He asked Benson's name. He did the same with Daniel, Alepho, and Lino. Their replies were in such soft voices that I'm sure Bob couldn't understand any of the unfamiliar names over the noise of the store. I liked Bob. He was serious and businesslike, but pleasant. I especially liked him for greeting each of the guys individually and so respectfully.

"Follow me," Bob said.

We went through a door near the front of the store and up a narrow, steep flight of stairs. At the top, we passed several small offices and entered a much larger one with an executive desk at the back of the room and a round conference table with four chairs.

"Have a seat," Bob said and pointed.

Looking unsure, each of the guys took a chair. They looked every bit as stiff and anxious as I felt. I sat in an extra office chair off to the side and Bob took a seat behind his desk.

Bob said to me, "My daughter was in Kenya on a mission."

In my barrage of background information to Bob on the phone, I'd mentioned that they'd come through a refugee camp in Kenya. Was that the connection, the vital piece, that had gotten us here? Maybe just curiosity. Whatever worked. "That's wonderful. Must have been a great experience for her. I'd like to go myself."

"Yes, she really enjoyed it. Life changing." A serious look came over him. "I don't know if I can use all four right now."

That he would even consider hiring one person had me over the moon.

"Will that be a problem?" he asked. "I don't want to cause a fight."

He was insightful and considerate too. "No," I said. "They

realize that. We discussed it. The oldest first. That was their choice."

Bob and I chatted for a few more minutes. I tried to turn toward the guys and speak clearly enough that they could follow, but I was sure they felt outside the whole conversation.

"So," Bob said, and turned toward the guys, "when did you get here?"

The question wasn't directed to any one of them in particular. No one responded. Come on, guys. They just looked at me like they were at the kids' table wondering if they were supposed to speak at all. I knew Bob didn't really care about the question. He was just trying to make conversation, to see how well they spoke English, see if they could interact with customers. "Daniel," I prompted, "you got here first, right?"

"Yes, I was the first," he said in perfect English but so softly there was no way Bob heard him.

Bob stood up and rolled his chair from behind his desk over to join the guys at the table. Daniel had still not answered Bob's original question. Bob was trying hard to make it work, and I liked him even more for it. I'd been so obsessed with getting them the job I hadn't focused on what it would be like once they had it. They needed an understanding, motivated manager like Bob.

"When did you arrive?" Bob asked again, now directing his question to Daniel.

"I arrive in March of 2001," Daniel said.

I looked at the others hoping they would offer an answer. Their politeness, nervousness, whatever it was that had sealed their lips, could be misconstrued that they didn't speak English. I smiled at them and did my best to put on a *go ahead and speak* look. No luck. My silent cheerleading wasn't working. No one said a thing. "Benson, Alepho, and Lino came together in August," I said. "Benson and Alepho are brothers. Lino is their cousin."

"Oh," Bob said in a concerned tone. "They can't work at the same store then. The brothers. Policy."

I cringed. Why had I offered that? *Shut up and let them talk.*

Bob looked over their applications. He would have seen that two of them had the same last names anyway. Even so, my interjections didn't help. Made them seem incapable.

Bob set the applications down. "I'd like to go around the table and talk to each person individually."

My stomach hadn't felt like this since I'd had to give an oral book report in ninth grade. It had all come down to this moment. I couldn't keep myself from talking for them, which would be counterproductive. I couldn't take it anymore. "Excuse me," I said. "I'm going to step out for a Coke." I didn't drink Coke.

SHE LEFT US

Alepho

Mr. Sullivan took us upstairs above the store. His big office looked so neat and clean. It smelled modern, like nothing I'd smelled before.

He allowed us to sit at a big table. I wasn't sure where to put my hands. Were we supposed to talk? What would I say?

Judy had conversation with Mr. Sullivan, speaking the native language so fast I had to cock up my ears like a hippopotamus to appear as someone who understood. I didn't want to seem like I'd just gotten out of a refugee camp and my English wasn't good. I nodded my head in agreement to everything. The truth was, I didn't understand a thing. Americans spoke fast and that made America seem so complex. Things just went in and out of my ears and remained a mystery. I wondered if one day I would speak as fast as they did.

Mr. Sullivan looked so important in his work attire of a white shirt with a tie and black pants. One day, maybe I could have my own office and dress up clean and neat. I wanted to be educated like this white man in front of me. He seemed so confident and well-versed in his language. I wanted that image of success and prestige.

Judy said this was a job interview, but it was going so differently from the training for job readiness at IRC. When was I supposed to introduce myself and look the boss in the eyes?

Judy and Mr. Bob Sullivan talked while he looked at the applications we had filled out. Nothing was going the way I'd learned and practiced.

Judy stood up and said she was leaving to get a Coke. Why was she leaving us? What was I supposed to do?

MALLS AND WIVES

Judy

Bob smiled when I said I needed to step out. He understood and was probably relieved. Now he could get done what he needed to do.

I paced around the store. *Relax. This is just one of the steps on the road to success. Whatever the outcome, it is progress. Part of the learning process. We all learn more from our mistakes than our successes. Blah, blah, blah.* The jittery feeling didn't go away.

A woman cleaning the freezer windows looked at me and asked, "I saw you all come into the store. Where are those boys from?"

I gave her some background.

"If they get the job, I'll look after them," she said.

That offer meant so much at that moment. This wasn't the first time people had been kind, but the accumulation of recent negative experiences made this positive one unexpected and especially nice. Maybe it was the post-911 mood. With rumors of new threats, people were scared. Especially of strangers. Fear and anger permeated the air. Yet, every night on the news there were reports of people pulling together and helping each other. A healthy response to hate and fear.

All I could do in the moment was wring my hands over the outcome of a wrapper interview. Having a minor breakthrough, even just a potential one, was so much better than the recent frustration. I couldn't do anything about a great battle between the world's cultures and religions, but a job in a store with more food than they'd ever seen, that would be something.

I wandered for ten more minutes and went back upstairs.

"They'll need to be drug tested," Bob said. "If that comes back negative, I can send them to training."

He said *them*. Yahoo. More than one. They must have finally spoken up after I left and won Bob over, like they did everyone who took the time to meet them. I wanted to jump up and down, but they looked puzzled. Bob mentioning a drug test might have had them totally freaked out, especially if that hadn't been covered in their job-readiness class. They wouldn't know it was standard procedure.

Bob turned around to get some forms out of a cabinet. I gave them a thumbs-up sign and mouthed, "Good job."

Smiles and relief all around.

Bob prepared their drug tests. Sitting at the round table, drug swabs sticking from their mouths, I wondered what they were thinking. It must have been a strange, confusing experience.

Bob filled out more forms and the longer it took, the more encouraged I became. He wouldn't go through this trouble if he didn't plan on hiring at least one of them. Still, it was possible that he tested them all so as not to hurt anyone's feelings. He seemed like that kind of a guy. Fine. One job was a big break and the others would be having their most positive job-hunting experience yet. Even if no one was hired, Bob Sullivan had made today a day we'd always remember.

"I'll call you," Bob said when all the requirements had been completed.

He probably wondered when I'd stop thanking him and let go of his hand. I wished I could thank his daughter too. Her mission to Africa might have been what opened the door in the first place.

When we were all back in the car and buckled in, I said, "You guys did a great job. Congratulations on your first interview."

Benson noticed my camera on the floor. "Can we take photos?"

"Of course." We took some under the Ralph's sign, some inside in various aisles and three in produce.

This was only a first step. I didn't want to be overoptimistic and have them be disappointed, but we had something to celebrate. "Shall we go to the zoo on Wednesday? You can invite Benjamin, too."

If they started work, we'd have little time for doing things like the zoo together. Hours in the grocery business were around the clock. They had to have jobs, but I'd miss being able to get together all at once.

"Yes, let's go to zoo on Wednesday."

My mind raced with the events of the day. It was Bush Senior who'd first spoken of the "thousand points of light." I'd run into those lights at Ralphs—Bob Sullivan, Dennis Murphy, and the woman cleaning the freezer doors. I thought back to when I'd been the one who hired people. I tried to recall if I had been brave enough to take a risk like they had. When I'd entered the computer business in 1970, I was the one who ran into one of those "points of light." Nineteen years old and female, I needed that break. I got one and stayed there nearly twenty years. A woman in business, especially management, was not a common thing at the time.

What had become clear to me walking beside the boys the past month was that it wasn't the rarer case of outright discrimination, but the more common and subtle tendency to favor those most like ourselves that had the greater impact on people like Benson, Alepho, and Lino.

• • •

After the Ralphs interview, we went to a mall to meet a friend of mine, Lucy, who'd offered to buy the guys some clothing at a store her husband frequented. Perfect timing. They would need black pants and shoes if they got the job.

"I'm excited about the job at Ralphs," Benson said as we passed stores.

"Me too, Benson, me too," I said. I just hoped there was a job. Bob didn't say whether he'd call the next day, the next week, or ever.

Spewing dolphin fountain sculptures caught their attention, but little else at La Jolla's largest mall did. We had a half hour to waste before meeting Lucy, and they weren't the least bit interested in the kiosks dripping with everything from jewelry to hairpieces or the storefronts filled with fashionably dressed mannequins. Nor were they as interested in the passing crowd—mostly white here—as the crowd appeared to be in them.

"Let's go watch the ice skaters," I suggested. We headed to the enclosed ice rink at the food court. They didn't want anything to eat or drink. The fajitas must have filled them up. We found a ringside table.

"Where are the sticks for their hands?" Alepho asked.

"Poles are used for skiing down a hill on snow."

"This is not snow?"

"No, that is ice. Very hard. For skating they don't use the poles. You'll see both skating and skiing this winter when the Olympics are on television."

The food court was a popular hangout for young people. Benson watched this crowd with more interest. "What do you think, Benson?"

"I want an American-style relationship with a woman."

"Really. What do you mean by 'American style'?"

"You know," he said, his expression serious, "some places in Africa, the women are not treated very fine."

I assumed he was referring to North Sudan, where they lived under Sharia law but he was too polite to be specific. "I've heard that. But from what I've read, the Dinka value women very much."

"This is true. They take care of their wives. If a man's brother dies, then he must marry his brother's wife."

"Not here. Only one wife. Or one husband."

"Just one the whole life?" Lino asked.

"Yes, one. Well, one at a time."

A disappointed "oh" chorused around the table.

Seemed to me we'd had this conversation before. Maybe the reality hadn't sunk in the first time.

"Yes, your whole life. Till death do you part. Choose carefully."

"Only one." Lino smiled. "I am going back to Africa to marry." They all laughed.

"One wife works out better in our society. Your wife is your partner, your best friend. Marriage is also a business contract."

Alepho gave me a skeptical look. "But what if you are president? Even the president has only one wife?"

"Yes, even the president. It is the law. To marry more than one person is a crime called bigamy in the US."

"But I read in a magazine that George Bush, he has a lady Laura and she is the first lady. Who then is the second lady?"

"She is the first lady of the country. George Bush only has one wife."

"Even the president, only one? I don't understand what happened with President Clinton and there was a girl."

"He had only one wife, Hillary. The girl was an affair outside his marriage."

They glanced at one another.

"My father had five wives," Benson said. He looked over at me for my reaction.

"Oh," I said as nonchalantly as I could, but thinking how complicated that could be.

"Our mother was the third wife."

How did that work out, all those women living together, sharing a husband? Hard to imagine peacefully sharing my husband with four other women. But maybe Paul could handle it. "Did you all live in the same house?"

"Each wife has a house with her children and my father have a big house."

"You had lots of other brothers and sisters to play with."

"Yes, many," he said. "Twenty or thirty. I miss that."

I bet he did. Great for the children, and the shared childcare duties sounded good to me. I would have enjoyed some help and especially companionship on those long solitary days when Cliff was an infant.

"Will an American girl marry a Sudanese man?" Alepho asked.

I wanted to just say yes, but the answer was more complex. He'd said American girl, not white girl. That could mean any color. I would have thought he'd ask, "Will a white girl marry a black man?" but this question indicated he saw it as more of a nationality issue. Or as a new American rather than a race, religion, or skin color issue. He'd seen many mixed-race couples in the inner city. Alepho was full of difficult questions. I made eye contact with him. "The simple answer is yes."

He raised his eyebrows. "Oh, that is good."

"The parents or family might object though." Brothers in the inner-city gangs came to mind. That discussion could wait. "I'm sure some of this is the same where you come from. Would a Dinka girl marry a Maasai man?"

They all laughed. No, her family would not approve of that, was the consensus.

"With Dinka," Benson explained, "a man may go with a girl who is not Dinka, but if a man has a daughter, the daughter cannot go with a man who is not Dinka."

"Aha! Double standard. We call that chauvinism."

"Chauvinism?" Alepho asked.

"Yes, you said it correctly. It's when men have rights women don't."

"Oh."

"More important is what kind of person you are," I added, wishing that it was more true than it was. "If you have a job, don't get in trouble, are a responsible citizen, those kinds of things, I don't think it matters whether you are a native-born American or not. Most of us, or our parents or grandparents, came from someplace else anyway, and we are now mixed up."

"There was very bad fighting in the camp," Benson said. "It was over a girl. Seven people died. They fight for two weeks."

"Two weeks? Didn't the police stop it?"

"The Kenyan police only stop after two hours. So, every day there is fighting for two hours, then they stop it."

This was a strange policy. Sounded like the police got their entertainment allotment before they shut it down.

"You can't fight here," I cautioned them. "It's called assault and it's a very bad crime, a felony. One hit and you can go to jail. As a refugee, you could be deported and sent back to Sudan."

I was uncomfortable lecturing, but a one-way ticket back to Sudan was a near-certain death sentence. I didn't know if they understood how a fight, even a grab or push, could lead to such huge ramifications for them. They'd come from an opposite situation.

"We know this," Alepho said. "But we are happy when you tell us these things."

I smiled, imagining Cliff thanking me for a lecture. But then he hadn't suffered the consequences first, like they had. They'd come to appreciate the value of prevention at an early age.

We met Lucy at the store. An hour later Benson, Alepho, and Lino had black pants and shoes, polo shirts, and new jackets. Surely those American girls would take notice now.

COMMUNITY MEETING

Alepho

After we survived the escape from Palataka, we found more fighting in Torit and ended up wandering for nearly a year, fleeing bombs, soldiers, and fighting. That was the year I found Benson and Benjamin in Kidepo. We were all together again, but then we were tricked and taken to another camp, a secret one called Natinga, where they trained boys to be soldiers.

Boys were always trying to escape Natinga, but they usually didn't succeed and were placed in a thorn pen, in the sun, in the center of camp. Benjamin ended up there two times for attempting escape.

I became sick with yellow fever. Benson kept me alive and put me on a truck to Kakuma Refugee Camp in Kenya for treatment. Once I made it to Kakuma and recovered from my illness, I started school again.

We went up into the hills to find a rock and brought it back to sit on under a huge tree. We found an old cardboard box and nailed it to the tree as our blackboard and made charcoal for the teacher to write with. We even found teachers among the adults in the camp and begged them to teach us. We learned to make our English letters by writing with our fingers in the sand.

After a while I lost interest in school. I never had enough food, my head hurt, it seemed that I was learning useless things. I was too old to believe in magic power anymore. There were no wizards. Besides, what good was school as long as I was stuck in Kakuma camp?

A few years later, when I was at a community meeting, an elder spoke to us boys. "Why do you think we lost our homes and families? Why is your own government killing you? Why have you been stranded in a refugee camp for almost ten years? It is because you don't have the magic. American people know the magic. They look up at the sky and understand the stars. They go to the moon and come back." He pointed down. "They even look under the ground and know what is there. We are being killed for the oil under our feet, and you don't even know it is there. Americans know because they have received the magic of education."

That man's message went to my heart. That power was real, and I needed to get that power.

After the meeting, I ran out to Kakuma Road and jumped toward the sky. I couldn't wait to go to school the next day, even if it meant sitting on a rock scratching letters in the sand.

The Lost Boys in Kakuma camp created a saying: *Education is your mother and your father.*

We'd lost everything. Our families, our homes, our lands. Everything had been taken from us. But once you had it, no one could take your education.

Now that I was in America and would soon have a job, my opportunity had arrived. I would go to school.

ZOO

Judy

When I'd first spoken with Joseph about meeting the Lost Boys, he'd said, "Just show them around San Diego. You know, the zoo or SeaWorld."

It'd taken a while to get around to this trip to the zoo, but that day had come.

When I arrived at their apartment, Benson opened the door and said, "In Dinka, *panda* means home. I want to see the panda."

"We will, for sure." They had on the clothes that Lucy had bought for them, including the brand-new wingtips and loafers. "Are those shoes comfortable? We'll be walking a lot."

They shrugged.

Right. Silly concern to someone who walked a thousand miles barefoot.

Benjamin came from the bedroom. I hadn't seen him since the day he'd arrived. He really was tall, at least four inches over his cousins.

"Hello, Ju … dee!" He gave my hand a hearty shake.

"You had a long trip to get here? How was it?"

"Oh!" He flashed that engaging smile and gave me a big powerful high five.

He sure wasn't as reserved as the others. Or soft-spoken.

"Yes, it was craaazy!" he went on. "I go to Nairobi and then to Brazil. When I come to New York, they do not permit us to land. They say, 'No, you must go to Canada.' We go to St. John's for three day. Very, very cold. Then we take bus to Buffalo, New York. Then other bus to Washington. I take plane to Dallas. That is in Texas. Then I take another plane to San Diego. I am here now."

He must have meant Brussels, not Brazil. He told it all as though he'd just returned from a Boy Scout outing. He didn't seem traumatized, that was for sure. "Wow. Quite a journey."

"I saw World Trade Center towers burning," he said flatly.

"What?"

"Yes. From my airplane window. I think they are oil towers on fire. Pilot say to look at the little screen. Airplanes fly into the buildings. I thought pilot telling us that we are flying into a building."

"Oh, no! That must have been the news you were watching. Wow, Benjamin, I don't know what to say. We're glad you're safe and have finally arrived."

"We go now?"

A man of action. "Absolutely, let's go."

It was a perfect autumn day for an outing. Perfect except that I hadn't heard from Bob at Ralphs yet. I wore a vest to keep my cell phone close in case he did call.

"May I drive your truck?" Benjamin asked.

The other guys didn't know how to put a seat belt on. "Uh, well, you need driving lessons and a license."

"I know how to drive."

How was that possible? From what I knew, he'd been with the rest of the guys. "Where did you learn?"

"I drove an ammunitions truck. They shot the driver. I drove."

That was hard to believe, but none of the other guys were responding, or scolding him for telling tall tales, just climbing in the car, like it was old news.

"How old were you?" This story didn't fit into what I thought I knew.

"Fourteen."

I thought he'd been in Kakuma camp then. There was so much about their stories I didn't know.

Benjamin climbed into the back seat with Alepho and Lino, his knees crammed against the seat in front of him.

"Okay, then, I see. You still need a license to drive here. We'll work on getting you that."

Benson, the eldest, sat up front as usual, and we headed out. I put in a reggae CD with some Jimmy Cliff and Bob Marley.

"Do you have Michael Jackson?" Benson asked.

"I might at home. I'll look for it."

"What happened to him?" Alepho asked from the back seat. "What did he do to himself?"

Another Alepho question. Although plastic surgery was simpler to address than the dating issue. Or Botox. Or SlimFast.

"He had a little too much surgery, but he also has vitiligo. It's a disease that causes the skin to lose its pigment."

"I saw people in the camp get that sickness," Alepho said.

That must have been interesting from their perspective. A person gets sick and turns white. What a contrast that would be. I'd never seen anyone as dark as they were. There wasn't even a lighter area on the underside of their arms. And Benjamin was the blackest, just as they'd said. "Do any of you remember the first time you saw a white person?"

"In Ethiopia," Benson said. "We were afraid because we were having rumors among us that white people took our people to their land. But it was just horror rumors created by the boys who have no knowledge about the world."

Or did know some history, I thought.

"The very first time I see them," Benson continued, "the two white men and three women were visiting us at Pugnido Refugee Camp. The women start crying when they see a lot of the boys are suffering and eating the grass soup. But we look at them and we ask ourselves, 'What is wrong with these people's skin? Are they sick?' After that the white people brought a lot of food to us, and we completely believe that they are very nice people. Every time they come they give us some candy and cookie, which we call biscuit, and some soaps. We tried to crowd around them a lot, but the teachers chased us away with sticks. Every time they visit we welcomed them by gathering in our schools and singing this song. 'We are very glad to see you today. All of our visitors.'"

He didn't seem the least bit inhibited about singing. I'd noticed in other situations that although Benson was not extroverted and did nothing to draw attention to himself, he was confident and self-assured in a way that suggested he didn't worry about what other people thought.

"This was repeated many times," he added. "They were the only people our lives were depending on. Someday you come to Africa. I will show it to you."

"Yes, I would like that very much." I'd always dreamed of going to Africa one day. It would be great to go with someone like Benson.

The zoo parking lot was nearly empty except for the usual

lineup of school buses. Tourists were still scared off by the threat of terrorism in public places.

As we waited in the ticket line, schoolchildren swarmed us. Benjamin looked especially tall surrounded by them. The kids were friendly and direct. Some asked if they could touch his skin. He seemed honored by the role reversal from the refugee camp.

Inside the gate, a flock of coral flamingos greeted us. They had been there ever since I could remember, and I'd been coming to the San Diego Zoo for at least forty-five years.

"I have never been to a zoo before," Benson said. "I want to see the great apes. In Sudan we only have baboons, and they are very aggressive."

"Great apes first then." We headed off to the ape enclosures. A male orangutan with jowls like dinner plates sat beside the glass apathetically watching the human crowd while two young-sters behind him wrestled over a stick. We took many pictures. Good thing I brought three rolls of film. After the gorillas, chim-panzees, and, according to the sign, "sex-crazed bonobos," we headed farther down the canyon and past smaller enclosures of a variety of species.

When we came to the cage of a medium size yellow-backed bird, Benson stopped and pointed. "That bird builds its nest of clay. It fishes in the river and puts the wriggling fish inside his nest. The fish flops all around and makes the nest smooth. When it is done, the bird puts the fish back in the river."

I read the sign below the cage. It said nothing about that amazing behavior Benson described. "Wow, a fish-recycling bird. Benson, you could teach our zoologists a few things about behav-iors." I loved hearing them describe the wildlife and culture of the place they'd left when still so young. The fondness in their voices left no doubt that their love for their homeland was bone deep.

We came upon some tough-looking, large, gray, short-legged birds with beaks like two machetes—the African gray hornbill.

"We catch those in Sudan," said Alepho. "You must be careful of the bill."

The whole bird looked scary, especially that bill. "You've eaten them?"

"Yes, we eat them. They are everywhere in Sudan and Kenya."

The San Diego Zoo lies across several hills with deep valleys in between. We wandered wherever the path took us. They showed interest in all the animals. I'd never noticed before that the majority in this zoo came from Africa. When we encountered signs that said, ETHIOPIAN EAGLE, or KENYAN COW, they became indignant. "This animal from Sudan," they told me. "I see this animal there." None of the signs credited Sudan. Years of war had done that. Just like it had been too dangerous for journalists, zoologists hadn't been there either. A whole land, its people and animals, lost to the rest of the world.

Atop Hoof Mesa, we came upon a beautiful large red antelope. Alepho said, "I know this animal. It eats snakes."

That sounded like the myth of the minotaur. Or as believable as their seven-foot-tall mother. "Antelopes are herbivores," I corrected.

"No," he insisted. "It make the sound of a snake at the entrance to the hole. When the snake comes to see, the antelope kills it and eats it."

Alepho was usually so sincere and logical. I searched out the description plaque on the antelope's enclosure to show him. *Known to kill and eat other small animals.* So much for book learning and hard and fast rules about herbivores. "You're right."

I checked my phone. No call from Bob.

We headed toward the new hippo enclosure. This was one of the few times besides the ball game that we'd ventured outside the diverse midcity area, where tall dark boys attracted little attention.

Here people looked, some even stared. Of course, as we stood by enclosures and they shared stories of fleeing from, hunting, or eating the creature on display, it was bound to attract attention. A few people asked questions.

Standing in the lower level of the enclosure, where only a piece of glass separated us and the swimming hippos, Benson said, "We know this animal. Hip-po-pah-to-mas. We eat them sometimes but you must be very, very careful when hunting. The hippo can bite a man in half with those teeth. If you swim underwater, they cannot get you, but then maybe the crocodile will."

Hippo or croc? I think I'd stay out of the water.

An older white woman sitting on a bench near us was listening. She leaned forward and asked Benjamin, "Where are you from?"

"I am from Africa," Benjamin said proudly.

She smiled. "Where in Africa?"

"Sudan."

"I thought so. Are you Dinka?"

"Yes, you know the Dinka?"

"I've traveled throughout Africa." Her tone was serious. "I know of the Dinka. It's a pleasure to meet you." She stood up and shook each of their hands. I introduced myself and she told us about her travels. When the time came to say goodbye, she clasped each of their hands warmly in hers. Tears welled in her eyes and she choked out, "I know what is going on in Sudan, and I'm glad you've come here. I wish you well in America."

As we walked away, I looked back. She was fumbling through her purse and pulled out a tissue and sunglasses.

We climbed to the top of another mesa and watched the polar bear cubs. Once again, schoolchildren swarmed us. A teacher gave me her card and insisted we visit her classroom. The school was an hour away. Maybe someday.

I checked my phone again. No Bob.

"The pandas?" Benson asked.

I pointed up. "Let's ride the sky buckets back to the entrance. They are that way."

They were hesitant at first about flying through the air in a bucket but finally agreed. Benson and Alepho joined me in the first car. It bumped and jerked against the platform. Their eyes grew wide and they grabbed the sides. As it settled on the cable, like a boat on water, and we swung high above the whole zoo, they relaxed and began to take in the spectacular view, locating enclosures we'd visited on foot.

"Have you heard of Disneyland?" I asked.

"No, what is this Disneyland?"

"Our next adventure." Hopefully we could arrange some days off work together. Hopefully they'd have work.

We had lunch at an outdoor place that was supposed to look like Africa. They didn't notice. Had the decorator missed the mark?

After we toured the snake house and visited the huge Galapagos turtles who reached their heads up for a scratch, Benson asked for the third time. "The pandas?"

"We're finally getting near."

I'd never seen the pandas either, because the line was usually longer than I wanted to stand in. We walked down the adjacent canyon to the panda line, which was unusually short due to terrorist threat. A large male slept beside the bamboo forest and a female with her back to us sat motionless. A sign said that the baby was on vacation.

"The pandas are just like their pictures," Benson said.

Alepho studied the chart describing their extraordinarily high-risk reproductive cycle.

"Miracle any survive," I said.

He smiled.

The pandas hadn't moved in ten minutes so we headed

farther down the canyon to the bear enclosures. They'd never seen one in person. No bear species in Africa. A bus passed. The large grizzly stood on his hind legs and gave a friendly wave. Huggable as a teddy. "They are actually really dangerous," I warned. As though they were at risk of encountering one.

We came to the lions' enclosure. I stopped to admire them and recalled the Lost Boy in the video talking about lions. Had these guys ever seen one on their journey?

Alepho came down the hill but kept going. As he passed, he said, "I hate lion," in a tone so profound it gave me shivers. In his honor, I walked on.

By the time we finished with the elephants, giraffes, and rhinos, and some creepy critters—like a scorpion the size of my hand that Benson said he'd been stung by a few times—I'd gone through two rolls of film. I checked my phone. No Bob. How long did it take to get drug-test results? When did I stop waiting and start contacting more stores?

It was almost three o'clock; I didn't want us to miss the seal show. They'd been surprised that my dog would leave the garage on command. I couldn't wait until they saw Rusty the seal.

At the stadium, we headed down the side aisle for some shady seats. Alepho entered the row first and the others followed.

Several empty seats beyond us a middle-aged woman made sure I saw her dirty look and rose, clutching her purse against herself with both hands, and moved away, across the stadium.

Really? Purse-snatchers in wingtips and golf shirts hang out at seal shows? Her behavior was as cliché as a *Saturday Night Live* skit.

Rusty's escapades made up for her rude behavior. I'd never seen anyone enjoy the seal show as much as my four companions.

Afterward, I went into the women's restroom. A pretty young

dark-haired woman approached me. "Are you with those boys?" she drawled in a thick Texan accent.

After the experience with the rude woman in the stands, I bristled at "those boys" in that accent and couldn't keep the sharpness out of my reply. "Yes, I am."

"I saw this *60 Minutes* special. Are they all some of those boys?"

"Yes, they are."

"Could you please give them my blessing?"

Oh, she was actually very sweet. How embarrassing. Served me right. I was just as capable of prejudging as the purse lady in the stadium. "I'd be happy to, but why don't I introduce you to them and you can give it to them yourself?"

She looked nervous and sort of surprised, like I'd just offered to introduce her to Brad Pitt. Her husband joined us. They told the boys they were visiting from Texas, and Benjamin shared his story of arriving in America and how he'd been in Dallas. More photos.

We called it a day and headed for the exit. On the way, we passed backdrops for photo ops. Benson wanted one with the panda. Alepho looked too weary. Another headache? How would he hold down a full-time job?

"Benjamin," I said. "Do you want a photo?" He turned and walked out into the passing crowd. No silly animal photos for him apparently. He stopped in the center of the main thorough-fare and waved his arms over his head. What was he doing now?

"American women, American women," he called out, "come, come for a picture!"

Oh my. The crowd parted. They didn't know what to make of him. Two women stopped for a moment and then tried to move on. He saw them. "Come! Come!" he insisted, flashing those bright teeth and herding them with his long arms. They gave in.

He organized them in front of the elephant with a crown and pulled them close. *Click. Click.*

"Save one picture," he said. "I must have one driving the car."

"You're not driving."

"I know, I know. I just sit for picture."

I saved two.

THEY HAD NO FIRE

Alepho

Judy asked us to go to the zoo. In the camp library, I had read that a zoo was a place where they kept animals. I'd never seen a zoo. I was excited to see what it looked like. How did they keep the animals?

Each cage had a description of the animal. Each animal had two names. One was the scientific name. I hadn't heard those before. Seeing those names made me think, wow, the people here are very educated.

Everyone around spoke English so fast. A little boy, not as high as my waist, ran to a machine and got a soda all by himself. People looked at us and somehow seemed to sense that we were new.

Many of the animals at the zoo were the same as the ones we had seen back in Africa. But they looked very different than the ones in the wild. They weren't alert or looking alive.

We said to each other in Dinka, "*Laai aci nyin ngong*," which means the animals are suffering. They all looked impotent. They had no fire. Even the lions.

The lions in Africa had fire. During my journey the nights on the road were dangerous, especially between villages, when we slept in the bush.

One night, while sleeping with a large group of boys, something warm and moist sniffed at my face. I swatted at it with my hand. Soft footsteps padded away. I fell back to sleep.

A boy's scream interrupted my dream. I sprang awake. Boys leapt to their feet and ran in all directions. A moonless night. We couldn't see a thing. What was happening? Who was screaming?

We found the injured boy. His cheek was gone, leaving a hole where we could see all the way into his mouth. Some wild animal, probably a lion, had bitten off part of his face. The same wild animal had sniffed me first. I shivered, thinking of what might have happened. The next few nights I couldn't sleep at all.

From then on, when we boys slept, we crowded toward the center like a pile of puppies competing for their mother's milk. No one wanted to be on the edge and carried away by a lion. All through the night we awoke and crawled back to the center of the pile.

Even with our precautions, a few nights later a sleeping boy was carried away. In the morning, we found his hand, legs, and head. The eyes were gone. My heart wanted to beat right out of my chest. I just wanted to be with my mother again. Sleeping safely beside her in our hut, not worrying about food or water or wild animals.

When we came to the cage with the lions at the zoo, I walked on. I didn't need to read the little sign. I knew all about lions.

HIRED!

Judy

When I arrived home from the zoo, Bob Sullivan had left a message on our answering machine. "The drug tests for the four applicants have come back negative." *Hallelujah!* "Please take them all for training Friday morning at seven, to the Encinitas Ralphs." The very store I'd shopped at for years. "Alepho and Daniel are on the schedule for next week." Next week. Wow. Two of them. *Thank you, Bob Sullivan.*

I needed groceries. I could ask who the trainer would be, say hello, and tell her a little about the students I'd be bringing for wrapper training. Couldn't hurt. I wished it wasn't so, but if people had some knowledge and appreciation of their background, like the two women at the zoo, their response to them was much more positive. It humanized the boys. They became individuals rather than very different-looking, possibly dangerous, outsiders.

The manager at Ralphs said that Karol would be the trainer.

He directed me to where she was cashiering. I got my groceries and went to her register. As Karol scanned my items, I introduced myself and gave her a quick background on the four new employees who would be in her training class.

"I heard about *that*," she said unpleasantly.

Her surliness startled me. Not even routine customer courtesy. I was speechless.

"Just be sure," she added, "they aren't late. I gotta get outta here. I'm going to Palm Desert at eleven."

I left the store stunned. What had that been about? Maybe saying something to her had been a bad idea. Maybe it was just that she'd have more students for training when she was in a rush to leave early. *Give her a break, don't jump to conclusions.* But we wouldn't be late, that was for sure.

"You're all going to training Friday morning," I told Benson on the phone.

"That is very good news." He sounded excited.

"I'll be there at 5:45 a.m. to pick you up." That was excessively early but Karol wasn't getting any excuse from me to fail them. "When should I call and wake you?" Four guys and one shower.

"Please call at 4:00 a.m. That way we can have a bit of tea. We will be waiting outside."

• • •

Friday morning I woke up before the alarm went off. Their big day had arrived. I was happy and relieved, but also so nervous. Karol had certainly added to that. Had I imagined or exaggerated her irritation? Maybe she'd had a bad day.

I called at 4:00 a.m. and James answered on the second ring. Figured. He was the only person in the house that didn't need to get up. The only one not getting this opportunity, and he needed it most.

The training store was just a mile or so from me, but I needed to pick them up and bring them back up north. At five I set out for their house in thick fog and surprisingly heavy traffic.

They were ready and waiting outside, dressed in their best. "You all look great."

"Thank you," Benson said. "We are honored for this opportunity."

They were always so gracious. They climbed in, taking their places in their usual seating arrangement.

The road wasn't visible beyond a car length. Good thing we'd gotten that early start.

"Is this winter?" Alepho asked. "It is so cold."

"This really isn't winter weather yet. When the ocean is warmer than the air, it evaporates and makes this fog. It's usually gone by the time you get up so you don't see it. When winter does come, it'll be colder than this. Do you have blankets?"

"Yes, we have a blanket," Alepho said. "Benson doesn't have one."

"I'll find more for all of you so that you don't have to heat the apartment." Which meant turning on that ancient radiator thing in the living room. I imagined it either blowing up or emitting carbon monoxide. Whichever, it scared the hell out of me. They wouldn't have the money to spend on energy bills anyway.

We arrived at the Encinitas store twenty minutes early and sat at a table near the front door to keep an eye out for Karol. Rigo, who worked in the bakery, recognized me and came over. I introduced the guys. He warmly welcomed them.

Except for the people stocking the shelves, the store was nearly empty. At five minutes to seven two more wrapper trainees joined us. I'd yet to see Karol, who wanted to be sure we weren't late.

At about seven, Karol came toward us. I nodded and started to say something but she acted as though she hadn't noticed us and headed around the corner to the coffee stand. Even if she didn't recognize me from the other day, who wouldn't notice them? Especially in this town.

Oh well, I'd get her attention on the way back and ask where the training would take place.

"That was Karol," I told the guys, hoping her rudeness had escaped their notice. "She will be training you today."

We waited for Karol to come back from getting coffee. We waited and waited. She had to come back this way. I walked around the corner looking for her, but she seemed to have disappeared. I asked one of the stockers if he knew where the training would be held and he shrugged.

We waited a few more minutes. I asked a cashier where the training might be but they knew nothing either. There was no one else to ask.

I'd come to make sure things went smoothly. How hard could that be? But it wasn't going smoothly. Someone was playing games.

A man came around the corner. TED and MANAGER on his tag. "Hi," he said. "Are you here for the wrapper class?"

Ted was nice, like Bob.

"It's meeting upstairs," he said.

Karol could have told me that on two occasions. Why couldn't someone like Ted or Bob be doing the training?

Ted gave us detailed directions on how to go up some stairs at the back of the store. The secret stairs Karol must have escaped up.

When we got to the conference room, fifteen or so other students were already seated and Karol had started the class. She didn't acknowledge our entrance, and went on with her instruction.

I directed the four guys and the two trainees who had joined us to the empty chairs in the back, waved goodbye like a mother dropping off her kindergartner, and tried my best to look cheery for them while resisting the urge to glare at Karol.

I went back down the stairs, spitting mad. Nervous sweat tingled my skin. Heat flooded my cheeks and flowed down my neck. Why was I so upset by a small thing? Because Karol could have told me yesterday we were to meet upstairs. She could have told me this morning when she walked right by us. The humiliation of being victimized and made a fool sent pricking heat to my ears. I'd failed when I knew better after going places with them these last weeks. The things I should have said and done to avert her subtle sabotage had come to me too late. I'd been a kindergartner mom in a moment when they needed a tiger mom.

At noon, Paul and I were driving to San Francisco for a wedding so I couldn't pick them up. Brianna at IRC had offered. I phoned her from the car and explained what happened with the trainer. "Am I imagining things?"

"I don't think so. But it's the trainer's loss."

Did she have to be so damn philosophical and forgiving?

Since meeting the guys in August I hadn't touched my novel. But the writing flame burned hotter than ever on a new subject. Some articles, perhaps. After all, the pen was mightier than the sword. Fortunately, I didn't have a sword.

NEVER DO WHAT I JUST DID

Judy

Monday afternoon I went to their apartment to hear how the training went. As I turned onto their street, Euclid Avenue, I saw it in a whole new way. The mothers with strollers and Laundromats and manicure shops were still there, but imagining Alepho and Daniel, and eventually the others, walking this street at night faded those things into the background. What remained were the houses with barred windows, dark vacant lots to hang out in and sell drugs, and the seedy bars that were closed now but would be open and rowdy when night came. Hopefully they'd start on the day shift. That would make their trip to the bus stop a lot safer. The neighborhood was diverse, more languages spoken than in any community in America, or so they claimed, but it also had the most gangs in San Diego, and the gangs might not be thrilled about newcomers. Who knew what lines were drawn in the sand by beer and bravado at night?

Alepho greeted me at the door.

"How did it go on Friday?" I inquired.

"Very fine. We were a little bit lost in the first. I couldn't understand. But it was fine."

They'd gotten through it. Two days away and I'd calmed down. Probably a good thing I hadn't picked them up that day.

Benson had a chair pulled up to the couch. His colored pencil set was out and he was working on a nearly completed drawing of a stick-legged boy in a pair of tattered red shorts with a rope around his waist holding them up. He was quite an artist, and a musician as well from what the others said.

"Is that you?" I asked.

"This look like everybody," Lino said.

"When bombs come," Alepho said, "we drop everything and just run. Our backpacks with books, clothes, blankets, everything. So we have nothing left. We all looked like this." He pulled a little piece of paper from his pocket. "This my schedule. I start work tomorrow. Daniel starts next week."

Maybe it was *me* the trainer hadn't liked. Or maybe she had had no choice. Maybe Bob had told her they were already hired, and her job was merely to do her best to train them. At any rate, she passed them and they were starting work. I added up the time. "They gave you twenty-three hours. That's very good for the first week."

"I am going to try very hard to do a good job." He looked so earnest, like the weight of the world was on his shoulders.

"I know you will, and you will do just fine."

"I am worried," Alepho said in a soft voice. "People do not understand me with my heavy accent."

"Your English is good. Your accent is nice. You only need to speak louder." I still didn't know if the soft voices were due to culture or embarrassment of their English. "This job is good for you because you will get lots of practice speaking to Americans."

"I will try. I am a little bit nervous."

For him to reveal that probably meant that he was a lot nervous.

"Don't worry. Bob knows you can do it. That's why he hired you. Just be sure to leave home early enough so that you're at work on time. Daniel is going to show you the bus route, right?"

"Yes."

"Be careful walking at night, okay?"

"Where are you going now?" he asked.

"You'll be careful, right?"

"Yes. Where you going now?"

"Well, I was heading home but now that I've come this far, I'm thinking about stopping by IRC." I wanted to speak with Joseph about making sure Alepho saw a doctor again. His medicine had been gone for a week and he wasn't feeling any better.

"May I come with you? I want to go to the bank."

"Of course."

Alepho brought some papers in the car and was writing something as I drove up their street and turned west onto University Avenue. I glanced over at him.

"I am translating email from Dinka to English," he said. "My friend send it. It has a little news about Sudan. You can read it."

"From Sudan. Does that make you homesick?"

"No, I have not been there for many years." His expression turned solemn. "I remember that night I was in the house. My mother was breastfeeding my little brother."

He'd never spoken about his personal experience before, mostly about conditions in the camp. I didn't know what provoked it, but I wasn't about to interrupt.

"You know the government gives the guns to the Murahilin horsemen. They attacked our village that night. When the attack come, my mother yelled at me. 'Alepho, what are you doing? Run!'" He shook his head, like he was ridding himself of the memory. His voice grew deeper. "I don't know why she yelled liked that. I ran and ran."

I looked over at him. He was looking out the window. That last image of his mother yelling at him to save his life had stuck in his mind all these years. Did a seven-year-old only hear the anger in her voice? Could he hear the fear? What she had feared most had come true. From what I read, many women and small children were burned inside their huts. As Cliff's mother, I could not even begin to grasp her state of mind. Two years earlier she'd lost Benson and never heard from him again. The baby in her arms was probably doomed. She was desperate to save Alepho.

"Was that the last time you saw her?"

"That was the last time."

"I think she yelled to save your life."

He looked right at me, which was rare, but I had to turn and look ahead to watch the traffic.

He said, "People say it is a civil war in Sudan. But it is not a civil war. It is more like Gomorrah from the Bible. They just kill the innocent people. All the people's bones are everywhere. Like an elephants' graveyard."

I didn't know much about the Bible and I'd never seen an elephants' graveyard, but he'd painted a vivid picture. I looked him in the eyes for a moment to show him I was listening and understanding, but too quickly I had to turn my attention again back to driving. I needed to make a left at the intersection ahead and there was no turn lane. Preparing, I pulled partially into the hectic intersection, eager to get back to our conversation. The oncoming traffic began to clear as the light turned yellow. I was about to make my left when a large panel truck came straight toward us. He wasn't slowing. He was accelerating. He'd never make the yellow. He was going to rush it anyway. I was stuck.

The light turned red, leaving us stranded in the middle of the intersection. Two seconds later the truck blasted through at full speed. Thank God I'd waited. So close.

"Whoa!" Alepho exclaimed.

He recognized the infraction even with his little experience. I completed my turn with the cars from the cross-traffic biting at my heels.

A cop was to our left at the corner of the cross street. He had to have seen it all. With a quick right turn he could nail the truck.

"Look at that!" I said. "They always say there is never a policeman when you need one, but he's right there. That guy in the truck is going to get a very expensive ticket."

I looked in my rearview. The cop was still at the corner.

"I am learning the patterns of the traffic," Alepho said.

"Yeah, I bet you are. That was not a good example. I read the other day that people running a red light are the biggest cause of traffic deaths. Don't even run yellows and always be careful if you are the first one to enter the intersection when the light turns green because some jerk like that truck might be coming the other way."

The mood of our prior conversation about the night he'd fled his home in Sudan had been irrevocably broken. I pulled into the bank parking lot. We exited the car and were walking toward the bank when a police car pulled up and blocked our path. The same one who had been at the corner. He wouldn't have had time to go after the truck. Why was he here?

The policeman jumped out and came around his patrol car straight toward us. I hadn't had a ticket in twenty-five years. I was respectful, appreciative, and a little scared of police, even though my fear had no basis except not wanting a ticket. Still reeling from the truck that almost ran us over and flabbergasted that the cop was here and not chasing the truck, I yelled, "I got stuck out there!" before he could utter a word and accuse *me* of running a red. "That guy was going fast. He ran the light intentionally. I didn't have a choice. You saw it. What could I do? It was green when I pulled out to make the turn. That guy went blasting through."

The policeman stiffened and looked slightly taken aback. We both stood there. He was middle-aged, white, and had a kindly face. He looked over at Alepho, who was dressed neatly and conservatively, as usual, and stood quietly by my side.

The policeman's shoulders relaxed a bit.

That gave me some courage. "Pulling into the intersection when it's green is legal, isn't it? I could see that guy in the truck was going to blast right through the red. He would have clobbered us if I'd turned. I couldn't stay in the intersection. I had to finish the turn on the red after he went through, didn't I?" I was pushing it, I knew it, but I'd go to court and protest if he ticketed me on this.

The policeman didn't answer me and didn't actually smile, but I sensed a smile below the surface. "Be careful," he said and walked back toward the driver's side of the patrol car. I waited while he went for the forms and to check my license plates. But he got in, shut the door, and put the car into reverse. He looked into his rearview at us. I mouthed, "Thank you," and wondered how it would have gone if I hadn't spoken first.

Then I told Alepho, "Never, never, never do what I just did. I was upset. That was a big mistake. You can't do that. I can do that because I'm an old lady, but I won't do it again. It's different if young guys behave badly like that." Especially young, tall, really black guys in this neighborhood. Or any neighborhood. They'd be stopped just walking down the street in mine.

Back in the car Alepho worked on translating the email. I looked over at him. Collared T-shirt, khakis, close-cropped hair, nothing gangster about him, but tall and black. Was he the reason the cop hadn't gone after the truck in the first place?

DOCTOR

Alepho

A truck almost hit Judy's car and she became angry at the police-man. Then she told me to never get angry at a policeman. I had no reason to be angry with the policemen in America. They were nice.

At IRC Judy spoke with Joseph Jok and told him about my problems. "Would you mind if I take Alepho to the doctor? He's starting work tomorrow and has stomachaches and headaches almost every day."

Joseph said, "Oh yes, please. That would be wonderful. Thank you."

Before she left me at IRC, Judy asked, "Please, practice taking the bus with Daniel this afternoon so you don't have a problem tomorrow." I told her that I would do that.

Judy called later and said, "I'm taking you to an internist. She's in east San Diego and has familiarity with tropical medicine, especially African. She's Nigerian."

Judy took me to the doctor's office. They gave me paperwork

to complete that was like a job application. We had heard that doctors in Egypt had people sign papers and the people didn't know what they were signing and that allowed the doctor to harvest their organs. I read every word before I signed that paper. I was happy that the doctor was from Nigeria and not Egypt.

They weighed me and put me in a room with Judy to wait.

Judy said, "Just tell the doctor how you've been feeling."

"My back hurts."

Judy said to touch my toes and stretch my back each day and she showed me how.

I did the same and put my hands on the floor.

"Yeah, like that," she said. "Maybe stiffness isn't your problem."

The doctor came in and examined me. She asked, "Do you have any problems?"

I told her about the back pain.

"Did it hurt when you were in the camp?" she asked.

"After they beat me."

"Beat you?"

"In '97 the Kenyan police beat me with clubs. My back very sore after that."

The doctor examined my back. "I don't see anything. Let's see how it does."

Judy asked, "Alepho, do you want to tell her about your stomachaches and headaches?"

I didn't need to tell the doctor now, Judy had just said it.

The doctor looked at me. "You might be still adjusting. I'll order some tests. Stop at the nurse on the way out."

The nurse said she would schedule the CAT scan and gave me a stool kit. What did a cat and a stool have to do with my problems?

PIECING IT TOGETHER

Judy

Never knowing what to expect, I settled on the couch with the most recent pages Benson and Alepho had given me. Their stories came to me in bits and not in any particular order. Sometimes computer generated, sometimes handwritten, they produced them double- and triple-folded from their pockets. Trying to piece together their lives, from their village through twelve or more years in exile, was like assembling a jigsaw puzzle without a picture as a guide. No references to dates, much less years, and they recounted incidents in towns and regions I couldn't locate on any map. The few maps I did find of Sudan were in Arabic or English and maybe they were referring to the Dinka names of places.

The most confusing part for me, and what was emerging as the most difficult for them, was hardly mentioned in the *60 Minutes* segment. After they were driven at gunpoint from the refugee camp in Ethiopia and forced to swim the Gilo River, they spent another year fleeing bombing raids by the government, two rebel armies who wanted to train them as future soldiers in various camps like Palataka and Natinga, ubiquitous hungry predators, and ever-present hunger and thirst. No wonder that what sounded like a hellhole to me, Kakuma Refugee Camp, had been a sanctuary for them.

So far, they hadn't written anything about being in America.

I'd never journaled or kept a diary of any kind in my life. I began to write. I didn't know what it would lead to, but my recent experiences had been so unique, I had to put them on paper.

CAT SCAN

Alepho

Judy said that a CAT scan was good and explained that it could look inside my head and see what was wrong. I was still confused.

She took me to the UCSD medical center. A nurse led me into a room and told me to take off my clothes and put on a shirt. The shirt had no back.

She led me to a room with a huge machine with a round hole. "Lie here," she said and put her hand on a narrow cot. I laid back and she put pillows beside my head. Then she strapped my head to the table.

"Now, lie very still," she said.

What could I do?

The cot began to move backward into the round hole of that big machine. That day my headache pounded inside, so I hoped the machine could see it.

Once my head was completely inside, the machine growled and clicked like teeth.

I'd been so stupid. Why had I agreed to go into that machine? Back in the refugee camp a guy had told me that some Americans were strange and ate people. When he'd been in the Pinyudo Refugee Camp in Ethiopia, the UN had brought them cans that said FISH. But when they opened the cans they found pieces of fingernails. Someone told him it was human meat put into the cans and FISH was written on it so that Africans wouldn't know. I didn't believe his story, but as I headed into that machine, I wondered if I would be ground up and put in the can and sent back to the refugee camps in Africa for people to feed on me. I almost changed my mind, but part of me thought the guy's story was not true. The Americans had traveled to the moon. They had amazing machines that could do almost anything. I hoped this one could look inside and find out why my head did not stop hurting. With this pain, I couldn't read. How could I go to school? I had to take this risk.

The machine whirred and clicked for a long time. My headache pain increased. I wanted to get out, so I thought about things to make the time pass. Some memories made me more unsure, like cautions the elders had given us about American men marrying only a single wife. That left many women who were not married and looking for husbands. Could my sponsor be selling me to one of those women? What did I know? I was an uneducated African. She could trick me into believing things I didn't understand.

All these things went through my mind in that machine.

The next day the doctor said the CAT scan showed nothing. I was disappointed. I wanted to find out why my head felt like it was going to explode.

SMILING

Alepho

I had begun my job at Ralphs. Learning about my new environment gave me some skills about food. I needed to know more. I'd received training, but I could not remember many things.

I stood at the check stand and said, "Paper or plastic?" but the customers did not hear me well.

The job trainer said that we must smile at the customer when we ask, "Paper or plastic?" In my culture, one does not smile unless one is happy. I practiced showing my teeth in the mirror.

I was told that soap could not be bagged with food, but many things were in boxes or bottles. How could I know what they were? I tried to memorize their names and what they looked like. The difficulties came when the customers brought things like Oreos or Ajax to the register that I was not familiar with yet. Were they soap or food? Customers became upset when I put the wrong things together so if I didn't know, I put them in a bag alone.

People sometimes asked where they could find an item. I liked helping people and these were good opportunities for me to learn where to find things, also. I led the customers on a search up and down the aisles. Some asked, "Are we getting close?" I couldn't answer them. I didn't know, unless it was soap they wanted, that aisle smelled nice. Some customers did not complete the journey and said, "Oh, never mind, I will find it." Most people were kind and thanked me for the assistance.

Ralphs was not a refugee camp. Customer satisfaction meant everything. If the customer was not pleased, I could lose my job.

One customer asked Daniel to find Kleenex. Daniel took the man outside and pointed across the parking lot. "The clinics might be over there in those tall buildings."

The customer became upset. Mr. Sullivan explained to Daniel and me that the man wanted Kleenex, not clinics. We didn't know it was tissue. Mr. Sullivan was always patient and kind to us.

Mr. Bob Sullivan's compassion saved me. If it were not for Mr. Sullivan, I would have been fired the first day.

NEGATIVE

Judy

Joseph explained the stool test to Alepho, and I picked up the container in its little white bag and took it to a lab. The results came back negative. Disappointing. I'd hoped they'd find something treatable and it would help the others as well. Word had gotten out that I'd taken a few guys to the doctor, so over the next weeks I began hearing from their friends with the same symptoms. Some worse.

What could it be? They'd been tested for the big stuff before they even left the camp, the things that could spread to us, AIDS, TB, etc. Who knew what they'd picked up in twenty years of not seeing a doctor and living in the conditions they had.

Alepho emailed me. *I'm very tired at work. I have a stomach paining. I want to delay my studying.*

For how long? He'd just started his ESL, English as a Second Language, classes. If he wanted to postpone his schooling, he really was feeling bad. So many times he'd said that education was the thing he wanted most. All of the Lost Boys did.

He said he'd had headaches in the camp, but he felt much worse here. How could that be? Stress? He had so many things to juggle: job, shopping, food preparation, sleep, laundry, and transportation to work. No wonder it seemed like he had little time for school, especially not feeling well. He also must have missed aspects of life in Africa, such as companionship and camaraderie. Benson had started working the day shift at the Ralphs in Hillcrest and Benjamin had just been hired as well.

From their writing, I'd learned that life had been difficult, hopeless, and cruel on their journey; they'd never known when they might starve to death or just get killed, but they were always together—thousands of boys. Together. Once they made it to Kakuma, they went to school and ate together once a day from a shared pot. They built their houses together. They played soccer with balls made from clothes wrapped around balloons, or grew vegetables together at the water tap. In the evening, without electricity, they sat outside, told stories, joked, played a five-string guitar, and sang. Whether it was working, having fun, or suffering, the experience was shared. America must have felt lonely.

PIRATES!

Judy

I'd had big plans for their first Thanksgiving, but when the schedules came out, all three were working Thanksgiving Day. New guys, made sense. Thank God they had jobs. I looked forward to celebrating their first Christmas in America.

We managed to organize a trip to Disneyland during the last week in November. I let Cliff skip school and he came along. A day with the guys would have more impact on him than a day in a classroom; he'd have plenty of those in his future. I was glad he still enjoyed palling around with them.

Even though the guys had been in America over three months now, the fun of discovering my world through their eyes hadn't diminished. Before coming, they may never have heard of McDonald's or Disneyland but knew our important presidents, states and their capitals, and appreciated the fundamental importance of things in our Constitution—like separation of church and state. The scads of stuff in our stores didn't interest or impress them. But they sure appreciated our educational opportunities and freedom. We'd see what they thought of Disneyland.

I'd assumed a weekday would mean the place would be empty. It wasn't. I asked Cliff, "Where shall we start?"

"Matterhorn!"

"Okay, let's do it."

When we came off the mountain, Benjamin and Lino said they'd liked it, but Alepho said the speed made him feel a bit dizzy.

"Hmm," I told Cliff, "maybe that wasn't the best choice for the first ride in their lives. How about something slower next?" I should have remembered that they'd asked me about some of the fast, dangerous sports they'd seen on TV, as though they'd been completely dumbfounded that people would do something like that for enjoyment. Or, they'd wondered why I liked to ski. Surely if I'd had adrenaline rushes from too many horrible experiences, I'd feel the same. "How about Pirates? Line is usually short. I think they'll like all the colorful animatronic figures."

"Sure."

I knew Cliff wouldn't say no to the Pirates of the Caribbean ride. After watching the *Peter Pan* movie when he was two, he'd become obsessed with pirates and spent his twos and threes running around in a bandanna with a sword.

We headed through Adventureland. "Oh," I laughed, "the Jungle Cruise. What would they think of that?"

"And Indiana Jones," Cliff said.

"Yea, that would be good too." Jeeps on a safari. Hadn't the search for the ark been somewhere in Ethiopia? Right next door to Sudan.

As I'd hoped, the line was short for Pirates of the Caribbean. They liked the talking mechanical parrot in front. Wait until they saw what was inside.

"First we go on a boat," I explained.

Alepho looked concerned.

"Don't worry, it's on a track."

"Track?"

"Totally safe. But don't be surprised when we go down two small waterfalls. That takes us to a river underground."

Benjamin and Lino leapt on board. Alepho, a bit hesitant, climbed in too. I loaded into the row behind them with Cliff and Benson, and we floated along past the restaurant to croaking frogs, banjo music, and fireflies. "I know those insects," Benson said.

Above the entrance to the underground cavern, a skull in a pirate hat told us to keep our limbs inside. "Here come the water drops," I said.

Enough other passengers screamed that I didn't know if the guys had, but we survived the falls and headed smoothly along to the cheerful "Yo-Ho" music.

Downriver the music slowed and morphed into a darker melody. A deep voice out of nowhere chanted, "Dead men tell no tales." I'd forgotten about that morbid warning.

Around the bend, a partially clothed pirate skeleton sprawled across the sand. Another skeleton had a sword run through his torso that pinned him to the wall. An animated giant crab fed on a third body.

Oh, my God. Dead people. *Stop the boat.* Please let me jump off right here and now and take my friends with me. How could I have forgotten about all the skeletons?

The boat didn't stop, of course. The ominous music played on and the voice that sounded like God kept chanting, "Dead men tell no tales." I hadn't forgotten. The aftermath of violence had just never meant anything to me before. Skeletons lying in sand. Could there be a worse image? Benson had given me a story he called "The Skeleton Tree" about a tree in the middle of a terrible desert crossing where so many people who couldn't go farther had stopped and never gotten up again. The ground was strewn with their bones.

I tensed. What would their reactions be? The three in front of us were talking amongst themselves in Dinka. I couldn't see Benson's expression, but if ever I'd felt vibrations of discomfort, it was then. I wanted the ride to be over.

But that was just the beginning. More skeletons, singing, steering a ship, drinking rum. At least the cute part was ahead with jolly pirates singing to cats, the dog with the jail key and the happy "Yo-Ho" song playing through it all.

Real-sounding explosions startled me. Cannonballs seemed to fly across our boat and strike the water. *Oh, get us out of here.*

When we got to the cute part, it wasn't cute. Pirates were ransacking a town, threatening to chop off a townsman's head, drowning someone else in a well, and capturing and selling women. Alepho had given me a story about his cousin who had been made a slave. A real slave trade still existed in Sudan. Their villages had been marauded by men on horseback, pirates of the desert. Such alive-looking figures made the whole thing worse. Skeletons were better.

What were my guests making of this whole experience? Americans had re-created some animatronic version of their childhood nightmare for entertainment? The ride seemed to go on forever.

Finally, the boat jerked, we climbed a water ladder, and emerged into the light of day. If they were shocked by it all, they were too polite to show it or comment. I was too afraid to ask.

We went on more rides with more benign themes, except the pile of skulls and hundred-foot python in Indiana Jones that also hadn't stuck in my mind from previous rides. Benjamin and

Lino loved the fast ones like Space Mountain, but Alepho didn't. Benson enjoyed the music and creative aspect of it all the most. We ended the day with A Small World.

I couldn't tell what they'd made of it all. Overwhelmed? Just wondering why? Too many fast rides and too much fast food?

Maybe I'd reacted to the skeletons and violence more than they had. But it had been a jolting reminder I was thankful for. I needed to be aware of things from their perspective as much as I could.

It had also made me wonder. Since it was a child's ride and represented the aftermath of so much violence, did some parents react the way I did when they took their children? And, what if there had been a bare breast somewhere in there? Would that symbol of life and sustenance have generated more outrage than all that depiction of death and destruction?

All in all, it had been a memorable day and Cliff had fun showing them around, but I doubted it had been near the adventure of our first day together at Walmart.

The next morning, I received an email from Benson:

Thank you for making me aware and awake in the world we are in and taking me to the land created by man wonder of brain technology. It gave me a lesson that man can do anything. Those Wonders of Disneyland will make me think for a week of the man who made such fun of real life excitement.

Had Walt Disney ever received a better compliment?

MORE GRANDER

Alepho

One day that we didn't work, Judy and Cliff took Benson, Lino, Benjamin, and me to a place called Disneyland. Judy put the car in a huge building and we rode a small train to the entrance.

We walked through a town with stores and different kinds of vehicles, even a bus pulled by a horse. Everything smelled so fresh, fresher than the American smell, so different, like another world I'd never experienced before. Judy and Cliff talked a lot about going on rides and which one. I was eager to find out what were these rides.

We came to a mountain and stood in a line. Judy said she was sorry for the large crowd, but the line was only a few minutes, not like the water line in the camp for hours or the ration line for a whole day.

Our turn came and we sat in these things that took off and went fast around the mountain and in the mountain. My belly jumped, like on the plane, but the plane only bumped a few times, this bumped and raced around the whole time.

Afterward, I sweated and was a little bit sick. Why did people want to subject their emotions to that?

We walked through the crowd. Cliff told us about the rides we passed. Things like small, fat elephants with wings that flew and coffee cups that spun around.

"Look," I said to Benson. "Adults and kids enjoy the same things together. That makes a family bond." I'd never experienced that in my life.

We went on a ride called Pirates of the Caribbean. This ride was slow and cool inside. We came to an area with skeletons wearing clothing and moving and doing things like they were alive. "Look," I told Benjamin, "dead people are a part of the culture here. The people are dead, but the bones are living." It was like a nightmare that I'd had on my journey where skulls talked to each other.

The boat floated through a town with large moving toy people and dogs and even a donkey. I wanted the boat to go slower. I couldn't see it all. This was something I could never imagine.

After that we went on a jeep ride and then a place for food. After the lunch, Cliff bought this giant colorful flower thing. He tried to get us to have one, but I'd never seen anything like that before. Cliff pulled off big pieces and put them in his mouth. "It's cotton candy," he said and offered me some.

Cotton? It filled my nose with something sweeter than honey. "No, thank you," I said. I turned to Benson. "That's white people food. I don't want to touch that one." Benson didn't want to touch it either, after I said this.

I'd never seen Cliff so excited as he was that day. We asked each other all day, "What is this place? It's so different. So fascinating." It was like the stadium or the zoo but more grander.

Americans organized things. They built amazing places. It made my brain feel small in my body. I felt so tiny.

At the end of the day, I'd had a great experience to see such a different world, but I wasn't sure if I would ever go to Disneyland again.

AM I HOT?

Alepho

Except for my stomach pains and headaches, my life progressed in my new environment. Everyone was so complex and educated. When they spoke English, my ears had to dance on my head in order to capture every word and understand what people meant. When I spoke, people responded with "What? I'm sorry, I can't hear you. Say that again." I didn't speak the good English they spoke. I couldn't wait to capture their accent and sound just like the white people speaking English. I was like the character in *The Gods Must Be Crazy* movie.

I took computer classes. Went on rides at Disneyland. Rode in cars on boulevards, streets, avenues, and freeways. I'd only known roads in Africa. I'd gone from a small village in South Sudan, to a refugee camp in Kenya, and now to this far side of the world, where I was getting acquainted with buses and trolleys in the metropolitan city of my destiny. San Diego was a saint city, as the named implied. What a privilege for me.

I liked my work at Ralphs. I'd learned to tell Tide from Froot

Loops. Don't bag those together! I didn't want to miss a day at work. I'd never called in sick.

The customers no longer made me nervous, until one day a pretty girl with long, silky dark hair came to the register. "Paper or plastic?" I asked.

She looked at my tag and tried to say my name but she could not. "How do you pronounce your name?"

"Alephonsion."

"Is it French?"

"No, it is not French, that is just my name."

"Can I call you Al?"

Her questions made me nervous. "Yes, you can call me anything."

"So where do you come from, Al?"

"Africa."

"I know," she said. "Where in Africa?"

"Sudan."

"Is it hot over there?"

"Sometimes." I had been told to make eye contact with customers, but in my country you only do that to make a point. It is aggressive. I bagged her groceries and tried to smile but I couldn't make the eye contact.

She picked up her bags and said, "Al, I think you are hot."

Hot? Heat flashed through my body. After she left the store, I lifted my arm and smelled my armpit. I smelled the other one. Neither one smelled hot.

I asked the cashier, "Am I hot?"

She said, "Uh-huh."

I excused myself and ran to the restroom. I'd showered that morning. I used deodorant like they showed us at IRC. I washed again.

The rest of the day I was so uncomfortable. Why were people rude in America?

I went home and showered twice to make sure that I wasn't hot. I dreaded going to work again.

The next day I wore two shirts under my Ralphs shirt. I became nervous when anyone came close to me. I did not want to be around people. I couldn't wait until my shift was over.

I asked Mr. Sullivan to transfer me to the midnight shift when the customers did not come.

GRAVEYARD

Judy

December was slipping by quickly and uneventfully. My hope for them to fulfill the American dream hadn't changed, but I'd been naive about the challenges newcomers faced. Day-to-day life struggles kept them from working on their future.

Sadly, everybody was scheduled to work on Christmas Day or evening. The next morning Cliff and Paul were busy, so I went down to the guys' apartment and we had a small celebration with some turkey, the traditional accompaniments, and a few gifts. A guitar for Benson and cameras for the others. They found my yams with marshmallows too sweet. I knew they would, but it was such an American tradition, I couldn't resist.

"Please greet Mr. Cliff and thank Dr. Paul," they said. They were always polite and gracious and seemed to understand that Paul was the one who made my time with them possible. I was thankful, too. I couldn't do any of this without his support.

Birth anniversaries weren't recognized in the Dinka culture.

When the Lost Boys came to America, they were assigned a birth date by the immigration service. For most of them that meant the best guess at the year they were born and the first of January as the day and month. On New Year's Day, I took a cake to their house. We placed it on a chair, gathered around, and lit the candles. They sang "Happy Birthday" for the first time, made a wish, and blew out the flames. Of course we took photos. I cut the cake into slices and added a scoop of ice cream. After the first bite—which it looked like they wanted to spit out—they hardly touched it. Too sweet and too cold, a clear consensus.

January was busy, but I tried to stay home at least one or two days a week. I was no longer writing my historical novel about a slave in the early 1500s. Now, living boys who had made an amazing journey were giving me inspiration and that writing felt more vital. I decided to collect their stories together and to organize mine as well. The other days, after I dropped Cliff at school, I headed down to their house. Something always needed to be done. Medical appointments, dental appointments, banking, financial assistance, signing up with the union, and, more and more rarely, doing something just for fun.

• • •

Bob Sullivan called me. In the nearly two months the guys had worked at Ralphs, he'd never called me before. Was someone sick or hurt?

"Alepho asked for graveyard. He doesn't seem like himself lately. I don't know what's going on. He was so excited and enthusiastic about the job and doing very well. Except for a few impatient people, the customers really liked him. He's smart. You know a guy like that could end up running the store. Now he's ripping cardboard."

The graveyard shift, oh no. That he'd no longer be with customers saddened me. That he'd have to make that mile walk down his street at night to the bus stop worried me. He'd seemed withdrawn recently. Sometimes when I gave him a ride to or from work, he'd have on sunglasses, earphones plugged into a cassette tape player, and his sweatshirt hood pulled down, like he was hiding. When I tried to make conversation, he'd politely take out the earphones and answer that question. I kept things light, hoping he'd engage. When he didn't, I hoped that was just his mood that day.

But graveyard? Damn. A real step backward.

• • •

One Saturday morning in early February I received an email from Alepho.

I have stomach paining. I don't know what happen last night. I wake up in back of store. Nobody know I lying there for some time. Me, Awer

Passing out was serious. His chronic discomfort and that of other Lost Boys had me worried. At a holiday party, I'd spoken to Stony, a friend and gastroenterologist. He'd said that their intestines would have to make a big adjustment from the high-fiber camp diet of hand-ground, dried corn to our high-fat and low-fiber refined carbohydrates. It could take time. But I wondered, how much time?

Fainting from pain or something worse was another story. Appendicitis? Who knew what other acute abdominal problem?

I called the apartment. No one answered.

I called Ralphs to see if they knew anything. "He left a while ago when his shift was over," Bob said. "He said he didn't feel well, and he didn't look good. What's wrong with Alepho?"

There was real caring in his voice, and it sounded like Alepho hadn't even told Bob about passing out. I didn't want to mention it if Alepho hadn't.

"I don't know. That's why I'm trying to reach him. He emailed me, so I know he got home."

I called again at the house and still no one answered. I had plans to go horseback riding with Susan, a friend, and then out to lunch. How could I? I canceled on her and hoped she'd understand.

When I arrived at Alepho's apartment, the screen door was shut but the door behind it was ajar a few inches. Weird. I'd warned them about the neighborhood and they'd always been good about keeping the front door locked.

I rapped on the screen door frame to generate a loud clatter. No one came. I walked down the balcony and banged on the window to the bedroom. No answer.

Silly at this point. He could have passed out again, but I felt uncomfortable just walking into their house.

I called from my cell phone. The living room phone rang. No one picked up.

I turned the screen-door knob and went inside. No one was in the living room or kitchen. The lights were off, the hallway dark. The door to Alepho's bedroom was open. The two beds against the walls on the left and right were empty and made up.

Under a single lightweight cover, in his bed that was crosswise between the other two, was someone. No head stuck out, and the body was so slight they were barely visible. How could it be him under there? "Alepho?"

No answer.

"Alepho."

Nothing.

Not knowing whether it would reveal a head or foot, I reached down and pulled back the blanket. Alepho faced me, asleep. He didn't look sick.

"Alepho," I said louder. Having a son, I knew how soundly young men could sleep. Even when Alepho had dozed in my car, it'd taken quite a bit of rousing sometimes to wake him up. Not yet time to panic.

"Alepho."

I shook his shoulder. He groaned. Whew. I shook harder. A hand popped out and flung itself over the edge of the bed.

Oh good, he was waking up.

James walked in from the next room looking groggy.

"Alepho was sick last night," I told him. "Did you see him this morning? Was he okay?"

"I didn't see him."

I put my hand on Alepho's forehead. He felt cool. I grasped the hand sticking out. It wasn't sweaty or too warm. "I don't know what to do." I shook his shoulder more forcefully.

"Alepho, wake up. Are you okay?"

He grumbled, "I am fine."

"I think we should take you to the doctor." I didn't want to say emergency room, but that's where I'd head.

"No. I am fine."

I'd heard that before, whether or not something was wrong. What should I do? It didn't feel right leaving. Not after what had happened the night before. I asked James, "Will you be around today?"

"Yes, I will be here," he answered sleepily and headed back into the other bedroom.

"Please check on him," I said after him. "Let me know if he doesn't feel well."

I couldn't leave right away. He looked okay and could probably use the sleep, but it felt wrong. I sat on the living room couch until that began to feel absurd. Should I wake him up fully and drive him to emergency? Or call 911 and be done with it?

He'd said no. I had to respect his wishes. He was a grown man, even if I didn't respect his judgment calls when it came to going to the doctor. Poking and prodding and doing tests in an ER might be stressful. If his intestines were adjusting, like Stony had said, maybe the extreme discomfort had passed.

I wrote a note on a piece of computer paper in case Alepho didn't remember that I'd come by, *Please call me. Judy,* and tucked it under his arm before leaving.

VALLEY VIEW

Judy

Alepho didn't call. I called the apartment over the weekend. His roommates answered and said he was sleeping. They also said he was fine. Of course. Their bar was low. You had to be dying not to be fine. I told each of them to contact me if he didn't get better. I emailed him but received no reply.

I finally reached him on Monday. "My stomach paining but I will go to work at midnight." He'd do anything not to miss work.

I'd do anything to figure out what was wrong. "I really think you should see a doctor again."

"It is getting better."

Tuesday morning, he called me as soon as he got home from work. "My stomach paining very much."

His voice was quiet and strained. I heard the suffering in it.

"Did you work all night?"

"I work but it was difficult."

"Okay, I'll be there in an hour."

I called Joseph. "Where do I take him?"

"Emergency room at Valley View Hospital. They take Medi-Cal."

Where the hell was Valley View Hospital? I thought I knew all the hospitals in San Diego.

Alepho was on the couch when I arrived. He moved slowly into his bedroom to get a sweatshirt. In the car he was quiet—so stoic that if it weren't for his knitted brow, I would not have known he was hurting.

At the top of a steep driveway, Valley View Hospital was a cluster of one-story barrack-style buildings. Alepho's walk was tenuous and stiff as we headed toward the door that read EMERGENCY. We filled out forms at the front desk and they put us in a tiny waiting room. Alepho leaned his head back against the wall and closed his eyes.

Any wait was too long, but I couldn't complain. In less than half an hour, they escorted us to a row of three beds divided by short flimsy curtains covered in prints I'd seen on men's boxers.

Alepho changed into a gown and climbed up onto his assigned bed with a hint of relief in his eyes that he was finally getting treatment.

A man in bright tropical-print surgical scrubs with a stethoscope around his neck came in. Was he a nurse or the doctor?

He introduced himself to Alepho. The doctor. He asked Alepho a series of questions in a mild African accent I couldn't identify. Alepho's answers were brief. He downplayed the severity of his symptoms, making it sound as though he'd come in with a mild case of heartburn.

I wanted him to do this on his own. I understood the tradition of bravery when you came from a place with no available help. But here in the ER? Complain. How could the doctor make a diagnosis if he didn't know the symptoms?

We weren't going home with Tums if I had anything to do

with it. "Look," I said, "he collapsed at work five days ago. The pain hasn't gotten any better. It's constant and severe."

The doctor raised his eyebrows and commenced a thorough examination of Alepho's belly. "I'm sending him to X-ray."

Alepho returned after a while and dozed on the ER bed.

A bit later, the doctor appeared through the curtain. "The X-ray didn't show anything. I'll give him a shot of Demerol for the pain."

Demerol? I didn't have formal medical training, but I'd learned a lot from Paul at the dinner table and from overhearing middle-of-the-night emergency calls. Masking abdominal distress with painkillers was dangerous. Besides, didn't they slow the digestive system, which would exacerbate a bowel blockage if that was the problem? What were we doing here? I should have taken him to the university hospital.

"Really?" I asked, not wanting to be rude or insulting but anxious about such a quick remedy. "Do you have any idea what is causing so much pain? Like the appendix?"

"Appendix looked normal. It's hard to tell, but you'd be surprised how many cases clear up with a shot of Demerol."

Good news that Alepho's suffering would be relieved, but I couldn't stop picturing an exploding appendix spewing deadly bacteria into his peritoneum.

Alepho got the shot and fell asleep. I wasn't leaving him alone. I sat in the chair for an hour until he woke up. He was groggy but said his stomach hurt less. "I want to go home."

I took him to the apartment and made sure someone would be there. He went to bed. When I called later that evening he said the pain was better.

"I want to work tomorrow night."

"There's no rush. You need to get better. I called Bob and told him you were in the emergency room today. Please, wait and see how you feel tomorrow."

I called the next afternoon. "How are you feeling today?"

"Better."

His voice was a little stronger, but not normal. "Is the pain all gone?"

"It is not gone, but it is less. I will work tonight."

"You should rest one more day."

"No, I will go to work."

He was adamant. I had to pick my fights. "If you don't feel up to it later, just call Bob. He'll understand."

"No, I must go to work. I can't get fired."

"You won't get fired for being sick."

"James and Lino got fired today."

"Fired?" They both worked at a factory up north. Poor Lino. How demoralizing. His first job and he was fired. "Why?"

"The IRC van broke down. They were stuck on freeway for seven hours. The workplace say they miss too many days."

Too many days? Were they sick too, or just car trouble? Oh God, seven hours on the freeway up in the suburbs of North County. I couldn't imagine the cars whizzing by—no doubt a few highway patrol as well—as eight or nine African men waited it out on the side of the road. Then they were fired on top of it. Lino was still eligible for food stamps, but James wasn't. The first of January, many of the boys had turned twenty-one and wouldn't be eligible for anything, not even Medi-Cal. Some days felt like quicksand. The struggling just sucked them down farther.

"Alepho, you won't get fired," I reassured him. "I'll talk with Bob. He cares about you. He knows you're really sick. Don't go if you don't feel well."

"I am fine."

Fine, of course. It had been a cold, foggy winter day. Night-time would be worse. He had to walk a mile up Euclid to the bus stop on University Avenue. Hopefully he was moving more easily than he had the day before. If only I didn't live thirty miles away and he hadn't switched to graveyard. Why did he do that? Would he ever switch back? It just seemed so lonely and depressing.

Diane, a friend and writer, called. "We're worried about you."

"Worried about me? Why? I'm fine."

"We haven't seen you in four months."

"Well, I've just been really busy. Things will slow down soon."

"Are you writing?"

Sneaky question. Another writer would know that question was the test of how smoothly one's life was going. She was asking about my novel, so I wasn't strictly lying when I replied, "Yes, I'm writing." I didn't say on something new.

"You should call Susan."

"Why? Is something wrong?"

"Nothing serious. I think she's just a little hurt that you forgot her birthday."

Damn, I totally spaced. So bad. "Oh God, that's right. That's why she wanted to go riding last Saturday. Then I canceled on her again. I feel terrible. I'll call her and set up something else."

When? I didn't want to end up canceling again. My scheduled activities were clashing with crises out of my control. A two-day excursion for Cliff to experience people from another life had snowballed into taking over my life.

That night I told Paul that Alepho's stomach pain seemed worse, not better, and it worried me to ignore it.

"Could be," Paul said, "that he didn't have fat in his diet for so many years. Might be spasms in the bile ducts coming from the gallbladder. The ducts atrophied and our fatty diet is suddenly stressing them. If he doesn't have a temperature, I'd give it a few more days. But if it gets worse, let me talk to Stony and some other docs to see what's going on."

THREE GRAY BULLIES

Alepho

"We must go," Daniel said. "Hurry."

I was taking a little longer to gather myself together after the day in the hospital. James and Lino had just been fired. Daniel was nervous about being late.

"Go," I said. "I will catch you on the way."

The night was foggy. My paining stomach kept me from moving fast. I didn't catch Daniel.

When I reached the corner and waited for the light, I saw the bus slithering off on that smooth road toward downtown. I crossed the street and sat on the bench to wait for the next bus. The chilling cold made me shiver. I covered my cold head with my hood.

Three gentlemen came to the bus stop. Two walked in front of where I sat. I pulled my feet back when one almost stepped on my toes. I thought they came to take the bus to their places or their jobs.

I looked to my left to see if a bus was approaching. A hard smack on my right jaw sent me plunging forward into the street.

What was that? My face hit the pavement. *Crack.* Pain shot into my brain. *Oh no, my front tooth!*

I jumped up. A foot came out of the dark and thudded into my stomach. I spiraled farther into the street and went down. A car screeched and went sideways. It had almost run over me. I quickly rolled toward my three assailants. Why were they doing this? I didn't know them. Did they want money?

I stood up clumsily. They came at me. One guy grabbed my hood and pulled it down over my face. I couldn't see. They kicked and punched me from all sides.

I screamed and screamed for someone to help. Cars slowed down and then drove off. But this was America. Why was no one coming to my aid? I stopped screaming.

Fend for yourself!

I rolled my fist and threw my right hand into the face of one guy. He crashed down like a landslide.

The shortest guy threw a bottle at me. I ducked and it missed and broke on the ground. He came at me with his fists raised. In the light I saw he had a dark mustache. I raised my leg and swung it at him. It knocked him to the ground. That opened some space for me. The third guy said, "Hey, you are good fighter." His hand came up. He had a knife.

I dashed off. Thankfully, my legs were okay. They saved me, I was able to get myself out of there.

I ran to the apartment, my body bruised and my face bloodied from the broken tooth. I didn't feel the excruciating pain of the tooth until my brother opened the door. "What happened?"

"Strangers attacked me."

He rushed to the kitchen for warm water and salt to ease my pain.

He first tried to call 911 but did not reach them.

I called Ralphs. "I can't come to work tonight." My tooth made it painful to talk. "Something happened." That was the first time I called in. I never wanted to call in. I felt terrible to miss work.

Benson tried his best to call who he thought would help me. We didn't know how to call the ambulance. The only thing we knew was to call 911 if any problem happened. He called again. They said the police would come.

While I waited for the police, I did what I used to do. I grew up in a war zone. There were no ambulances or emergency rooms there. I nursed the pain in my head by sleeping on it. If you got hurt, you coped with it until it healed itself. That was how you survived.

The police came four hours later.

PART THREE

FEBRUARY 7, 2002–JUNE 2002

BEAT UP

Judy

Before sunrise I sat down with that precious first cup of coffee and opened my email. Benson had sent one during the night.

Dear Judy,

I'm writing by this very late time at night because of Alepho. He was going to work but as you know that he is sick he could not run to the bus. He is attacked by three men at the bus stop.

What? Oh my God, was he all right? I read on.

They kicked him in the stomach and broke his upper tooth and his hand is sprained. He fought back and only run away when the men brought out their knives. He just lay on the floor and hold his stomach when he reach the house, and I think he is fainting. I don't know if to call 911. I try to call you but you might have sleep because no one answered the phone.

Thank you, Benson

My heart slammed inside my chest. Three men. Knives. Kicked in the stomach. That was six hours ago. Where was he now? I checked the "new mail" list again. No more emails from Benson. He wouldn't have been able to call our home phone because of the long-distance call limit on theirs. I unplugged my cell phone from the charger down in the kitchen and turned it on. There was a message from James at about the same time as the email from Benson and with the same information. I called their house.

Alepho answered on the first ring. Relief flooded through me at the sound of his voice.

"Are you okay?"

"I was beaten."

"I'm so sorry. Where are you hurt?"

"They kicked me in the stomach." He spoke slowly, clearly an effort to get the words out.

"Have you been to the hospital?"

"No."

"I'll come down and take you to the doctor."

"No. I want to go to the dentist. My front tooth, it is broken."

Oh damn, not his front tooth. He was already self-conscious and hesitant to smile just because of the gap between them and the discolored one. Now one was broken. "What about your stomach? Benson said they kicked you. Shouldn't you see a doctor first?"

"No. I need dentist. It pain very badly."

"The dentist probably doesn't open until nine. I'll be there right after I drop Cliff at school. Can you wait until then?"

"I will wait."

Alepho was standing on the balcony when I arrived. He pointed to the dangling front tooth with bloody knuckles.

"You fought back, didn't you?"

"They wouldn't let me go. I fought a long time. They were three grown men. I almost beat them. I knock one man down. The short man with mustache threw his bottle at me. I moved and it missed me. He said, 'Hey, you are good fighter.' He pulled out his knife. That is when I run home."

"Thank God you did. Did they ask for money? Were they trying to steal your wallet or something?"

"No."

Not a theft. Hmm. Just drunks? Sport fighters? Three on one. How sporting. *What assholes!* Or was the attack due to a worse motivation?

"How is your stomach? You sure you don't want to have a doctor look at it?"

"No. The dentist, please."

The dentist said he needed a root canal and that she could do it immediately. I wasted the first hour running unnecessary errands and spent the next one in the dentist's parking lot, unable to concentrate enough to read the magazine in my lap. My panic over his physical wounds was subsiding. A buzzing rage and sickening ache of profound shame that this unprovoked attack had happened to him here, in our country, remained. How did he see it? What was he feeling? It had to be some horrendous mix of humiliation and hopelessness.

When he emerged from the dentist, the broken tooth had been splinted to the teeth on either side in hopes that it would grow back into the bone. On the ride home he didn't say anything and stared straight ahead. What words would be soothing? Did the whole world feel chaotic and violent? Was America no different from the war zone where he'd been except that it had more food, which he didn't like anyway? He must have wondered if his life would ever be different. Would he be welcome anywhere?

Everything I thought of to say sounded like false assurances.

"I'm really sorry," I told him.

He said softly, "You have no reason to be sorry."

"I am sorry. Things like this shouldn't happen. I've lived here my whole life, and I've never been beaten up."

He looked at me out of the corner of his eye. "Why would they beat you?"

No answer was needed for that question. He understood more than I'd hoped he ever would about life here.

As I was preparing to turn left onto Euclid, he pointed down University Avenue and yelled, "That look like the man. There. There."

A stocky, dark-haired man went into the taco place near the corner, about thirty feet from the bus stop where Alepho had been attacked. I aborted my left turn and drove slowly past the restaurant. No one was visible inside. The man must have gone back toward the kitchen. I pulled around the corner and waited where we could watch the shop from the car.

A DOG AND A CAMEL

Alepho

My broken front tooth pained like a spear in my head. I went outside the apartment and waited for Judy at the stairs.

When we'd first arrived in America, Diar from IRC had taken us to see a dentist even though we told him our teeth were good because in the camp we'd always cleaned them with sticks. Still, Diar insisted we go. That dentist drilled holes in four of my teeth and filled them with metal. This happened to all the boys. "They are making money from the government," we said to each other.

I didn't want to go to the dentist for my broken tooth, but it hurt so much that I didn't know another solution. Judy arrived and said she would take me to a dentist that I could trust.

The woman dentist from Asia gave me a shot. The pain went away. She connected my broken tooth to the other teeth until it could become strong again. She didn't drill anything.

On our way back to the apartment in Judy's car, I saw a man walking at the corner where I'd been attacked. He looked like one of the men who had beaten me the night before. "That look like the man," I told her.

The man went into a restaurant. Judy put the car where we could wait and watch the door to see if he came back out.

I had not expected such a violent physical attack in this land, America, that I held in highest esteem. On my outings, I'd never seen anyone look at me with disdain. People looked at me, but I assumed that was curiosity written on their faces. As children in Africa, when white people came, we swarmed around those creatures who looked like us except that they were white. My mind couldn't conceive of what to make of them. I admired them innocently.

Now I lived in their land. I thought that to Americans I must be a black version of the white person who visited Africa.

My survival-self hadn't adjusted completely to this place with tall buildings, smooth paved streets, and everyone driving new cars. Everything looked so fresh and smelled perfumed. My senses were seduced. I'd been the newcomer enticed to believe all was flowers. Everything seemed safe. After being beaten up, the concept in my mind of my new home changed from sweet to reality.

When a problem comes to visit you, it doesn't warn you that it is coming your way. The reality was that there were good people and bad people everywhere. At first in America, I hadn't thought that. I thought if there were bad people here, there weren't many because there was law and order. Everything was under control. I didn't know people would come out at night and attack for no reason.

Those three gray bullies who beat me were my awakening welcome to the new land. I would be alert in the future. It was a matter of always being careful, just like where I'd come from.

I'd had many experiences with bullies. But the one that taught me the greatest lesson was when I was the bully.

In Palataka camp they had made us boys work hard for the soldiers. All day we built their houses, grew their food, and dug their toilets. We had to find our own food. Lizards, leaves, roots, and rats.

One boy, who didn't hear well, never accompanied us boys who went out and worked all day. He stayed back and gathered dirt into a pile and sifted through it, collecting discarded grains into another pile. This bothered me. Why didn't he have to work hard like the rest of us? We all had some sort of wound or injury. What was special about him? People called me deaf too, because pus and blood dripped from my left ear and I couldn't hear out of it. I'd been bullied for so long, I thought I'd bully someone else, someone who I thought couldn't fight back. Hunger had made me angry.

At the end of one hot day of work, I went up to the half-deaf boy. "Why don't you work with the rest of us?" I demanded and kicked down his grain pile.

His eyes were on my face. I knew he understood even if he couldn't hear me well.

"*Imoosaba*," he said. Be careful.

The next day, he didn't join us in work again. I kicked down his grain pile.

"*Imoosaba*."

"You don't scare me," I said, mouthing the words. He was skinny except for a big head.

The third day, before I could knock down his pile, his arm came from behind and swooped me off my feet. I landed on my back. My head slammed against the earth. Air whooshed out of my chest. My breath wouldn't come back in. I tried to get up and fell right back down. The ground spun under me. I tried to raise up again and fell back.

Staring at the trees swirling against the sky, I realized that skinny boy could have beat me more, but he just continued his business. When he'd separated out all the grain, he washed out the last of the dirt in the river, and a small child joined him. Together they cooked those grains and shared them.

Sprawled in the dirt, watching the two of them, I recalled a saying from my culture. *A dog barks loudly at a camel, but the camel gracefully walks on.* A camel didn't care what a dog said. He didn't pay attention to small annoying things that didn't matter. He continued his walk, carrying his dignity with him.

I'd been nothing but a barking dog when the skinny boy just wanted to go about his business of surviving and helping a small child. He'd warned me twice. I hadn't listened. That skinny, deaf boy was wise and clever and kind to a small child. He didn't allow an annoyance like me to change his course.

Bullying was senseless and cowardly. Dangerous, too.

Those three gray bullies who had attacked me at the bus stop were annoying dogs. It was better to walk on with my dignity like the camel.

I asked Judy, "Can we go now?"

WHERE THEY FROM?

Judy

No one had come back out of the restaurant. Alepho sat in silence, like he so often did lately, his brow a fixed wrinkle. He'd only been here four months and he'd been beaten. Perhaps he was thinking life was better in the camp where he knew what to expect.

It could even be seething anger on his face. I'd assumed we would call the police if he identified the guy. That's what I would do, but what if he leapt out of the car to confront him? I'd begun to think waiting was a really bad idea when he asked, "Can we go now?"

What a relief. "Of course, yes, let's get you home. You can file a report with the police."

"Maybe."

His *maybe* was as close to a *no* as it could have been. "I also think we should look for a new apartment."

"Okay."

It wasn't much, but there was more enthusiasm in that

response than I'd heard from him in a month. "Until then, please never walk alone to the bus at night. Even if it means two of you walk with whoever is going to work. Just make sure no one walks that street alone to the bus stop or back."

I dropped Alepho at his apartment and headed for home, ruminating on all that had happened, when a reality dawned on me. I'd been thinking that since it appeared to have been a senseless random beating, three drunks sport fighting, or perhaps even a hate crime, it probably wouldn't happen again. That was naive. Alepho had knocked down two of the attackers. They could be out for revenge. No matter how many roommates Alepho walked with, they might be ambushed by even more guys. Being in a group might be their best defensive strategy, but to someone else it could look like a Sudanese gang, albeit in button-down shirts and belted khakis, moving in on someone's territory. Worse, if fighting broke out, they might be blamed and arrested. For a refugee, a felony arrest meant deportation back to Sudan.

They were deep in the gang-dominated part of San Diego. There were no other bus stops within walking distance. They had to get out of that neighborhood right away.

• • •

I'd learned from job searching to do research before getting the guys involved. The next morning, with pad and paper in hand, I scanned the classifieds and made a potential list of apartments for rent staying within the window of affordability, safety, and location for their jobs. I'd call first, make an appointment to see it alone, negotiate on the rent, then take them for the final decision.

I started with the best option. "Hi, I'm calling regarding the two-bedroom apartment on Alabama Street. I was wondering if it had a laundry and security gate."

"Rented it this morning."

The next one was rented too.

"Hi, I'm calling about the—"

"Caaarrlll!" a woman's voice screeched.

I pulled the phone away from my ear.

"Yeah," a gruff voice said.

"The two-bedroom apartment on Kansas. Is it still available?"

"It's a house. No singles. No pets. Are you married?"

"Yes, I'm married, but … never mind."

Only a handful left on the state streets and then it would be the number streets, not as safe an area. "Hi. The two bedroom on Ohio. Is it still available?"

"Yes."

The accent was foreign. Maybe they'd be more understanding. "Does it have a laundry or security gate?"

"It have ziss."

"Oh, that's great. Could I see it? Maybe tomorrow?"

"Who ziss for?"

"Well, I'm a mentor through the International Rescue Committee …"

"Who zat?"

"The … It's for five students."

"No, couple only. No kids."

Oh boy, who knew it would be this hard. Didn't they want customers like every other business? One more on Ohio. "Hi, I'm calling about the two bedroom. Is it still available?"

"No student."

Did I sound like a student?

Thinking I could bargain on the rent had been naive. I was

already prepared to beg or bribe. "Hi, I'm calling about the two bedroom on Illinois. Do you still have it?"

"I have eet."

Couldn't identify that accent. "I'm looking for an apartment for five really great young men who are students."

"What country they from?"

"Excuse me?"

"Where they from?"

"I don't think you can ask that."

Click.

Those landlords and managers didn't know what great tenants they were missing out on. They worked, they studied, they read. A dominoes game was the wildest thing I'd seen.

"The apartment on Illinois. Is it still available?"

"Yes, it's still available."

The man's voice was direct if not pleasant.

"Does it have a laundry or a security gate?"

"Both. It's upstairs."

"Great." Best to get past the couple thing right away. "It's for five students. Young men."

"Students?"

"Yes, and these guys are the best. They're very quiet. They just go to work and to school and study. Honestly."

"That's fine. I don't discriminate in any way. It has to be only one lease though. If one moves out, I don't want to be chasing them down for rent."

"I understand. That's okay. It doesn't matter, does it? One lease?"

"No. Just as long as one of them earns three times the rent to qualify."

"Oh."

"If you want to see it I'm showing it to two other people at ten tomorrow morning."

"Sure, ten. We'll try to be there." I sighed. Even if we were the first ones there, it was unlikely they'd be selected as tenants.

And three times rent? Not one of them even made one times rent. The landlords knew all the tricks.

I called Joseph Jok at IRC. "I'm so worried. They have to move out of that neighborhood. But how do you find apartments for these guys?"

"It's difficult. You have to go to the property managers. Sometimes you encounter, uh … discrimination."

I sighed. "I haven't even gotten that far."

CONFLICT HERE?

Alepho

After I was beat up, people had many opinions about what I should do.

Some people said, "When you are scared, you have to fight back."

Why did that big man from Africa run from another man? I wondered if people were really asking that in their heads. That was my pride talking. Pride could get me killed.

I stayed inside the house when I wasn't at work. When we were all in the front room one day, Benson said, "You need to go outside of the house. If anybody says a bad word to you, just walk away."

"Some people tell me I must fight back here."

"Don't try to fight back," Benson said. "This is a foreign land and you don't know what they can do to you. Anybody can just kill you with a knife or a gun, take your life. Nobody is going to ask them about it. You will just disappear in this jungle. Do you see the helicopters that fly around this area? They are looking for people who do bad things. If you do something, they will find you."

That scared me. I didn't know how Benson knew about the helicopters. I'd been thinking that I needed to fight to the end.

Lino just sat on the couch and listened to us. I didn't know if he agreed. He'd never fought in the camp even though he was taller and stronger than both of us.

Benson said, "You are in a place like you have never been before. When a dog goes to another village and he is attacked by other dogs, the first thing the dog does is put his tail between legs. It is only then that the other dogs will leave this dog alone. If the dog is not submissive, they will kill that dog."

I said, "Some people will violate you. You have to stand up for yourself."

Benson said, "Use your wisdom."

Benson was always good at using his wisdom. "That is helpful," I said. "Mostly I have to be extra careful."

"Groups here don't get along," James said.

I didn't know James had been listening. I thought he was watching the TV.

"There is conflict between blacks and Mexicans."

That seemed so strange. Why would groups here have conflict? In a war or camp people fought for a place to live, or food or water. In America, they paid rent and bought food. Nobody fought us for those things. They watched TV and went to movies and shopping with girlfriends. So many good things. People didn't get to do those kinds of things in Sudan or countries I had been in. Maybe in Kenya we'd heard that they went on safari, but I doubt many Kenyans could go on safari, just visitors. Only a few people in Africa got to do things like they do in America. Now we were doing them, too. What did groups have to fight about when there was so much to do?

I listened to Benson's advice, but still I was angry. I felt helpless. The wise best thing to do was to take my pride and swallow it. But it felt like a rock going down.

STARVING IN CHINA

Judy

In the month since Alepho had been beaten, I'd stopped in every property management office in the area and put their names on the wait list. When I called their house, Alepho never answered. "He's sleeping," I was always told. He didn't answer my emails for days at a time, and then the answers were brief. He hadn't given me anything that he'd written in months, so I assumed he wasn't writing. I had no idea if he was reading, but he hadn't asked for books. If I did manage to get him out for some made-up errand, he hardly spoke. Pushing him to talk never worked, but I let him know I was available, or I could find him someone who was more qualified.

Within weeks, two other Lost Boys were attacked in a similar manner. One sustained a serious head injury.

Even so, I wasn't positive that that was what had put Alepho in such a funk. He'd been depressed and solitary before the attack, too. I'd read that post-traumatic stress could come back at any time. Maybe it never went away. It also didn't help that none of them had found relief from the head and stomach pains.

To make matters worse, Benson told me that people had phone cards now and calls were pouring in from Africa, constantly reminding all of them that the suffering back home went on. Due to the time difference, the calls came at night, disturbing everyone's sleep. Brothers, cousins, uncles, friends—they all desperately needed help and now had a "rich" relative in America. The attack on New York had completely shut down refugee resettlement. The rations in Kakuma camp had recently been cut in half. Just a few American dollars would buy food there for a week. Their little brother, Peter, left the camp for Nairobi in hopes there was something there. There was nothing for a Sudanese refugee, not even food and water, and now he had no way to earn the money to get back. Their uncle was still stuck in Uganda with no way to get to or help his children. Now he was sick with typhoid fever.

They'd taken to unplugging the phone at night, but the guilt must have been overwhelming. No wonder Alepho hid from it all by sleeping. He'd quit going to school, and I worried that he'd begin missing work as well, even get fired. Half of his roommates were already out of work again. Daniel and James lamented that they'd been here a year and saw no progress in their lives. It did seem like for every step forward, they slipped two back. I reminded them that they'd passed the GED and their entry-level jobs should motivate them to go to college or learn a trade. "We know," they said, but the frustration and discouragement were evident in their sighs and body language.

I'd begun to feel the same. I even asked myself: *Are they really better off here?* How could I give them hope when sometimes I had so little myself?

At the dinner table one evening, Cliff wasn't eating his food. I told him, "Eat the chicken and beans, too." All he'd touched was the buttered rice.

"I don't like this brown stuff on it. Can I just have some chicken soup?"

"No. Eat what's on your plate. You're not going to waste food."

"I know," he said in that snippy voice teenagers have mastered, "children are starving in China."

I didn't acknowledge his disrespect.

"Or Suuudaan."

I stood. The chair skidded loudly across the tile floor. Startled fright rose in Cliff's eyes. "I'll show you Sudan," I said. I took his plate, walked to the back door, and dumped its contents outside for two very excited and appreciative Labradors. "Now, go do your homework."

Cliff stomped down the hall. His door shut quietly. My outburst had made some impression. I wanted to stomp off to some room too, but I sat back down and Paul and I finished the meal in silence. I might have made him a bit nervous as well.

"Are you down about something?" he asked tactfully after dinner.

I appreciated that he hadn't asked flat out why I was so bitchy. "Down, discouraged, disillusioned. Who knows? One of those *d*-words."

"Something not going well?"

"Unemployment and no health care are one thing. But getting beat up just because of how someone looks really sucks. I still haven't found them a better apartment. I'm not sure what's possible anymore."

"You have to expect setbacks."

Paul could be so logical. "I know that. I still believe in the opportunities here, but I'm not so sure anymore that they are available to everyone. I thought I could make a difference in someone's life, but I feel like a naive idealist."

"I like idealists."

I didn't smile. His timing sucked if he was trying to be charming. "It's not about me."

"Look at it this way," he said. "What you're doing is a lot like practicing medicine."

"It's not at all like medicine. You actually help people."

"Some people get better, but others we can't help—no matter how hard we try."

I didn't answer. He hadn't experienced all the setbacks with them, felt the frustration, seen the disappointment. He was a problem solver and good at it. I understood that, but that somehow made my problems feel small. I wished he'd just listen and agree.

"Ask yourself," he said, "what if you weren't there at all?"

"I wasn't. And it didn't keep Alepho from getting beat up."

WERE THEY LOOKING AT ME?

Alepho

I returned to work, but everyone felt like strangers. Before the pretty girl had told me that I was hot, I'd been the laughing and smiling person, enjoying the job.

Bob switched me to graveyard shift, and at first, I enjoyed ripping the boxes. The hard work felt good. That job really did make me sweat.

After the beating, people said, "Al, you're not smiling anymore. Are you all right?"

Some people were kind and tried to cheer me up. That made me feel better.

But, later I'd see them talking and laughing with others. I knew they were talking about me and laughing because I was hot. I became alert and suspicious of everyone. Were they looking at me?

My sweating grew worse. I was sure everyone could smell me. I tried a deodorant that had scent. People said, "You have too much deodorant." I sweated more.

One day at work a group of employees were talking in the other aisle. One said, "I can't believe he works here."

They didn't say a name, but I knew they were talking about me. Everybody knew I smelled. They were wondering why the manager allowed this smelly person to work there.

Everyone who had thought of me as a good person, now thought of me as a bad person, a smelly person. Everyone was saying, "This African boy smells in the supermarket." Even the customers.

When people came near me or, worse, walked up behind me, I became stiff and held my arms at my sides very tight over my armpits. If they came closer, I moved away. My only peace was my day off. I relaxed. But even then, when I thought about it, with just my roommates there, I began to sweat. I couldn't go to the St. Luke's Church. Except for work, I stopped going out at all.

Even at night I sweated. Nightmares came every night. Gunships were shooting people as they ran for cover. Sometimes I felt like I was shot and was screaming. I'd fall out of the bed all wet. I began sleeping on the floor, but that didn't stop the nightmares or the sweating.

Everywhere I went people looked at me. I understood that before the men beat me, I had been like a child, thinking people were curious about me. Now I knew they were looking to see if I was from here. If I didn't look like someone who belonged, I was not welcome.

I backed away from everyone. I told Benjamin that I didn't trust anyone. He said, "You are stupid. You should trust Judy. She is your sponsor."

I said, "You are the one that does not understand. How can I trust someone that I just met? What is she up to?"

"You *are* stupid," Benjamin said. "You have a trust problem."

I felt like my world was falling apart. I had everything to lose and I was mad at everyone in the world for that.

I wondered if I should go back to Africa. Where would I go? I couldn't go back to the camp. They would say, you went to the US and now you are back. Why did you come back? I'd say because I was hot and I sweat. They would laugh and say that's such a strange thing. What do you mean you're hot and that you sweat? Everybody sweats. That's normal. Why would that make you leave the country?

A little thing had gotten into my mind and made a hill into a mountain.

I went online to see how to get rid of being hot.

I read an article that asked who was hotter, Brad Pitt or George Clooney. It seemed that being hot was a big issue in America. There were many products for the problem. I even read about injections of Botox to make the sweating go away. They said they were expensive, but I didn't care. I needed it.

I said to Bob at work, "This is not enough money I get paid. No one appreciates me."

Bob looked at me strangely. "Are you all right? You okay?"

I said, "Yes, I'm okay."

"Maybe we should give you a couple of days off. Maybe you're working too hard."

I was working six days a week. I paid the rent and the food and wired the rest of the money back to the camp. I couldn't eat extra money. I had promised my friends and family I'd help them. When I'd found out there was no money in the pillows, I felt like I'd lied to them. They didn't have enough food in the camp and things had gotten worse. I had to do something.

The people in Africa didn't say thank you when I sent that money. People in America said thank you more than they did in Africa, but they didn't talk to you. I always said hello to our American neighbor and he never said anything. He just walked past like I was a dead person. I decided I shouldn't say hello anymore because I didn't know what he'd do. I must have offended him by greeting him too much. It was hard to know how to read the people in this new land.

We'd been told to thank the customers at Ralphs. Some said, "Oh, anytime." Some said, "My pleasure." Some did not respond at all.

A man said, "You bet!"

I didn't understand. Did he say, *you black* or *you bad*?

I decided to make my face hard all the time to show that I was a bad person. *Stay away from me. Don't talk to me. You might say something strange, and I am going to explode.*

OUT OF AFRICA

Judy

An obsidian scorpion the size of a lobster cornered me in the kitchen of the house I grew up in. Paul was down the hall. I screamed. No sound came out. I tried again and again. He didn't look my way. A hum grew to a roar. Antonovs. If I could hear them, their bombs were already falling. Flames exploded in the orchard.

I awoke in a sweat. This was the second dream I'd had that could have been in Africa but was at home, or a place similar to my home. In the first dream a lion had chased me, and I ran as though through molasses; I'd awakened just as he leapt.

The dreams were unsettling, but illuminating. I'd been told that Alepho had taken to sleeping on the floor because he fell out of his bed during nightmares. If I had bad dreams from just hearing about their experiences, I couldn't imagine how real and horrible all of theirs could be.

Joseph Jok called midmorning. "The property management

company on Adams has a couple of apartments for you to look at."

I went by the Euclid apartment to see if I could get Alepho to come with me. He'd been excited when I mentioned moving.

Benson answered the door. "He's sleeping."

Again? He hadn't even worked the night before. "Is Alepho still going to his GED classes?"

"I don't see him go. Sometimes he is sleeping."

Sometimes?

Benson attended morning classes but Alepho had been going to the evening ones because he went home to sleep after the graveyard shift. I didn't blame Alepho for no longer wanting to venture out at night, but for him to miss school saddened me, and the excessive sleeping was worrying. Surely, this was post-traumatic stress—or whatever one called it when the trauma hadn't ever stopped.

Benson agreed to come, and we met Joseph Jok at the property management company just down the block from the IRC offices. If only they'd find them a place in that neighborhood. We picked up two keys for vacant units and headed over to check them out. The apartments, however, were not farther from their Euclid one and closer to Van Dyke Avenue, the gang more well-known than the street itself.

"Please," I begged the woman at the property management office, "find us something in this area."

Another day when I arrived at Euclid, Alepho was on the couch. I convinced him to go grocery shopping. On the way back to his apartment, I decided to stop by the property management office to see if there was anything new on the list. Alepho had brought his algebra book with him, probably a device to keep from talking to me, and absently stared at the open pages sprawled across his lap while I drove.

I stopped at the property management company, but they didn't have any new apartments that were either affordable or in the right area. The rest of the way home Alepho seemed to be in some far-off place, like he was wishing he was anywhere but where he was.

• • •

Whenever I was in town, I stopped by the property management company and checked in with Candace—we were now on a first name basis—to see if any apartments had become available. She assured me that she'd call if they did. I had doubts, but figured she might eventually just want to get rid of me.

Classified ads still bore as much fruit as a rock.

I searched out articles on the internet, talked to experts, and read books by experts in a quest to know more about people who had suffered trauma. *Get out of the house, break the cycle*, was the general consensus. That was something I could actually help with. Whether it had been Alepho's recent beating at the bus stop, a lifetime of trauma, or the adjustment to a new place and culture that had neutralized his zest for life, I couldn't be sure. Maybe he didn't know either. I rarely understood what caused my own low spirits that could, at times, require a superhuman effort just to start the day.

To the point of irritating him, I'd often mentioned that professional counselors or doctors were available to him or any of the other Lost Boys. Thanks to a local nonprofit, Survivors of Torture, International, it was easier to get psychological treatment than medical treatment.

I did my best to explain the concept. Still, Alepho wasn't interested. A psychiatrist friend enlightened me. "Talk therapy is a Western thing. Many cultures would find talking about your pain a worse torture. As do many Americans."

When I wasn't with Alepho or the others, I tried to keep from getting overwhelmed by it all myself. Not with great success. Their struggles were always on my mind.

One Monday, when Cliff had after-school activities, I was free for the day. Alepho hadn't worked the night before, so I called him around eleven. "Hello." He sounded like I'd woken him up.

"How about doing something like the museums or a movie?"

"I'm really, really tired."

It would have been so easy to just say, *Okay, fine, some other time.* But he needed to get out. "Please, Alepho. Let's go do something fun. Just for an hour or two. It's your day off."

When I picked him up he was wearing a dark sweatshirt with the hood up over his head, sunglasses, and earphones to his cassette player. The beat of traditional Dinka music leaked out.

I drove to Balboa Park. "Let's see what's playing at the natural history museum. You will need to leave the music in the car."

He reluctantly removed the earplugs and cassette player and put them on the car floor. We watched two documentaries on the museum's massive new screen. The second one on Baja California had such breathtaking photography I wanted to move five hundred miles south to somewhere on the Sea of Cortez.

"I really liked that movie," Alepho said as we walked out.

That tidbit of enthusiasm was like a cup of cool water. "Yeah, wasn't that amazing," I gushed. "I love that area. So beautiful. Really spectacular."

"Can we go home now?"

My heart sank. "Oh, sure. Of course." Our excursion had been disappointingly short, but if I didn't oblige him now, he might not go out again.

I arrived home after dropping Alepho off and listened to a message on my answering machine from my father, who said he had waited at our favorite restaurant until twelve thirty. "Did I have the wrong day?" he asked.

No. He didn't have the wrong day, and it was so totally like my father to assume fault.

I was the one who had forgotten. A disturbing image of him at the table alone assuming it was his mistake only made my rudeness feel worse. *Unforgivable.* Next it could be Cliff waiting on the curb somewhere.

STRONG WORDS

Alepho

Everybody tried to irritate me, to make me angry. I played Dinka traditional music whenever I was at home. It helped me to think of other things.

One day James said, "Turn off the music. It disturbs my studying."

"You're stupid," I said.

"Sit down."

I sat on the couch as James requested. He was older and a military man. I respected him for that.

He stood over me and looked down. "You are just my roommate. They brought you here to this apartment. You were a good guy, but now I don't know who you are anymore. I don't know what you've been through. I don't know what you're going through now. What you said to me, calling me stupid, that is wrong because I never said anything wrong to you."

James had never spoken to me like that. He was always

laughing and making jokes. His strong words surprised me. They upset me more. "You're stupid and you don't care."

James didn't respond. He threw up his arms and went into his room.

At first, anger burned inside me. Then I thought more about what James had said. I'd gone down in my feelings and in my mind. I didn't approach my roommates nicely. Small comments made me lash out at everybody.

Reacting to my environment was why I was still alive. In the war, the boys who hadn't reacted, the ones who went into shock or just sat down, were the ones who died. Antonovs bombed us, soldiers shot at us. You had to either lie down or jump in a trench. Sometimes bombs landed in the trench and those people were buried. Either way, you weren't sure about your protection. My spirit had always been jittery and shivering.

In America, I was having that same nervous reaction. I sweated and my heart raced when someone came close or I just thought about it. Sleep offered no peace. Nightmares sent me right back into war. Even though I was in America, these things were constant reminders of my past.

I didn't know what to do or where to go. Sudan still had war. The camp had no hope.

EXASPERATION

Judy

Reading to fall asleep was a lifelong habit. I propped my pillow against the headboard and opened up a thriller romance. Delicious escapism from real problems.

Paul climbed into bed, opened his medical journal, and looked over his glasses at me. "What's that?"

Did he have to comment? "A novel."

"You finished your research on Sudan?"

"What's the point? Taking a break."

"What are you doing tomorrow?"

He didn't usually ask me that. "Going for a run with the dogs and then running some errands. Working in the yard. Running some more. I don't know."

"Not going to town. You're kidding."

"I'm not kidding." My response came out snappy. My frustration wasn't with him. I softened my tone. "I'm tired of walking around in a fog. I've learned a lesson the hard way. You can't get emotionally involved. I'm going to do what I started out to do in the beginning—fun excursions. I can't solve all their problems." I didn't mention leaving my father alone in a restaurant. I was too ashamed.

"What's so unsolvable?"

"Jobs, apartments, school. Medical. Post-traumatic stress disorder. The list goes on." No reason to mention being stopped by that cop or the recent beatings. He wouldn't understand and might not want me down there at all. I wasn't in danger because I wasn't a threat—unless it looked like the North County soccer moms had formed a gang and were moving in. If Paul insisted I shouldn't be in that neighborhood, it would add another complication and I had enough of those.

"Then who's going to help the guys?"

I didn't answer.

"You just seem happier when you're involved."

"Happier? Lying awake worrying that someone might get fired or become homeless or get beaten, and there's nothing I can do about it. How is that happy?"

"Call it fulfilled then."

"It's only fulfilling if I can accomplish something." The second that was out of my mouth, I knew how horribly empty and selfish it sounded and that my fulfillment was never the point. A swell rose in my chest and up into my throat. "I ... left my father sitting alone in a restaurant waiting for me."

Paul smiled. I was close to sobbing, and he smiled.

"Did you really?"

"Yes."

"You're overreacting. Your dad is cool. Plus, that's easy to solve. Read your calendar. Or better yet, get a PalmPilot."

I shook my head. It figured he'd have a solution, and that it would involve technology. *A PalmPilot.* Another time I might have laughed. "Seriously. I'm not qualified to really help them and I've made mistakes. My expectations were too high."

"So what does that mean?"

"I'll help them with their English, or take them to the beach or on a hike." What I really yearned to do was go on a long road trip. Up Highway 1 to Big Sur or across the Southwest. Alone. My life was the ideal and dream of most of the world. Where was this feeling coming from? Flee what? Responsibilities? The people I loved?

Paul gave me a disbelieving look. "Yeah, right, the beach, huh? I've never known you to do things half-ass."

I gave him my dirtiest look. It had been a compliment, but I wasn't in a reasonable state.

"You used to work as many hours as I did," he went on. "You're not happy when you're idle."

Persistence was one of his virtues. An admirable trait when it wasn't applied to me. I just wanted to get under the covers, but insulting him wasn't a way to say goodnight. "I didn't say idle. I'm just going back to my original commitment. I might have been a dedicated mom, I might have worked hard in computers, but I kept my priorities. This time I feel like I've walked out of my life."

"Are you sure you didn't just walk *into* your life?"

• • •

Alepho emailed the next afternoon. *Do you think they should bring refugees to this country?*

Typical tough Alepho question. Maybe the answer depended on whether your mentor was competent or a floundering failure.

That evening I made a three-course dinner from scratch. Paul hadn't eaten like that in a while.

"So," he said, "looks like you stayed home."

"Do you remember how I told you that Alepho always asks me the really hard questions?"

"Yeah," he said, discreetly trying to chew the brisket.

"Today he had one that I couldn't even begin to address."

"What was that?"

"He asked me if I thought it was a good thing to bring refugees to this country."

"It has to be better than where they were."

"We like to believe that. Of course, they have more food, but it hasn't been all that safe. In the camp, they went to school all day; now they ride the damn bus and work. They used to play soccer. They don't have time much less a place to do that here. They're lonely, I can see it. I used to think that they would have hope for a better life. But life in the city is so different from ours. They try, but everything seems to knock them back down."

"Did you really think things would come together in less than a year?"

"Bottom line is, I made a mistake going beyond showing them San Diego. It's a never-ending battle, and the worst thing is I've created false hope for a dream that can't come true."

WHAT TO DO WITH PAIN

Alepho

My roommates, brother, and cousin said they saw a bad change in me. I wasn't the same person I had been when we came to America. They scolded me and advised me.

"What are you doing?" Benson asked. "You are doing nothing. Remember your past. You survived greater challenges."

When I wasn't working, I stayed in my room. People had tried to talk to me. They told me I was different now. I knew that. I felt different. Judy asked me if I wanted to see a doctor. I didn't need a doctor; I wasn't sick or bleeding. Judy took me to a museum and movie. I knew she was trying to get me to be out of the house. I wasn't comfortable outside. People stared at me, but now I understood that it was not because they were curious like we had been as kids about the white people, it was because I was an ugly person or I didn't smell good.

There was still a breath of life in me, but I hurt deeply. Not like the pain of my stomachaches or headaches. Those were not serious pains. I knew how to live with those pains. This was something in my heart or my soul. It was in my chest like a weight. No one could feel my pain. They could not understand. I did not understand.

I didn't want anyone to sympathize with me. This was my own problem. I'd known much worse physical pain and suffering. Now I was mostly sad. But why? I was in the best country in the world with a job, a place to live with a bed, a couch, and even a refrigerator and television. These were things that I had never imagined having.

I wasn't afraid of pain. Pain is an interesting thing because it causes people to change. Some quit or give up. Some, like me, become angry or sad. Others improve.

At times pain had raised me to a new level in life. When things had knocked me down—a war, hunger, or even a bully—I became less prideful or arrogant. Less judgmental of others. I saw more of myself and the world around me, like never before. A light came into me. Deep pain had made me rise above my human defects of character, like being selfish or judgmental. It had forced me to do something and given me discipline.

But I'd also seen pain make good people do bad things. Parents trying to save their child! I saw pain expose the precious nature of people's beings. Suffering people helped those who were suffering more. The jewels, the pearls, the very being of people could shine through pain.

I didn't want to be the person who gave up or gave in or became cruel. I wanted to be the one who shined.

Whenever I was in pain, my heart told me to go home. Where was that? My mind wasn't reasoning well. My heart was caught in a trap, and I wanted to figure a way out. I tried to be better each day. I tried to make myself busy. I tried to be with people so that I wouldn't feel alone and disconnected. But amidst people, I felt that gap more. The pain hurt deeply, but I could handle that. Sadness stopped me now.

Change was a process. I'd been through it before. Survival had been what forced me to do things, but I didn't need to search for food or run from bombs anymore. Now I worried about things like how people looked at me or how I smelled.

I'd read on the internet that they could inject a person with Botox to stop the sweating. I called Judy to ask her about that. She didn't answer. I didn't leave a message.

I couldn't find the thing to start the process of change. I used to love books. I'd waited for weeks in the camp to have a book for one night. Now I had books all around my bed, but they didn't interest me. I no longer wanted to walk or explore my new surroundings. Some days I didn't even care if I escaped the feelings that kept me back. Was I just a lazy person?

WORMS

Judy

I met my understanding father at his favorite restaurant. He didn't bring up the missed lunch the week before, so I did. "I'm making changes," I said.

My cell phone rang while we were eating. Caller ID showed the apartment on Euclid. I ignored the call. They'd leave a message if it was urgent.

• • •

A week went by. I checked emails to make sure there were no emergencies and stuck to my original plan of showing the guys around, not getting involved in all of their struggles.

Paul and I attended a medical meeting over the weekend. At the cocktail hour, teetering on heels, balancing a gin and tonic in one hand and carrot sticks in another, I shared with a microbiologist who worked at the university the symptoms so many of the Lost Boys were suffering from.

She shook her head and smiled. "Definitely parasites."

"You've got to be kidding. How could that be? I've been running around with little white bags of poop samples for months and the results all come back negative."

"You can't go to those commercial labs. They always put the newest person on stool samples. None of them here know how to look for the eggs anyway. Every parasite is different. Some shed eggs one day in six months."

"How do I guess that day?"

"You can't. Treat them prophylactically."

Hmm. No doctor had suggested that before. What did it mean exactly?

We sat down at a table with a white cloth, china, and three sets of glasses. The parasite conversation continued and spread. Only physicians could discuss those miniature monsters and their science-fictional relationships with humans over a pasta appetizer.

A doctor across the table got everyone's attention. "Tapeworms, pinworms, roundworms, they've got a real zoo over there in East Africa. Can't leave out river blindness, the evil Medusa. But her three-foot-long cousin, the guinea worm, is the one that creeps me out. Emerges through the skin like a strand of this angel-hair pasta." He pointed to his plate. "You have to wind it up on a stick to keep it intact until it has completely left the body or you'll have one nasty infection. Or schistosomiasis, that's the sneaky one; it's calcified the liver by the time you have symptoms."

I whispered to Paul, "What's his specialty?"

"Infectious disease."

I leaned over. "They mostly have migraines and intestinal

symptoms. The weird thing is that they've gotten worse since they arrived here."

"You said they were in a camp for some time, right? Just imagine, they were all starving. Now the worms are eating too. You've got an exploding parasite population pooping in their gut. Think of the toxins. That'll give you one hell of a headache."

"Yes, so many of them have headaches, but no doctor has explained this before."

He smiled in a knowing way. "Most of the parasites will die eventually without their reproductive vectors here, which is usually some specific insect. But others, like onchocerciasis, can live for eighteen years."

Yikes. I needed to do some more googling about all this when I got home.

A gastroenterologist beside me added, "In Mexico, they give worm medicine to the kids every six months. It's harmless to humans. Just affects the sugar uptake of the parasite."

"What's it called?"

"Mebendazole or albendazole, depends on the country. Don't know if you can get it here."

"Where can you get it?"

"Mexico."

We had friends who went to Tijuana every day for their work. Worm medicine I could get. I finished off my pasta pomodoro with a newfound enthusiasm.

• • •

Several days later, I went to the Euclid apartment. Blistering sunbeams streamed through the bare front windows. "Where are your curtains?" I asked.

"The Bols have family visiting," Benson said. "They needed both apartments."

"Your sofa cushion covers are gone too."

"They said they need good cleaning."

"They" no doubt meant the pretty Bol daughters. These five young men would, of course, oblige any of their requests. I hoped the girls knew that curtain and cushion fabrics were not designed to be washed like a pair of jeans. Looked like I'd arrived too late to save them from what would surely be their ultimate demise at the Laundromat down the street. I sat down on a bare foam inner cushion on the sofa and bit my tongue, knowing the destroyed items would come out of the guys' security deposit.

The two Bol girls came back up and began to unplug the computer equipment. "Hey, wait, not that," I said. We compromised by shoving the computer table into the corner.

Alepho came from the back bedroom. "Hey," I said, "I think I found a medicine for your headaches and stomachaches."

His lips pressed together. No response. I thought he'd be ecstatic.

"Wouldn't it be great to feel better?"

"Is it pills?"

"Yes, I think so."

"I don't take pills. I need the natural medicines my mother used to make."

Exasperation nearly made me throw my arms into the air, but I held them at my sides and said nothing. I guess this was a good indicator that he wouldn't be interested in Zoloft for PTSD or depression either, even if I could get him to see someone. A friend was getting me the worm pills. Maybe the other guys with the same symptoms would take them.

Lino plopped down next to me on the couch where there was no cushion at all. It felt strange for him to be six inches lower. He handed me a pamphlet. "What do you think?"

The brochure was for Job Corps, a federally funded program where young people looking for a new start could learn a trade or skill—all free, if they qualified. "I think it's a great idea."

I'd heard that a few of the Lost Boys had gone there with mixed results. The vocational and educational programs were excellent, but the instant immersion into a rough American crowd had been brutal. The natives took it out on the foreigners, like leaving bananas in condoms on their dinner plates or greetings like, "Hey, asshole." Some of the Lost Boys left, but a few stuck it out and would graduate in the coming months. One of their friends would soon finish the yearlong office-skills program and complete his GED there as well. Then two more years of free tuition and board at the local junior college were available to him.

"Which one should I choose?" Lino asked, pointing to the categories under construction and looking more enthusiastic than I'd seen him in months. "I like masonry and carpentry. What's this mean? Drywall?"

"That's this white stuff on the inside walls. Like the mud for your huts. Brianna suggested that you try a few different things before making a final decision."

"Oh, that is good. But you get no money."

"You don't need money. Everything is free, room and board included, and you come out with a valuable skill. Construction pays well." Lino was smart, tough, and independent, very good with his hands and mathematics. If he could handle the crowd at Job Corps, the construction industry might work well for him. "Why don't you take the tour with Brianna?" I put my arm around his shoulders. "This could be a really good opportunity. I know you'll do well there."

Benjamin burst through the front door. "Ju … dee," he said and grabbed me in a hug. He'd been working at the Ralphs in Hillcrest for a few months and seemed happy with his job, but Job Corps would give him a skill. Benjamin could tolerate the crowd; he could handle any group. He looked over the brochures.

"Are you interested?" I asked.

"Ju … dee, I work and work, no time for school. I study American culture. What I need to be is a movie star."

I almost started into a list of reasons why Hollywood was not a good choice but stopped myself. Why discourage him? What were his chances anyway?

• • •

Nothing had yet materialized in their quest to find a safer place to live, so a few days later Benson and I stopped by the property management office again.

"We need to find something farther west," I explained to Candace at the front desk for the umpteenth time. "More out this way."

"There's the list," she said, pointing to the other counter. "There's a new list of available units every week."

I knew that. I'd been picking up the list for a month.

A young white man walked out from behind the partition and asked Benson, "Do you know Alepho or Daniel?"

Benson looked taken aback and didn't answer.

"Meet Benson," I said. "Alepho is his brother."

"I'm Derek," the young man said and shook Benson's hand and mine. "Alepho and Daniel and I work together at Ralphs. They're great guys."

I glanced over at Candace to see if she'd heard that personal recommendation from her own office mate. "That's who needs an apartment," I said loudly enough for Candace to hear. "Benson lives with Daniel and Alepho. Alepho got beat up in his neighborhood out by Euclid. They really need to move over this way."

"Oh man, that sucked when he got beat up," Derek said. "They're real nice guys."

Candace was still listening. "It was great meeting you," I told Derek. "I'll tell Alepho and Daniel that we ran into you here. And thank you, Candace. We really appreciate anything you can do."

"I'll call you if one comes up," she said. "We're always looking for good tenants."

CALM SPIRIT

Alepho

Benson's words came back to me over and over. "Remember your past. You survived greater challenges." His words shamed me. The only person I hadn't lashed out at was Benson. I respected him for his calm spirit. Whatever problem presented itself, Benson wouldn't react. If you pinched Benson's finger he would just look at you like, *Why did you do that?* If you pinched my finger, I'd scream and be angry with you.

Benson was right, I had survived challenges. I understood how to fight hunger and disease or run from danger, like a lion or guns. But in America the challenges were unknown. How did I fight them? This was the first world, the new world. A new environment for me. It even had a new energy. The energy in Africa was different from the energy in America. People woke up in America and they had things to do. In Africa, we'd woken up and said there is nothing to do. There was no hope or opportunity. Americans had a clear sense of purpose. In the camp, our sense of purpose was what to eat, what to drink, where to sleep. In America people were thinking beyond those things. *How do I make more money? How do I buy a house? A better car?* I didn't think of those things. They seemed so far away from what I could do.

Those conversations with my brother and roommates made me realize I needed a way to think and survive in this new world.

Responding to a threat had been my survival for so long. In San Diego, there was not a lot of threat. I realized that I had just been in the wrong place at the wrong time that night. I would avoid those kinds of places. We needed to find a safe apartment, and I needed to find better survival skills.

My first challenge was to adapt to the American standard. I had to look nice, smell good, and be successful. Those things were not the standard I had been used to. They contradicted my survival thinking. I'd failed at those American standards. I needed a solution to the sweating so that I could go out like Americans and smell nice and look good. I saw the commercials on TV for soaps, sprays, and deodorants that made a person feel fresh and smell good for others. I would try more kinds.

When we'd first arrived in America, we'd heard that some people lived on the street. We could not believe that at first. Then we saw with our own eyes. People without homes carried their possessions with them like refugees. They had not adapted to the survival in this country. We sat down and talked. We tried to identify the problem.

Now we faced some of those challenges when we tried to get a new apartment. They wanted us to have a credit history. How did we get that? Food was easy to get, but some things, like a place to live, they made difficult.

FIVE PLATES

Judy

Candace called. "Hey, I've got an apartment available on Adams."

Adams Street, west of the 805 freeway. Great location. Once again, a connection had given them the break they needed, but this time the connection had been through someone *they* knew. That meant all the difference.

We took a look. The apartment was small and in a good area. After some debate about affording it, they gave notice on Euclid.

• • •

On moving day, I arrived at the old Euclid apartment early. Outside their door, boxes and bags waited to be loaded. I opened the back of my SUV and picked up a box.

James was flinging things from a box into the large trash bin. "No, no," he shouted, "is trash."

"But these are the plates and kitchen things."

"Five guys. We need only five plates, five forks, five knives." He resumed sailing things into the bin.

A bowl I'd given them was about to lose its useful life. "Wait, wait, I gave that to you."

"We don't need, is extra."

I stood back and watched without feeling a smidgen of the cultural sensitivity I usually tried to apply. When he tossed the instructions for the camera I'd given him at Christmas, I said, "Wait, you might need those."

"I throw camera away too. My friend tell me these things distract. I must concentrate on my school."

Remember, pick your battles, I told myself. I stayed to watch more and more "extras" meet their demise just in case something indispensable was at risk. As items flew into the trash bin, my own cabinets, cluttered with unused items, came to mind. Did I really need that set of used, chipped, brown stoneware dishes? Or a dozen other wedding gifts I'd never used? Could they be useful for someone else?

I hoped America didn't change James' priorities too much. But next time, I'd encourage him to take his discards to Goodwill.

The move to the new Adams Street apartment took only two trips. They decided they needed a sofa bed for weekend visitors. Weekend visitors, huh. I bit my tongue and hoped they liked sharing the five remaining plates.

We found the perfect pullout couch at a thrift store.

"Now this is the really tricky part," I told them once we'd unloaded it from the truck. "See the twine it's tied up with? We have to tip it to get it through the door. You don't want these babies to open up, so it's tied closed."

Benson and Alepho each lifted an end. The particularly deep-seated sofa bed wasn't cooperating with their narrow door. "Okay, now tilt it as little as possible to get it through." A screen door reduced the opening further. They tilted and tilted and tilted. No good. Still wouldn't fit.

"More," I said.

The sofa bed flew open like a jack-in-the-box and jammed in the door frame.

Damn. That happened every time I'd moved one of those things. I burst out laughing. From the expression on their faces, nothing was funny.

"Ju … dee!" Benjamin yelled, coming into their courtyard. "I got callback."

Did he say callback? "Benjamin. Glad you're here."

"You take me?"

"First, hurry. Grab this end."

With four sets of hands we wrangled the sofa closed without losing any fingers, got it the rest of the way through the door and arranged against the wall.

I took a deep breath and brushed the dust off my pants. "What did you say you need to go to?"

"I have callback at four o'clock. Can you come and talk with these people?"

"You mean like a second movie audition? How did you get that?"

"Paper say all African men come. I go and they take my picture and make video. They call and they say, 'Benjamin. Come back at four o'clock. The director want you.'"

Boy, had I been wrong thinking he would have no chance with Hollywood. He sure was resourceful. The meaning of his Dinka name, Akuectoc, came to mind. The self-reliant one.

"They say I have to go for three week."

"Three weeks? Really. What movie?" I'd heard a student had been following him around with a movie camera for several days and disrupting his work.

"I don't know movie. They say I go to Mexico."

"Mexico? You've got to be careful. We better find out what they pay and stuff. Who are they? Sometimes these movie companies don't really have money, so I don't want you to lose your job for nothing."

Or be in a porn film.

It wasn't all that surprising someone had discovered him. He was tall, stunning in appearance, and full of charisma, charm, and confidence.

"No, I cannot lose my job at Ralphs. You take me then?"

"We need to get the other sofa section at the store, and then I have to pick up Cliff from school."

What was I saying? I had to go with Benjamin. Who knew what these people were up to. He could not go alone.

"Never mind, Benjamin. Cliff can go home with a friend. I'll pick you up at your apartment at three forty-five."

• • •

Benjamin was waiting in front of his apartment in a white golf shirt tucked into black jeans. He squeezed into the front seat. "You look nice," I said. "How do you like Benson and Alepho's new apartment?"

"It is good."

"I think it will be safer. I hope you're always careful."

Creasing his brow, he said, "I was attacked too."

"Attacked? What do you mean? When?"

"Nobody believe me. Before Alepho beat up, one night when I get off work at Ralphs, like eleven o'clock in the night. I just waiting at the bus stop on University and two men, they speak Spanish to each other. In English they say, 'You want to fight?' and they attack me."

"What happened?"

"They attack me and I knock them down. They didn't get up; they just lay there. When the bus came, the driver is African American. He say, 'Hey, what the hell's going on here?' I show him my Ralphs badge." Benjamin grabbed his shirt where the badge would be, as though he were showing it to me. "And I say, 'These men, they attack me.' The bus driver say, 'Come on, get in.'"

"Your Ralphs badge saved you." I'd never thought of him as a fighter, or even able to fight, he was so sweet and joyful, but I realized that was naive considering what he'd survived.

"My friend Santino attacked too," he said.

What? "Benjamin, you'll have to tell me about that later. We're at the audition."

CASTING

Judy

Benjamin and I entered the lobby where a young man, about thirty, had a badge and a fancy camera. He extended his hand. "Hi, I'm Tom, the assistant casting director."

"I'm Judy, Benjamin's mentor. I came along to get more information about the movie. Who's making it, where are you filming, that sort of thing. Benjamin told me it would require three weeks."

"Three weeks for extras. Actually, for Benjamin, it would be five months."

"Five months? Where's it being made?"

"In Rosarito Beach. Mexico."

"Benjamin, it's five months in Mexico."

"I cannot do that," he said.

"Who's making this movie?" I asked. If it was some martial arts thing from overseas, I just didn't think it was worth it. Porn was out of the question.

"The director is Peter Weir."

Peter Weir. He'd directed three of my all-time favorite movies: *Gallipoli*, *Dead Poets Society*, and *Witness*. I was listening.

"We're shooting at Fox Studios, where *Titanic* was made. Russell Crowe is starring, and we want Benjamin to be in the core group."

"Oh." Damn. Russell Crowe, *Titanic* set.

Tom handed me a brochure. "Fifty core-group actors will be living here." He pointed to the picture of a new ten-story hotel on the beach with a glass elevator and pool. "The movie is based on a Patrick O'Brian novel. It's working title is *The Far Side of the World*, and it takes place during the Napoleonic Wars. We brought a tall sailing ship from Boston through the Panama Canal. The core group will have two weeks of training at sea on the ship, learning to sail, shoot cannons, and handle a sword."

Tom seemed professional. He directed his explanation to Benjamin. Benjamin listened carefully and looked over frequently for my reaction. The pay per hour was actually less than minimum wage but Tom said they'd work more than forty hours per week; and with a food allowance and free housing, Benjamin should make more than his current job.

What a lifetime experience that could be. Besides, learning to sail a tall ship, fire a cannon, and sword fight, it would be instant assimilation. Into what though? Rosarito Beach, Mexican border town, seedy bars, center of the drug market, and fifty young actors?

Benjamin was only nineteen and hadn't been in this country a full year. Still, his prior experiences had been like boot camp for adversity. If he wasn't prepared to handle something like being on a movie set, who would be?

I turned to Benjamin. "It's a big movie. A good movie. And it's being made by one of the world's best directors." I doubted he knew what a director was at this point, but he'd know soon if he ended up in the movie.

"We auditioned here for extras," Tom explained. "But when Peter Weir saw Benjamin's tape he wanted him in the core group."

Wow. Peter Weir personally wanted him. I nonchalantly said, "I'm not surprised."

"So, Benjamin," Tom said, "do you want to do the movie?"

Benjamin sat up straighter, and in a serious tone with that self-assured bearing that came naturally to him, said, "I don't know. I must talk with my manager first."

Tom looked taken aback. I was taken aback. *Manager? What manager?* He'd found the audition on his own, but he had a manager too? He was a man of many surprises. One day he'd announced he had his driver's license and I didn't even know he'd been practicing. Akuectoc, the self-reliant one.

Tom asked, "Can you speak with your manager soon?"

"Yes," I said, having no idea what the situation was but not wanting to interfere with something Benjamin had arranged. "We'll call you."

"So, Benjamin," I asked on the way out to the car. "What do you think?"

He shrugged and climbed into the front seat. "I will do it only if my manager say is okay."

"Who is your manager?"

He gave me an impatient look. "Judee. You know. Please, will you call Mr. Wood and ask him for me."

"Mr. Wood?"

"Judee," he said, "you know Mr. Wood."

The name was familiar. I smiled as it dawned on me. Mike Wood, his manager at Ralphs. "Okay, yes, I will call him."

I pulled out onto University Avenue and my cell phone rang.

I answered it. This woman said, "Hi, this is Judy Bouley, casting director for *The Far Side of the World*. What is it going to take to get Benjamin in the movie?"

The casting director. Tom must have called her the minute we walked out. I felt like I was in a movie. "He wants me to—"

"I know, his manager. Who is this manager? Should I call him? What is it going to take? Does the manager want a part in the movie? What does he look like? Maybe his son wants to act?"

Oh my. Benjamin sure held the cards. "I don't think that will be necessary. Let me talk to him. Benjamin doesn't want to lose his job."

"Job?"

"Yes, he needs the insurance."

"Okay. You'll talk to him and call me right back? I want Benjamin on this movie. Peter wants Benjamin on this movie. And let's do lunch. You and Benjamin. I'll be in town next week. I'll call you."

She was all Hollywood-style business, but I liked her. Something in her voice. I liked Tom too. I smiled. "Benjamin, we just have to get it by your manager, maybe put him in the movie too. Then we can all do lunch."

Benjamin tilted his head and gave me a quizzical look.

"I'll talk to Mr. Wood," I said. "I'm sure it will be fine and you can get your job back."

I was happy to see that was a priority for him over the movie. I couldn't wait to get home and tell Paul the whole unbelievable story. He'd get a good laugh about the manager part. "Can I ask you something, Benjamin?"

"Sure."

"A year ago, when you were in Kakuma, what did you think you would be doing in America? Did you ever think that you might be working in a Hollywood movie?"

"No. I think that I be able to go to school for free."

Yeah, that would be a real dream come true.

"I just want you to think about living down in Mexico for five months. Rosarito is a wild border town. I know it sounds glamorous living in a fancy hotel, but I'm not sure you can come back to visit once you cross the border. We have to find out how long it will take to get you a travel visa."

"I can do it."

"This movie is about a battle between these ships. There's going to be shooting and fighting and blood and all. Is that going to bother you?"

"Judee, you see, only one thing is important."

"What's that?"

"Money."

I was glad I knew him well enough to know it was not greed or materialism motivating him. Seven guys were in his two-bedroom, one-bath apartment, and three weren't working. He wasn't thinking of a flashy car, a cell phone, or a new wardrobe when he said money.

"My friends," he said, "all night, they call from Africa."

"I know, Benjamin, I know."

LIVING INSIDE ME

Alepho

I had no idea beasts lived inside me. Those worms ate my stomach lining and left severe potholes, which caused me so much pain and sent toxins through my body and brain cells, which caused the severe headaches. I'd had them for so long that I'd forgotten what it felt like to feel normal.

Judy said she had pills to kill the worms. I didn't want to take them. Then some other Lost Boys took them and felt better. So, I took them too.

After a few weeks, my headaches and stomachaches reduced. Even my sweating seemed less.

I told Benson that a girl at work had said to me, "You are hot," and that I was still upset by her rudeness.

He said, "You must learn the culture before you react to things."

I asked Judy what it meant to be hot. She said, "That's a compliment. It means that you are attractive."

I didn't believe the girl was saying I was attractive. Like many words in English, "hot" had more than one meaning.

• • •

Small pains don't change a person. It takes a deep gully of a wound, like a crack in Mother Earth kind of pain. Only if you were still alive after you'd gone through that furnace did the mind wake up and begin to question. Life had plowed us through seemingly unnecessary challenges in order to move us ahead. Through pain I'd learned about the preciousness hidden in us. Our faith, power, strength, and hope. These things had gone into hiding in me, but pain was beginning to expose them again. The bigger the pain, the more light that entered after. I wasn't through all my pain, but the sadness was leaving, and I wanted to begin the process of changing in my new world. I wanted a great light to enter me.

SOMETHING TO SMILE ABOUT

Judy

"What are you smiling about?" Paul asked over the pizza I'd picked up on the way home, which was no longer hot enough to be really good.

I wiped my mouth. "You won't believe it."

"What?"

"First let me tell you the rest. The guys' new apartment is smaller, but definitely in a safer area. James got a job at Ralphs and he just registered at City College. Lino went down to Job Corps ..."

"What won't I believe?"

"Benjamin has two jobs now."

"Ralphs, right? What's the other one?"

"He just got a part in a Peter Weir movie."

Paul put his pizza down. "Peter Weir? Really?"

"Really. And Russell Crowe is starring. They're filming on the *Titanic* set."

"Damn. That's amazing." He smirked, like he'd been right about something. "So everybody is good?"

Alepho popped into my head. "Pretty much. Even the medicine seems to be helping with the parasites. Took a few weeks, but most of them have said their headaches are nearly gone. You know the two that had river blindness? They finally got what they need to treat it. Ivermectin. I gave that to my horses. It's like five dollars a pill and twenty million people around the world are blind because they can't get it."

Paul shook his head. "That's probably one of a hundred medicines you could say that about. Imagine how many things like that keep people from functioning."

"Functioning and dreaming. Alepho said something today that hadn't occurred to me. He said everyone in America asks him what is his dream. He said he doesn't know yet because he came from a place where they were just trying to stay alive and that nobody dreamed. Now he said he understands that America has possibilities and he's going to find his dream." I looked up at Paul. "I was happy to hear that. Having possibilities. That's what it's all about."

A possibility of another sort had been bubbling up in my mind. I'd read their stories over and over. What they'd survived and achieved was extraordinary, and as a writer, I appreciated their fresh metaphors and lush lyrical voices that evoked a world so totally foreign to mine. They made me smile and cry and inspired me. I sensed they'd do that for others. But I was too emotionally involved to judge their merit. I decided to email one or two stories to Roslyn in the morning and get her opinion. She was the best writer I knew, and she lived four thousand miles away and had never met them. She would be objective.

Has to be your next book, Roslyn emailed back.

AFRICAN PRINCE

Judy

I called Benjamin. "There's a cast party at a yacht club, and we're going to meet all the other actors for the first time. I would wear something nice."

"You?"

"No, I meant you. Sorry. Using 'I' is a polite way of suggesting what you should wear."

When I arrived at his apartment, I didn't recognize him at first. He stood on the sidewalk in an elegant long white tunic, matching balloon pants, and a traditional African pillbox hat, all embroidered in gold. Nice, all right. He could have been an African prince.

"We go," he said.

"We go."

Benjamin hadn't yet arrived in America the day I took the other guys to Coronado, the small, flat island directly across the bay from downtown San Diego. When I was a child, it was only accessible by ferry. We drove up onto that swish of blue that now arced across the harbor.

"Wow," Benjamin said as we reached the apex where the bridge was tall enough to allow America's Cup racing yachts to pass below.

The yacht club was down a long driveway, behind a gate and nestled in a cove on the harbor. Traditional white clapboard siding accented by hunter-green shutters made it feel like Cape Cod. Beyond it, tall masts danced in the breeze against the sunset.

"I want to see the boats," Benjamin said.

We detoured down to the docks and watched a class of Lasers, single-man racing sailboats, shove off with clean-cut adolescents tending rudders, unfurling sails, and staring back up at Benjamin.

After lingering for a while on the docks in the gentle late-afternoon breeze, we entered the clubhouse through double-beveled crystal doors, gliding over green velvet carpets, past burnished mahogany furniture and shimmering trophy cups in glass cases. Middle-aged, white, mostly male yachters in crisp, serious-looking navy-and-white windbreakers and deck shoes made me feel starkly urban in my black leather jacket. Benjamin, towering above me, looked like someone from another land entirely. He strode through the formal dining room with the confidence of a visiting dignitary, ignoring the surreptitious glances coming from below captain's caps.

Outside at the barbecue area, twenty or so young men, easily recognizable as cast members by their long hair and muttonchops, looked as though they'd been transported here in a time machine. A pretty blonde spotted us—how could she not?—and rushed over to greet us warmly. Judy Bouley, the head casting director. In person, she was just as warm and fun as she had been on the phone. I hoped we would "do" lunch one day.

Benjamin and I cruised around, sampled appetizers, and admired the sunset. I thought everyone was meeting everyone else for the first time, but it felt like everyone already knew each other, and no one came over to meet Benjamin, which ticked me off and made me sad for him.

Dinner was announced. Benjamin and I were seated in separate areas. Actors in one, family in another. Judy Bouley introduced the staff and gave more detail on the training and filming for the next five months.

A thunderous explosion interrupted her. I jumped. Three military jets in a triangular formation approached as though they were coming straight for us. I could even make out the pilots.

Benjamin ducked. I could only guess at the memories of Russian Antonovs flashing through his mind. He turned toward me with a worried look. I read on his lips, "What's that?"

"Our planes. It's okay," I mouthed back, wishing I were beside him, and made a mental note to warn him again about the simulated battle scenes he'd be shooting on the movie set.

• • •

Several weeks later, a fellow writer and passionate ship aficionado, Ed Jones, drove Benjamin and me down to the movie set at Fox Studios just south of Rosarito Beach.

This time Benjamin wore a black T-shirt and jeans. Several actors we'd seen at the yacht club came over. "Wow, dude, was that you?" It seems they barely recognized him without the traditional African attire.

After completing some paperwork, we headed to the hotel on the north side of town. Like the brochure promised, a glass elevator and lovely pool with a waterfall were only yards from a broad beach with strings of rental horses. As Benjamin settled into his room, he looked a bit lost. "I'll call you tonight," I told him. I doubted his loneliness would last long.

REALLY, YOU TOO?

Alepho

Benjamin left San Diego to work on a movie in Mexico. One afternoon, when my roommates were out and Judy wasn't around, I forced myself to walk around our new neighborhood. I passed coffee shops and restaurants and ninety-nine-cent stores. The people did not look like the ones who'd lived near our old Euclid apartment. Here, many people had tattoos and rings through their noses and ears. Like a different tribe.

I went into a grocery store. Looking at all the things brought back the memory of how nervous I'd been when I first began working at Ralphs. I hadn't known anything at all about so much American stuff.

I walked down the laundry soap aisle, enjoying the smell coming from each package. A worker was stocking shelves. "Can I help you?" he asked in his American voice.

"No, thank you," I said. "I'm fine."

"Okay," he said. "There are so many varieties I get confused myself."

I started laughing. "Really, you too?"

"Yes."

I couldn't believe my ears. I thought all Americans knew everything about everything. I was kind of shocked that this American native was confused, too. That was a surprise to me.

The story of my life had been filled with surprises. I had thought I would grow up in my village and raise many cows and children like my father. War surprised me. I survived war when most of the boys died. That surprised me too. I thought I'd never get out of the hopeless refugee camp, then my chance came to go to the greatest country in the first world. What a surprise that had been. It seemed that any day could hold a surprise. How could I be sad and stuck in a small place when I had no idea what surprises waited for me?

MISSION TRAILS

Judy

The following week, I called the new apartment. Alepho answered. "Would you guys like to go on a hike?"

Silence. Maybe a hike wasn't enticing for guys who'd walked a thousand miles.

"It's a park near you. A beautiful place where we can walk." I sensed that still hadn't sealed the deal so I added a white lie. "Please. I'm really not comfortable hiking alone."

"Okay," he said.

"Do you want to ask Benson, or any of the other guys to join us?"

"No one is here."

"Okay, that's fine. Wear comfortable shoes." Who was I kidding, he always wore the same shoes, the ones we'd bought at Walmart that first day. Pretty much the same couple of shirts and pants too, always clean and pressed. "I'll be there in an hour."

Getting out of the city would be good for him and his PTSD or depression or cultural adaptation struggles, whatever it was that had him hiding from life. Technically, the park wasn't *outside* the city, but the biggest one *inside* a city in the country. Five thousand acres of wild hills and canyons. Convenient, yet it felt remote.

Alepho was waiting out front in his sweatshirt with the hood up over his head when I arrived. He climbed into the front seat and sat with slumped shoulders. I ignored his lack of enthusiasm—at least he wasn't wearing earphones—and pulled out of their driveway.

We left the car in a dirt lot and started out along a path cut into the side of the hill. We'd gone about a half mile when I stopped at a spot where steep, rocky slopes framed rolling hills that were not yet terraced for homes or crisscrossed by poles and wires. Even the air was untainted by the out-of-sight, highly populated valley below, and mountains fifty miles in the distance could be seen. I loved that middle-of-nowhere feeling. "This is my favorite view," I said. "From right here I can only see nature. Not one sign of humanity in my entire field of vision."

Alepho didn't respond at first and then turned to me with a look of surprise. "This looks like Sudan!" he burst out as though he were suddenly somewhere else.

"Really? I pictured it flatter."

"The south has many hills. We crossed Imatong Mountains on the way to Lokupar."

Lokupar? I hadn't even read about that one yet.

"Everywhere is green. Huge mango trees."

"Must be beautiful. I can tell you miss it."

"I smell water."

"Smell water? How can you—"

Without another word, he bounded off the trail and down into the steep ravine like a California mule deer.

"You have to stay on the trails," I shouted. "Watch for snakes."

What was he doing? He could fall, get lost, get bitten, or surprise a mountain lion. Besides, the water was up ahead, opposite the direction he just took off in.

Damn it. I waited a few minutes, deciding what to do. Why couldn't he just follow the rules? I looked around—no rangers or witnesses—and took off in the direction he'd gone. The descent was steep. Dirt and loose gravel crumbled beneath my feet. I took small steps, sliding with each one, even in my hiking shoes. How had Alepho run down so fast in his crummy ones?

He was nowhere to be seen. I followed a sort of animal trail, no wider than what rabbits might use, overgrown and disappearing in places, pushing through bushes that scraped my legs and made snakes invisible. About halfway down, I came out on the top of a large boulder. Any detour around was too steep and overgrown with impassable shrubs. Alepho must have gotten down though. Determined not to be shown up by youth or gender, I sat and scooted. The last part was vertical, and I jumped to the dirt below.

I called out. No answer. I continued downward, pushing through shoulder-height sumac bushes. Near the bottom, the ground flattened out and knee-high grass grew beneath oak trees. From somewhere within, I heard the gurgle and trickle of a stream. He'd been right about the water.

Downstream a few yards, Alepho stood next to the creek, his sweatshirt hood off, his head tilted back, his arms in the air like a sun worshipper.

"You were right. How did you smell this?" I puffed, trying to catch my breath.

"You don't smell it?"

"Uh, no." I didn't think a colorless, odorless liquid could be smelled.

"Stand right here." He stepped aside and took in a deep breath as though the aroma rivaled that of baking pizza.

I took his position, closed my eyes, flared my nostrils, and gave it my all. At most, a faint whiff of sumac baked by the hot sun. Fresh water didn't stand a chance of triggering my olfactory system. I was about to ask him if he'd smelled the sumac when he turned and hurtled back up the ravine in the same fashion he'd come down. So much for restful contemplation. I took a moment to recover and started back up at my own pace. He'd have to wait at the top because I had the car keys.

My footholds gave way in the loose dirt and rock, quadrupling the effort. I stopped about a third of the way to the top to let my lungs catch up. When I resumed, the way grew steeper. At the halfway point, I reached the boulder. Oh crap. In my haste, I'd not given a thought to getting back up.

Tall, thorny bushes hugged both sides. I wasn't climbing through that. A small crack on the lower vertical face looked like a potential foothold. I crammed in the edge of my shoe but it slipped out. A higher crack looked promising as a handhold, hopefully too small for a nesting rattler. I tried pulling myself up, but my arms weren't strong enough and my feet just couldn't get any purchase. I picked the pebbles from my bloodied palms. I would have to be Spider-Man to get up that.

Why couldn't he have stayed on the paved trail? Another crazy escapade, exactly what I'd been doing too much of recently. I closed my eyes, gritted my teeth, and held in a frustrated scream.

"Hey."

I looked up. The blinding sun silhouetted Alepho lying on his stomach at the top of the boulder with his arm extended toward me.

"Take my hand," he said.

I hesitated. He kept his hand out. I gave in and reached up.

He grabbed my hand and pulled me upward. I tried to help with my other hand and both feet and still didn't find much traction. He was surprisingly strong and lifted me anyway. He wouldn't let go until I stood safely on the top of the boulder.

Depending on him felt foreign. How awkward to be so out of my element.

"Thank you," I said, averting my eyes, which were instantly awash in a confusion of feelings. I sorted through regret for my exasperation, thankfulness, forgiveness, and something else. Discomfort with being dependent on him? His whole life in America had been out of his element. Did he feel like this all of the time?

"Ready?" he asked.

I pretended to gaze at the view. If I looked at him at that moment the moisture already in my eyes would well over, and he wouldn't have any idea why. Nor did I exactly, but I began to think the overwhelming feeling was shame for not understanding and stepping away from someone in greater need than myself.

"We're already halfway," he insisted.

He was encouraging *me*. "Okay. As Benjamin would say, 'we go.'"

Alepho stayed beside me and told me stories. There was a bounce in his walk that I hadn't seen in a long time. If I were ever in trouble, he was the kind of person to have around when the going got rough. Exactly like I needed to be for him and his brothers and cousins. Not a quitter and a coward in the hard parts.

In the car, I turned on the air-conditioning and handed him a bottle of water. A grin that he couldn't seem to contain spread across his face. I hadn't seen that smile in such a long time. He'd come far, but he still had a long journey ahead of him. If he was willing, so was I.

"Hey," I said. "Tell me how we wire the money to your uncle so he can return to his family."

Policies and plans had their place and time. So did tolerance, flexibility, and compassion.

SMELLING WATER

Alepho

I don't know why Judy thought about doing it, but she asked me to go for a hike. I wasn't sure what that meant, but it sounded like we would drive the car somewhere to walk, and she didn't like to go alone.

She drove us to a place where there was nothing, and we left the car in a field. As we walked toward the hills on a small road, she showed me the plants that were poisonous, the ones that were good, and the ones I shouldn't touch. There was a lot of learning, but at the same time I began to feel a sense of freedom. I was liberated, no longer locked in a tiny place of worrying about sweating all the time.

We came to an area that looked out through the hills to the valley below and she stopped. "This is my favorite place," she said. She just stood there looking at the hills.

I closed my eyes and felt the earth under my feet. Instead of streets and cars, I smelled leaves, dirt, and flowers. For the first time in so long, I could breathe. I opened my eyes and looked out at the hills. "This is like Sudan," I said.

Between the earth, dried weeds, and sun-cooked leaves, something smelled familiar. *Water.* "I smell water," I shouted and ran down the hill like a young goat released from its corral. I touched rocks. I hugged a tree. I ran through the bush. So many good things out there.

At the bottom, I reached a small stream. I closed my eyes. The smell of the water, the trees, the wet earth was alive, and it brought back my good memories of Sudan. I felt completely free and happy. And strong, like the day I'd been the boy who found water on our journey. I lifted my arms. At that moment, a new spirit entered me.

After a while, Judy came down to the water. She still could not smell it. On the way back up the hill, she couldn't climb a rock. I went back to help her, but when I reached her I could see that she wasn't happy. I gave her my hand, and she climbed up but she still seemed upset. Maybe that was why she didn't like to go out there alone. I hadn't seen other dangers, like lions or hyenas, not even snakes.

Judy remained quiet on our walk. I wondered if she felt badly that she couldn't smell the water or maybe that she couldn't climb the rock. "Once in Sudan," I said, "when we escaped Palataka, we were walking and didn't have water. We became so thirsty we couldn't talk. Then, I smelled it. The water. Like today. I told the other guys. Just like you, they couldn't smell it either. But they didn't want to listen to me because they were older."

"What happened?"

"I convinced them to follow my lead. We came to a stream in two hours. I laid down in that water and drank like a cow."

"You saved their lives," Judy said.

"Many times we helped each other to cross streams or climb rocks."

Judy smiled.

I said, "My father could smell water."

"What was your father's name?"

"Deng. Deng means 'rain' in Dinka. Very popular name."

"What does Awer mean again?"

"In Dinka language it mean window, like where the light comes in. Dinka is like English, some words have many meanings. In Bar el-Ghazal region where I am from, Awer also mean 'lovely wild dove.' Names are very significant in Dinka culture. There is legend in my subclan that an ancient spiritual prophet named Awer Jongar conquered and subdued the lion's kingdom and brought back the durra crops hidden in his long African hair. I also heard the midwives gave me the name Awer because they saw something in me like that prophet at the delivery time."

"I bet you have many amazing stories."

"I have many," I said. "But some I will never tell."

• • •

Back at the car, Judy gave me a bottle of water. She looked happy again. She must have liked the stories I told her. Then she told me that she wanted to send the money to help my uncle get back to his family in Sudan. That gave me so much relief. I'd been the lucky one to come to America. But I hadn't been able to help my family back home. I had not even helped myself. I put myself into darkness.

Now I felt life coming back into me. I saw that there was

much more for me to do than just hide in that small cage I had created for myself. Judy came as a rescuer. She opened the door. She'd opened the door many times before. This time I was ready to move ahead through that opening.

AMERICAN BOY

Judy

A week after our hike, I stopped by the guys' new apartment. Alepho was in the front room on the new sofa reading *Of Mice and Men*. He could have been reading *Goosebumps* and I would have been thrilled. Although still quiet, restored curiosity lit his eyes.

On my way home that afternoon, Judy Bouley called. "Benjamin is doing great. He was made captain of the cannon and received an A in rowing. Do you know of any other Sudanese who would like to join the core group?"

I hesitated. "Let me give that some thought. Can I get back to you?"

"Sure. No later than tomorrow, please. We need someone by next week."

I'd learned that Benjamin's travel document wouldn't arrive for months and even that was uncertain. He couldn't come back into the US until it did. Judy Bouley had assured me they would have access to good health care. But what if someone needed to return sooner for other reasons? Also, many guys had just started jobs or classes. Running off to be in a movie wasn't necessarily a smart choice.

Cliff, Paul, and I sat down to dinner. "Judy Bouley called me today," I said. "She needs another actor. Everyone is in classes or something, so I was thinking it might be an opportunity for Alepho."

"Cool," Cliff said.

"There's a lot to consider." I explained the dilemma of the delayed travel document.

Paul said, "If I were twenty years old and fit the bill, I'd jump at it. What's the worst that could happen?"

Cliff said, "Doesn't she want an American boy too?"

• • •

I called Alepho the next morning and explained the opportunity. He expressed interest. There wasn't much time for decisions. I headed down to their apartment so we could talk in person about all the things that would need to be done, including speaking to Bob Sullivan at Ralphs about getting his job back in six months.

Alepho met me at the door in mirrored sunglasses. He must have been wearing them inside. His latest device to hide from the world?

When I'd finished explaining the details, he said, "It would be good to see how they make the movies. In the videos in the camp, I didn't know what was real and what they made up. Now I can learn about that."

I called Judy Bouley and let her know Benjamin's cousin was

available. "Can I audition him on Friday?" she asked. "If it works out, can you get him down to the set soon?"

"Sure," I said, not having any idea how we'd arrange everything, especially transportation. I wasn't comfortable driving in Mexico, and Rosarito was a long taxi ride from the border.

Right after I hung up, Sharon called from the IRC. "There's a reporter in town from the *Los Angeles Times* on Friday afternoon. Would you mind bringing Benson and Alepho to the office for an interview?"

CORE GROUP

Alepho

Judy came to me at our new apartment. "There's another job on the movie Benjamin is working on. You would be in the core group."

I didn't know what that meant. I'd seen movies, but what would a movie job be?

Judy said, "You will live in a nice hotel and they will give you the food."

If there was food and a place to sleep, that was great. Those were the things I always worried about.

She said, "You will get paid about the same as at Ralphs."

That sounded good because all the money from my Ralphs job paid for food and rent. What I earned on the movie would be extra if they paid for the hotel and food. I could send some to my friends and family like I had promised them.

Judy said, "Sometimes you will be working on a ship for fourteen hours a day. If you work those extra hours, they will pay you more money."

My excitement really built then. I'd been thinking about how to move my life forward, and I recalled the elder back in Kakuma camp who'd told us that we needed education to change our lives, to change the situation in Sudan. Education had the magic power that would let me do those things. It was clear to me after nearly a year that I needed education to improve my own life in America and to help my family and friends back home. I understood now that to go to school, I needed money. The movie job was a life surprise that I had never expected. My opportunity to move forward had arrived.

On Friday morning Judy picked me up in her car. "They might be auditioning lots of people," she said, "so don't be disappointed if you don't get chosen."

I understood. I would do my best even though I did not know what a person did for an audition. Would it be like the Ralphs interview?

"And, if you have any doubts about doing this, now is the time. Once you are down in Mexico you can't come back until your travel document arrives."

"Yes, I know." If I got the movie job, I didn't need to come back until that work was done. That was okay with me, but Judy seemed to be worried.

We arrived at some offices and a lady named Judy Bouley, who looked like Judy Bernstein, took me into a room. "Take off your sunglasses, please," she said. She turned on a video camera and wanted me to pretend that I was a sailor and a captain on a ship. I repeated the words she asked me to say. I'd never been on a ship so I wasn't sure if I did it well.

We went back out where Judy Bernstein was waiting. Judy Bouley asked, "Can you have him on set Sunday?" I wasn't sure what the set was, but I thought that meant I had the job.

"Great," Judy Bernstein said. "Will do."

OVER RAVIOLI

Judy

Judy Bouley wanted Alepho in the movie, and we had two days to figure it out. In the meantime, I'd promised Sharon I'd bring Alepho and Benson to meet the reporter. We picked up Benson at the apartment and headed over to the IRC.

The reporter, about forty with thick strawberry-blond hair, a kind face, and wearing dark green khaki pants and tan shirt that screamed *National Geographic,* waited in Sharon's office.

"Hi. David Weddle," he said and shook hands with each of us.

We went into a small conference room and settled into chairs around a long table. David explained his assignment: a piece about the Lost Boys for the *Los Angeles Times* Sunday magazine.

He began by asking Benson and Alepho questions about their lives in Africa. I'd been unsure about how they would respond in an interview situation, but they appeared comfortable and answered enthusiastically. David moved on to their experience in

San Diego and listened intently even when their answers went off track and were difficult to follow.

Two hours flew by. Benson needed to be at work. Not wanting to be rude to David, I asked, "Would you like to come with us to Ralphs?"

"That would be great," he said, as though I'd just invited him to the Oscars, not to watch a wrapper at a grocery store.

Alepho remained at the IRC, he'd take the bus home later, while Benson and I headed to Ralphs with David following us in his car. He observed Benson at work, talked to Mike Woods, the store manager, and took copious notes. Somehow, we'd missed lunch, which didn't seem to bother the guys, but by late afternoon I was faint from hunger. "How about something to eat?" I suggested to David.

Over ravioli, I told him about Benjamin and Alepho's new job on the movie. As I was saying it, it dawned on me that a potential ride sat right across the table. Reporters went into war zones and stuff, right? What was a drive to a movie set across the border?

OWN KIND OF STAR

Judy

David graciously drove us to the Rosarito Beach studio on Sunday. Judy Bouley, who I liked more each time I met her, offered us a tour of the entire set. She'd also offered two guys I really cared about a chance in her movie.

We toured through several buildings where they'd constructed a full-size replica of a ship and various cabins within that were so realistic it was like Disneyland on steroids. Outside, while she explained how a huge tank had underwater hydraulics that moved the ship while the jet engines along the pool's edges simulated storms, Alepho, who had been quietly listening, wandered away along the edge of the pool and stood by one of the huge engines, gazing out at the ocean beyond. He looked so intense. What was he thinking?

"How long will you be here on set?" I asked Judy, concerned that Alepho was feeling overwhelmed in another country already.

"Until they wrap."

"The whole movie? I thought once all the actors were hired,

the casting agent's work was done." I'd been imagining her at an office somewhere with a couch.

"Casting director," she corrected me. "It's my job to make sure those fifty actors are on the set every morning. Some days we'll start at 4:00 a.m. Believe me, there are plenty of distractions at night for young men in Rosarito."

"Sounds more like a camp counselor job. Is it just you?"

"And Tommy, my assistant, who you met the first day."

"Personally, I'm really glad to hear you'll be here. This will be a big adjustment for Alepho and Benjamin. Please let me know right away if you don't think either one is doing well. Benjamin's really outgoing, but Alepho is more, uh, introverted."

"Don't worry," she said. "I've got your number."

I knew that, but would she notice with so many young men and so much responsibility? Would she call if it could mean losing an actor? "Excuse me a minute," I said, and left her talking with David.

I went to Alepho and looked into his mirrored sunglasses. "I hope you enjoy this." I couldn't stop worrying. He'd said the pills had helped with his head and stomach pain, but I still wasn't sure about his state of mind. He kept so much inside. Now he'd be far away in Mexico and adapting to a whole new culture again. "This movie set is pretty amazing, isn't it?" I added, hoping it would inspire him to share what he was thinking.

He took off his glasses and looked me directly in the eyes. "When I get back to San Diego, I will write more."

I hadn't expected that. "Good. Writing is a great way—"

"I need to make a book about my life."

The positive signs just kept coming. "Wonderful." I hadn't heard such hopeful things from him in so long. I especially liked the way he used "need" where we typically said "want." More necessity, more urgency that way. A book had been simmering within me as well. Could we somehow do one together?

He stepped back and looked out toward the ocean. "First, I need to find my family. I need to know if my mother is still alive. Will you help me?"

I stared at him for a long moment. "Yes," I said, committing without having any idea to what. "We will try." Where and how did one begin searching for a person in a war zone? But then, I hadn't been accomplished at searching for jobs, housing, or killing parasites either, but the experience had shown me that willingness to try was what mattered. "When we find them," he said, looking directly at me, "I need to build a school and a clinic in my village."

A school. A clinic. Big undertakings. Until the war ended, maybe impossible. But who knew what was possible? If Alepho, who had come from such dire circumstances and started over here with nothing—who still had almost nothing by our standards— wanted to help the people back home, I wanted to help them too. "Yes, yes, we will."

He exuded that same excitement and confidence that had lit his eyes the first day at IRC. He'd be fine down here. He was resilient, otherwise he wouldn't have survived in the first place.

"The border wait is a couple of hours on Sunday afternoon," I said. "We need to get on the road."

We hugged and said goodbye. I reassured him we'd work on those projects when he returned to San Diego. "I'll be back to visit," I said and left him there in his thoughts and dreams, in a kind of dizzying combination of happiness and sadness myself, maybe like what I would experience one day when Cliff took off to college. It had been for Cliff's sake that I'd originally said yes to meeting three extraordinary young men in the first place. I hoped that it had expanded Cliff's world in some memorable way, and most of all, that it had given him an appreciation for the comfort in our lives.

A cool breeze rippled the tank water. I stopped for another moment to take in the immensity of the movie set and the infinite sparkling blue of the Pacific beyond. My friend Aida liked to say, "Empathy can save you." The last year had put so many aspects of my own life in perspective. A traffic jam might be annoying; it wasn't a tragedy. It was a chance to take a sip of water, enjoy the music, and remind myself of the amazing young men who'd crossed the vast African plains barefoot as children. A chance to be thankful that it hadn't been my child, and to do what I could so that no children suffered such horrors again. Maybe an even bigger reason to write a book.

Benson once shared a Dinka saying with me: *When two elephants fight, it's the grass that gets trampled.* So apropos. The Lost Boys had been trampled by forces beyond their understanding or control. Learning about their way through the world had allowed me to see so many aspects of mine with greater clarity. Not only had I come to know and better understand what people faced in troubled places—as well as the challenges here for those who came to escape—but I'd been awakened to the struggles within my own city that were faced by those who weren't as fortunate as myself.

I looked back to where Alepho stood, gazing out. What a journey he'd made. Dusty refugee camp to Hollywood movie set. And his journey wasn't finished. He wanted to share his story, build a school and clinic, and most of all, find his family. I didn't know how much of that was possible, but trying was the only way to find out. Behind those mirrored glasses, Awer was his own kind of star, and in that moment his possibilities seemed endless.

DINKALAND TO MOVIELAND

Alepho

Mr. David Weddle drove us to Mexico and he asked me more questions along the way. Only a month ago, I might not have liked those questions. I would have been angry and suspicious of why he was asking. Now, his questions made me feel important. The same way I'd felt leaving Kakuma camp and walking up the airplane stairs like a president. I hadn't felt like that for a long time.

We crossed the border into Mexico and went through the city of Tijuana. South of there the towns became smaller, with dirt streets, simple square buildings of cinder block, and dogs running loose. It looked like so many towns I'd passed through on my journey, but without the war. Mexico reminded me of Africa; I became excited to explore it. Mexican food had become my favorite, especially carne asada burritos.

Judy Bouley showed us around the movie studio that was as big as a city. She took us to a building larger than Walmart. "That's a duplicate ship they're building," she explained. "The real one is docked down in Ensenada, about an hour south of here."

I didn't understand why they needed more than one ship to make the movie, but I didn't understand a lot of what Judy Bouley was saying.

She showed us another ship. "That's the French ship. The two battle it out off the coast of South America."

South America? I liked the way she spoke, but I wasn't sure what was the movie and what was real. What would be my job here? *Relax,* I told myself. The grocery store had felt this big and strange at first. I would learn.

We crossed the lot to a tank that was the size of twenty swimming pools like the one at Judy Bernstein's house. I couldn't see the bottom. "This tank held the *Titanic* replica," Judy Bouley said. "That was nearly full size. Under the water, hydraulic arms lift the ship, and those jet engines along the edge simulate storms." She pointed to a big field of cement that was next to the ocean. "They filled that with water, and the whole thing blends against the ocean. We'll do the same."

I'd never imagined anything like this when we'd watched the videos in the camp and tried to figure out how the people were in the small box. I walked along the edge of that huge, deep pool of water and stood beside a jet engine. I looked out to the ocean and took a big breath of the air.

I'd been lost in the dark for so long, not trusting anyone, not seeing a way in my new world. In the refugee camp, they'd told me that I'd be given a pillowcase filled with money to make my life in America. I knew how silly that was now. Benjamin had been right: to be guided from fire, it was people I needed to trust. Like our sponsor, Judy Bernstein. She was skinny and not rich, but she knew how to make things happen. My headaches and stomachaches were much better with the pills that she had convinced me to take. She got us a new place to live and found the Ralphs and movie jobs for us. In the future, I would listen to the counsel of those who tried to help me, learn to trust them. They were the money in the pillowcase.

Now, here I was in another country, standing on a movie set, looking out at the Pacific Ocean. A journalist from an important newspaper had come along just to write about me, a boy no one had wanted for so long. I would never stop trying to move my life forward. I needed to find my family and help the people back home. In Sudan we said, *It takes two hands clapping to make a noise.* Judy said that she would help.

If darkness came again and I was lost, I would take time to smell the water. I would not forget that challenges made me stronger and life was sure to present another one of its surprises.

THE END

AFTERWORD

BY ALEPHONSION DENG

For the nine years that I lived in Kakuma camp there was no news about my family in Sudan. I did not know who may have survived. When we arrived in America I had access to a phone and the internet. People in Africa were also acquiring these technologies. In 2004 a call came. A soldier told us that he had traveled through our village and had seen our mother. Benson and I gathered some money and paid that brave soldier to go back, into the war, and let our mother know that her two sons were alive in America.

One day, a few months later, some photos and an audio tape arrived in the mail. We saw our mother sitting in front of a hut next to a palm tree that I remembered from my childhood in the village. After eighteen years, I heard her voice. That was a day I will never forget.

Working on the movie in Mexico, which became called *Master and Commander*, was an amazing experience. Fortunately, our travel documents arrived the same week the movie wrapped, and Judy brought Benjamin and me "home" to San Diego.

Several months later I secured a job in the medical records department of Kaiser Hospital, where I worked for five years.

Being a refugee can feel like an invasion of another nation's economy, resources, culture, and space. I have come to understand how some people feel negatively about people being brought to their homeland. They fear that their way of life will be threatened.

I understand those feelings because as a refugee I am a person whose own way of life was violated in my native land. I experienced the harsh realities of war and its consequences; loss of family, loss of home and land, violence, abuse, exploitation, abject poverty, and the resulting serious health issues.

My love goes to the Lost Boys who perished before my eyes. Boys with whom I had shared yams and leaf soup, whose legs and feet could not take them farther, whose hearts faded out as they gave in to their fate.

People say refugees are resilient. I was resilient at first because I had created a sense of hope about coming to my new country. Years of brutality had taught me to cope in simple ways. Things like singing, dancing, praying, ceremonies, familiar rites, habits, and food kept me going. I lived in a dream that one day I would wake up and everything would be peaceful, secure, perfect. I had created a false hope in order to survive.

Soon I realized that my magical kind of thinking from living in war and camps where I had no control over my life did not serve me well in America. My false hopes needed to be replaced with real hopes and real goals. I had to become practical and self-reliant. Rather than hoping my luck would give me a fish, I needed to learn to fish.

Those fishing lessons took many years. I did not know that the effects of childhood trauma can linger long after a person reaches a safe and secure home. I didn't understand this PTSD, post-traumatic stress disorder, until I embarked upon a healing process of rehabilitation and reconciliation. My faith in humanity needed to be restored before I could trust others and accept support. I now realize the impact that violence and trauma can have on a person in so many ways. I see that even many Americans struggle with the same issues from abuse or going to war.

My love goes to all of the refugees and displaced persons in the world who lost their home for reasons beyond their control. No one wants to leave home. We are all homesick.

Sharing my story has helped me. Our writings that began in the composition books we purchased at Walmart that first day we met Judy evolved into our book *They Poured Fire on Us from the Sky: The True Story of Three Lost Boys from Sudan*, published in 2005. Since then, we have spoken at hundreds of schools, universities, organizations, and corporations across the country.

I'm told that I'm an inspiration. But the people I meet in my new country inspire me. I hope this book has accurately reflected the ordeals and dreams so many of us share and has inspired you as well.

My love and gratitude go to all Americans for offering me the opportunity for a new life.

Please visit us at our website: TheyPouredFireBooks.com

ACKNOWLEDGMENTS

BY JUDY A. BERNSTEIN

It's often said that writing is a solitary act. That hasn't been my experience. Writing has given me new and lifelong friendships and a supportive community and has taken me places I never would have been.

Thank you, Joni Evans. You saw something and took a chance on new writers.

Thank you, Clive Priddle at Public Affairs Books, for shaping our story into what it needed to be.

Thank you, Cynthia Cannell, Charlotte Kelly, and Nico Brown at Cynthia Cannell Literary Agency, for giving us more support than we ever dreamed possible.

Thank you, Madeline Hopkins and Ember Hood for such careful and thoughtful edits.

Thank you, Blackstone Publishing, for taking us on this journey.

Storytelling comes more naturally for some, like my coauthor, Alepho. For me it has been a long process of learning the craft. I could not have accomplished that without the wonderful people and help I found in writers' groups. Twenty-five years ago, I confided in my sister, Tamara, that I was writing in the closet. She'd majored in literature, so I asked her to read some of my work. "You need a book doctor," she wisely advised. Warwick's bookstore in La Jolla sent me to Mike Sirota, and I joined his writers group.

For twenty years I received patience, encouragement, support, and some painful critiques from the Asilomar Writers Group. Thank you, Jerry Hannah and all of the Asilomar writers, for founding, gathering, and inspiring such a dedicated and talented group of writers in one extraordinary locale.

Horses brought the Riding Writers together, but writing still keeps us going. Susan Union and Diane Lee Wilson, for twenty years your time and input has been invaluable; your friendship is precious.

Every Thursday afternoon I look out over rolling hills of avocados and vineyards where I'm joined by the De Luz Writers group, a tireless bunch sharing tales; some fiction, some real, and some real masquerading as fiction. Thank you, Mary St. John Putnam, and David Putnam—your crime novels are proof that you lived what you write about.

The staff at the San Diego Office of the International Rescue Committee works tirelessly to assist refugees in adapting to their new country. Thank you, Bob Montgomery, Sharon Kennedy, and Joseph Jok for assisting me as well.

None of this would have been possible without my wonderful husband, Paul. He has dedicated his life to helping others and supported my work and my writing. He's a surgeon, an author, an innovator, a great husband and father, and a beacon who is familiar with the sacrifices and rewards of hard work.

In the beginning, Cliff was the motivation for the whole

endeavor that led to meeting the amazing young men from South Sudan. Cliff's excitement and enthusiasm inspired me to do more. Cliff, and his lovely wife, Kristy, still inspire me. They both work to make this world a better place.

Everything pales beside what my dear friend and writing partner, Alephonsion Deng, has contributed to this project. He walked the walk no child should ever experience. Since those years of suffering, when it would have been so easy to hide away with the pain, he instead made the courageous choice to do what he can to prevent others from suffering similarly. It can't be easy to write or speak about the most painful aspects of one's life, yet he does it over and over, sharing his story with thousands. Alepho, your message enriches us all.